Praise for *Awakened*

Too many believers view the coming age with fear and avoidance. Ralph Plumb has laid out the who, the how, and the why and given us the tools we need to be prepared and to be victorious. *Awaken: Embracing Freedom in Times of Peril* is a thorough, well-grounded overview that reminds us to be alert and engaged, but never intimidated. This is a must read for every believer.

– Kay Edwards
CEO, Outsight Network, Mequon, WI
Author, *Hunt with Your Pack - Why Networking Alone Isn't Enough*

We have had the privilege of working with Ralph over a number of years in connection with The Lovelady Center, a faith-based prison re-entry and addiction recovery haven for women and their children. What we have witnessed over that time is Ralph's deep commitment to serve people in need. We trust the validity of his Kingdom "large assignment" to rescue at-risk children described in Chapter 13. We recommend this book to all who understand the biblical admonition to "be in this world but not of it". You may not fully align with all the complex issues dealt with in "Awakened," but everything points back to God, the author and finisher of our faith. *This book will "awaken" and encourage you.* It calls us all to action in support of the will and purpose of our Heavenly Father.

– John McNeil
Chairman/COO The Lovelady Center, Birmingham, AL

– Beverly McNeil
Founder, Portraits of Hope, Birmingham, AL

This book offers valuable information on how pervasively the "enemy" has corrupted every center of influence in America and the entire world. Ralph's view that only God is the solution aligns fully with my own. True believers, obedient disciples of Jesus Christ, must be *awakened* and become active warriors of the Holy Word. As we repent and receive His grace, revival and transformation in our public square and local communities, will result. Believers are called to be "salt and light" in this kingdom age. *Awakened* reminds us of God's grand design, how He empowers us to embrace freedom and that He expects each of us to "occupy" here on earth until Jesus returns.

> **– Lloyd Mize**
> A disciple of Christ
> Real Estate Broker, Temecula, CA

I have known Ralph for over 40 years as a man who walks with God and commits significant energy in every mission of great significance and eternal importance. The whole of Ralph's work in this book reflects thoughtful and thorough research coupled with a presentation that provides an intersection of theology, leadership, justice and compassion.

> **– Ron Maines**
> Principal, Crossroads Leaders, Russellville, AR
> "Working alongside leaders to get from where they are to where they need to be"

Dr. Plumb's latest book, *Awakened: Embracing Freedom in Times of Peril* could become an instant classic with amaranthine proportions. This book serves as a GPS for a rigorous journey rather than a handbook for living with a singular destination. His ability to articulate present-day challenges, leading the reader through a minefield of complex obstacles, is exemplary. He keeps the ultimate goal of Christ's return in the forefront and points to it throughout the book, not losing sight of the goal. This book demonstrates the age-old adage that "in order to change the world, we've got to change the narrative". *Awaken* leads us to the precipice of a new narrative.

– David Weston
   An abiding love for Jesus, longing for His return
   Last Reached Initiative, Greenville, SC

This book, Ralph's 7th published, gives both present context and historical perspective to the deep darkness that has come upon the earth. Yet it offers great hope through the emergence of kingdom solutions that will bring even greater light. His chapter on Kingdom Alliances offers a biblical template from which we can rebuild and repair, with our eyes collectively on Jesus, the master architect and finisher of our faith stories.

As longstanding strongholds and root structures are dismantled and broken down through continued exposure of evil, new kingdom builders are rising up with innovative, entrepreneurial kingdom building blueprints that have been vetted in the secret place. This is a time for accelerated kingdom collaboration!

– Leslie Mahre
   Prophetic Intercessor, Kansas City, MO

Author's Note: I have listed these greatly appreciated endorsements in the chronological order that they were received.

AWAKENED

*Embracing Freedom
in Times of Peril*

RALPH EDWARD PLUMB

MCHENRY PRESS

Awakened

Copyright © 2024 by Ralph Plumb

Published by

McHenry Press

www.McHenreyPress.com

"Let's bring your book to life!"

Paperback ISBN: 978-1-964251-23-3

Cover design by Debbie Lewis

Printed in the United States of America

Dedication

My sheep listen to my voice;
I know them, and they follow me.

—John 10:25

This book was written by your watchman on the wall. It is offered with humility to the awakened and those about to be. With our imperfect human understanding we see through a glass darkly, yet illuminated in faith by your Holy Spirit, I commit this book, for such a time as this, to you . . . Jesus.

Your Name is power

Your Name is Healing

Your Name is life!

Contents

Contents

Introduction

AWAKENED: EMBRACING FREEDOM in Times of Peril offers a serious message . . . to a specific audience . . . for an intentional reason . . . at this precise time in salvation history. I do not proclaim this with a complete sense of foreknowledge but with humility, sensing that these are extraordinary and prophecy-fulfilling days. This message is for "the remnant," the *ekklesia* (called-out ones), the *qahal* (congregation, assembly)—every follower of Yeshua who worships and prays, within and outside of formal structures. May we all, the bride of Christ, God's end-times warriors, those who have been *awakened*, who pray as watchmen, receive this exhortation. *Two words of caution*: This book is not a "light" read. And, if, for some readers, these terms do not resonate with you or you feel no affinity with them, this book may represent unfamiliar territory. I wrote this book to bring specific awareness to the origin of our present circumstances and to call for accelerated engagement and intercessory prayer from those who can make a redemptive difference.

My favorite books are full of personal, motivational narrative and dialogue. Jesus taught in parables, which communicated most effectively. But given the range of complex topics included here, I have done my best to document, with Endnotes, persons of authority or with direct knowledge. Everyone senses that bad things have happened in America and the world. This book will shed some light on how we got "here". I trust Holy Spirit will speak to you, to discern what He intends. And for the prophetic intercessors, I pray this book will give deeper insight to help tear down strongholds! May you be motivated to think carefully, pray fervently, and act accordingly.

This is a season for boldness. Silent thoughts do not change culture. In war, especially in spiritual warfare, there is no room for hesitant combatants or timid responses to evil. More than any time in history, our efforts must be determined and sustained. The decade ahead is not for the faint of heart or the hesitant of faith! The uninformed and disinterested have no framework for why the stability of life we have grown accustomed to seems to be imploding. Trust has been lost in the leaders of virtually *every* sector of society. But why? We're living in an enveloping evil—wars and civil conflicts, cancellation and control, gender perversion, assault on our children and the traditional family, blatant corruption, climate hysteria, the next "planned-demic" with suffocating mandates, tyranny undermining true justice, and a new world order in the making, just for starters. It is time for America, for every nation that has tasted freedom, to wake up.

Thank you, Eric Metaxas and Jack Hibbs, among many others, for your voices of urgency. Most people can recognize evil. Far fewer understand where it really comes from, how it cleverly manifests in all elements of life, and therefore, how to overcome it.

So, what do we do now? In times of peril, you cannot overcome if you don't know the adversary. It is absolutely necessary to understand that the source of all that is good, God—who is eternal, omniscient, omnipotent, and omnipresent—is dethroning the personification of evil, Satan, who possesses none of these traits. This enemy is the primordial force at the core of *all* our earthly trials and brokenness. During this end of the church age and the dawn of the kingdom age, our mortal enemy is frantically active, but running out of time. This is a *kairos*, a divinely appointed time in history, and we are privileged to live in this era. No generation has or will experience what is about to take place, *on an accelerated basis*, for an unknown period of years. While this disruption and the infiltration of evil undermines every "mountain of influence" in our global societies, nevertheless God is doing something new and powerful! We who listen to His voice and know Him can rest in this confidence.

What years lie ahead defy a precise chronology. "But about that day or hour no one knows, not even the angels in heaven, nor the Son, but only the Father" (Matt. 24:36).

America's Judeo-Christian constitutional republic, and the greater spectrum of democratic countries worldwide, are facing three *external* existential threats converging on us simultaneously:

1. Radical jihadist Islam who demand fealty to their *god* or be killed
2. Globalist secular humanism, which has as its goal to delude and replace *God* in all things

3. *God-less* Chinese communist hegemony with a one-hundred-year plan to subvert, then subjugate

These are three of the enemy's conscripted forces. But our true enemy is Satan, behind the people and institutions who have allowed him dominion. The ultimate goal of this great deceiver is to supplant everything of God and to separate humankind from Him.

America faces a serious *internal* existential threat as well. Virtually all of our institutions have been taken over by a prevailing evil that is intentionally trying to destroy us. Therefore, now more than ever we must look intentionally, with fresh spiritual discernment . . . *at everything*— history, science, government, politics, corporations, economics, political parties, social movements, thought leaders, controllers of messaging in the public domain, and more. Simply stated, *anything* that denies the Word of God comes out of an antichrist spirit of deception, a lying spirit. This is the Occam's razor of this book. Randy Clark shares this further wisdom:

> In this new millennium, we Christians no longer find ourselves in a predominantly Christian culture. We now find ourselves in a pagan culture in much of the world. We find more similarities in our culture to the first two centuries after the crucifixion and resurrection of Jesus than at any other time. If the Church is to be the leaven that leavens the whole lump, if we are to see the Kingdom of God ever expanding, then we will not be able to trust in our might or power, but must rely on the Spirit of God, "'Not by might nor by power, but by my Spirit,' says the Lord Almighty" (Zech. 4:6).[1]

This book is divided into three sections. The first four chapters summarize God's original intent and grand design; Satan's opposition to everything of God everywhere; current examples of perversion, corruption, and treason; and a sampling of prophetic guideposts including those that foretell *some* of what is about to happen. Many uplifting and prophetic declarations have been made in faith for the immediate years ahead, that God will not allow the United States to be consumed by the fallen angels of darkness and their demon doctrines. After this time of shaking, God *will* restore America to its covenant roots, and the *ekklesia* will experience a time of abundance, favor, and blessing. *Yet, we are living in a finite period of repentance and restoration.* We must remember the culmination of God's redemptive plan outlined in Scripture.

The next eight chapters identify specific ways in which evil has corrupted the good. I use as a framework the familiar term (to some) the seven "mountains" or "centers" of societal influence—religion, family, education, government, business, media/technology, and arts/entertainment. I also have embedded in these chapters the destructive influences and outcomes in a range of very important topics—the military, direct social media and government collusion, artificial intelligence, "Big Pharma," racism, diversity, equity, and inclusion, gender confusion, abortion, climate nonsense, and the end of a cash-based system replaced by a centrally controlled digital one in much of the world. I also compare true biblical justice to currently espoused social justice. This section ends with the tangible plans being made by the "dark side" to continue to build a new world order. This is Satan's last futile effort to create the ultimate global counterfeit to God's plan. But the enemy is the forever loser! Thank you, Tim Sheets, for this accurate depiction. What *will* happen after this fiery period ends is the ushering in of a new heaven and earth, as proclaimed in Revelation 21:1.

The remaining four chapters offer resources to assist us to embrace freedom during times of peril. *After all the bad news, this book is intended to encourage.* These chapters identify some unique applications of kingdom wealth creation, transfer, and provision. "Wealth" does not refer only to financial resources, but rather drawing down on the provisions that have been "stored up" by God for His people in this ordained time. These resources include human, intellectual, and financial capital (as described in a business context); or supernaturally provided relationships, knowledge, and "manna," using different language. One specific model that will be explained is the emergence of *Kingdom alliances*—intercessory prayer originating covenantal communities that will be part of God's stewards of the greatest transfer of wealth in human history. This has been a "calling" and a burden on my heart for some time now.

Finally, as you read this book, please keep these points in mind:

1. This author understands that there is no universal agreement on every topic among the faith community. Each of us hold strong views on politics and matters of faith. I am perfectly comfortable articulating my

position while trusting you will understand the specialized focus of this book and why it was written, without rejecting the whole on the basis of any specific point(s) of difference.

2. The emphasis of this book is on what God is doing in the spiritual dimension concurrent with what we see and experience in the natural realm. These realities are not always discerned in our temporal, time-bound life. In sections I have used specific names of political figures and others despite the intense divisiveness that exists, because I believe being "nice" or neutral is not what is needed at this time. You can draw your own conclusions about specific events which happened under certain leaders or influencers and, thus, the spiritual consequences for their actions.

3. This book is only a synopsis of the many deeply complex issues included here. I have endeavored to provide well-researched information gleaned from a divergent range of sources, for you to prayerfully consider. Please remember, every reference or Endnote is time-sensitive and will wax or wane in importance as the months advance past our publishing date. Yet I value the gleaned wisdom contained herein from "many advisers" (Prov. 15:22), whom I have chosen to highlight.

4. Our enemy—Satan, the god of this age, deceiver of the whole world, the father of lies, *is* constructing a one-world order and whose servant will proclaim the ultimate blasphemy. Will this happen in our living years? Only God knows. This is why I have included resources for when living in freedom becomes most difficult indeed. *And it will!* Therefore . . .

Be strong and courageous. Do not be terrified; do not be discouraged,
   for the Lord your God will be with you wherever you go. (Josh. 1:9)

Ralph Edward Plumb

GOOD OR EVIL—

In All Matters,
There Are Only Two Options

CHAPTER 1

God's Original Intent and Grand Design

IT TAKES ENORMOUS "faith" to believe the predominant dogma that over untold millennia our evolutionary ancestors crawled out of a pond after earth was enigmatically created from a cosmic explosion.

> The Big Bang Theory is the leading explanation for how the universe began. Simply put, it says the universe as we know it started with an infinitely hot and dense single point that inflated and stretched—first at unimaginable speeds, and then at a more measurable rate—over the next 13.7 billion years to the still-expanding cosmos that we know today.
>
> Since existing technology doesn't yet allow astronomers to literally peer back at the universe's birth, much of what we understand about the Big Bang comes from mathematical formulas and models. Astronomers can, however, see the "echo" of the expansion through a phenomenon known as the cosmic microwave background.[1]

To clarify this further, parallax trigonometry can only accurately measure a few hundred light years of distance. (Another source indicates 100 parsecs, roughly 326 light years.) Thus, begins a very shaky cornerstone for the remainder of evolutionary theory.

The next spawn of this macro-conjecture is the explanation for the "evolution" of the earth and its inhabitants. The theory of evolution is now the fully accepted "enlightenment" position of the majority of our Western *and* Eastern political and academic institutions. It's science, right? *We must remember that this, too, is still a theory!* Many voices influenced the contemporary origins of the universe and humankind taught in our schools and universities, but by whom and from what realm? Who has elevated this false counter-position to God creating the heavens and the earth?

One contributor is writer and philosopher Ayn Rand, founder of Objectivism. She declared, 'Reason is the only objective means of communication and of understanding.' At least this is the prevailing worldview of the majority outside of communities of faith which, *without proof*, deny that a Creator exists. Other specific individuals who contributed to the various tentacles of this hydra called evolution, *all faith-hostile*, include James Hutton, Charles Lyell, Charles Darwin, and Ernest Haeckle. In Chapter 2, I will attribute this counterfeit narrative to its true source.

Here is a research recommendation for you, *if* you wish to penetrate the carefully constructed "scientific" history of the origin of our universe, with planet Earth having a supposed age of 4.543 billion years:

> *Ocean salinity*—The average sea surface salinity is 35 PPT (parts per thousand), between 3.1% and 3.8%. Increasing salinity decreases CO_2, and affects evaporation and formation of sea ice. "Records show that the saltier parts of the ocean increased their salinity by 4% in the 50 years between 1950 and 2000."[2] Consider this mathematical construct if applied over the alleged 4.5-plus-billion-year age of the earth.

> *Depletion of the sun*—Our singular solar system power source burns 4.21 million tons of its mass per second ($m=E/c^2$). This equates to a rate of shrinkage in its radius of 2.5 feet per hour, from a total radius of 7×10^8 and a mass of 2×10^{30} kg. Other mathematical constructs suggest the sun has a burn rate of five or six feet per hour. No matter. Do the math based on a multiple-billion-year life cycle. Over this time period the sun would have had such a massive gravitation pull it would have obliterated our entire solar system.

> *Moon's orbit*—The moon is spinning out of the earth's orbit at about 1.49 inches (3.78 centimeters) per year. There are 63,360 inches in a mile. Therefore, the moon will have moved one mile in 42,523 years. The earth is currently 238,900 miles from the moon. Does the math come anywhere close to 4.5+ billion years?

Carbon dating—Carbon-14 (C-14) dating is built on a series of necessarily interconnected assumptions, suggested as scientific hypothesis. These include: a constant rate of C-14 formation and decay, decay of the earth's magnetic field, radiometric techniques occurring in a "closed system," and many other *complex* issues. In short, the C-14 dating technique does not work when considering fluctuations in the amount of C-14 in the atmosphere and rates of diffusion over time.

Geologic column—This is a helpful methodology for studying different layers or strata of rock, sediments, and other substances to determine more about the geologic history of certain regions. Studying stratigraphic geochronology has some value, but there have been assumptions inserted in this process that undermine the full representations of this "science." One most important example is arbitrarily assigning X years (without proof) to these strata. This philosophical orientation came from Scottish geologist Charles Lyell (1797–1875), author of the three-volume *The Principles of Geology*. His aim was to "Free the science from Moses."

We *must* take into account the spiritual orientation and, therefore, the hidden (or blatantly transparent) motivation of each major player who has influenced, if not corrupted, every "mountain of societal influence." Again, this information was given simply as an opportunity for you to research if interested.

It is important for the ardent person of faith—or no faith—to understand the arbitrary assignment of epochs of millions of years, vis-a-vis Lyell's hypothesis of uniformitarianism explaining the geologic formation of the various strata of the earth's crust. There is no "scientific" validation for his doing so. Lyell was also hostile to the Christian faith, intent on removing any notion of divine creation. He had documentable influence on Charles Dawin—and thus the slippery slope of accepted "science" that prevails in most of our postmodern enlightenment world of scholarship.

The Christian faith community seems to embrace two positions on the origins of the earth. Either 1) The earth was created in six days (but what constitutes a "day"), as described in Genesis 1:1–2:4; or, 2) The earth evolved over multiple billions of years, without fully knowing how to explain the gap between the two. Similarly, the Christian faith community seems to take two positions on the origin of life: 1) "God created mankind in his own image . . . male and female he created them" (Gen. 1:26); and, "Then the LORD God formed a man from the dust of the ground and breathed into his nostrils the breath of life, and the man became a living being" (Gen. 2:7); or, 2) Some vague explanation that somewhere during the evolution of hominids God breathed life into that sequence of beings. Once again, two fundamentally incompatible choices.

Alleged hominid development

One of the top ten nano-scientists (chemist, nanotechnologist, and nanoengineer) in the world is Dr. James Tour, who conducts research and teaches at Rice University in Houston. A web search or YouTube will provide ample information—one video in particular, "Dr. Tour Exposes the False Science Behind Origin of Life Research." His challenge to the prevailing position of abiogenesis (that life arose from nonlife—of its own volition) has yet to be proven wrong. He promulgates an explanation of adaptation rather than evolution—disproving the sequence of random variation, mutation, genetic variation and natural selection, upon which evolutionary theory depends

His forthright scientific investigations have been excoriated by others in his professional community. "I have seen a saddening progression at several institutions, witnessed unfair treatment upon scientists that do not accept macroevolutionary arguments regarding the examination of Darwinian theory... When the power-holders permit no contrary discussion, can a vibrant academy be maintained? University means 'unity in diversity.' Could it be that the National Academy of Sciences itself has turned a blind eye to the disenfranchisement that is manifest upon those holding a skeptical view based upon the scientific data?"[3] Dr. Marcus Ross, vertebrate paleontologist and young-earth creationist, also provides excellent reading in his books, including *The Heavens and the Earth* as well as *The Geology of the Post-Flood World*.

As some "authorities" moved incrementally in the right direction, they postulated the allegedly 'pseudo-scientific' theory of Intelligent Design. "Intelligent Design is the theory that life, or the universe, cannot have arisen by chance and was designed and created by some intelligent entity. Proponents say that theories other than evolution must be considered."[4] One small step for man; but here is the truth, one giant step for mankind, *for those who discern*.

> In the beginning God created the heavens and the earth (Gen. 1:1).

> You alone are the LORD. You have made the heavens, even the highest heavens with all their starry host, the earth and all that is on it, the seas and all that is in them. You give life to everything (Neh. 9:6).

> It is I who made the earth and created mankind upon it. My own hands stretched out the heavens; I marshalled the starry hosts (Isa. 45:12).

> In the beginning was the Word, and the Word was with God and, the Word was God. He was with God in the beginning. Through him all things were made; without him nothing was made that has been made. In him was life, and that life was the light of men. The light shines in the darkness, but the darkness has not overcome [understood] it (John 1:1–5).

We have access to approximately six thousand years of recorded history. There are pre-Noahic references in Scripture to creatures we can construe as "dinosaurs" such as Leviathan and Behemoth (Job 40–

41), or great sea creatures and beasts (Gen. 1:21, 25). The discovery in the early 1900s of porous channels of ultramafic rock comprising 84% of the earth's volume, and the presence of large reservoirs of water under the earth's crust, bring better understanding to the "great flood." The earth was not simply deluged by rain or a "regional flood" of some type, but was a catastrophic, completely global event. When you fully investigate these disparate elements of the larger creation story—God did create *everything* by the breath of his mouth—scientific description is not a deterrent to faith. Second Peter 3:3–7 reminds us that in these latter days, scoffers who "willingly are ignorant" of creation will deny its divine origin, deny the flood, as well as reject global events as God's judgment. Whichever track you believe in faith is a matter between you and God. But for those who reject God because they believe we exist outside of His created order— well, that also is between you and God!

Having presented this, my book is not intended to serve either as an apologetic or polemic. We will invest most of the remainder of this chapter to address the truly amazing precision, numerical meaning, significance, and interconnectivity (which is *discoverable*) in the grand design of His creation. But we will first consider, in a necessarily rudimentary manner, God's original intent for His creating. Within the Father's larger created order in the universe, which we cannot possibly fully comprehend, the two elements of creation we will reference briefly are *human beings* and *spiritual beings*. Both have an ordained purpose for existence. Libraries full of books have been written on each of these topics; we only offer this as a simple starting point.

The original intent of God to create mankind was for His pleasure; and our purpose, in response, is to give glory to His majesty, to live in intimate communion with and to enjoy Him forever. "Martin Luther said that if he could understand the first two words of the Lord's Prayer as Christ did, the rest of his life in Christ would fall into place. Luther's observation shows that it is easy to *use* God's words, but much more difficult to grasp the reality they signify. This is true with regard to the "image of God." Most believers have heard of this concept, but few grasp the profound significance of its meaning. The image of God (*imago Dei*) is a foundational concept for understanding our significance and purpose. Understanding how we are made in God's image helps us see the basis for the dignity and purpose of our life and work."[5]

God created us as tripartite beings—a fancy word for "composed of three parts" or, more accurately, elements. He created our bodies out of dust (*soma*). Then, unlike any other animals on earth or created beings in the universe, He breathed into us two elements that made us into the "image" of God—not because of arms or legs or a corporeal body, but rather two elements that exist in the spiritual realm: a soul (*psyche*), better understood as our distinct identity including our intellectual and emotional essence; and a spirit (Greek *pneuma*, Hebrew *ruach*, or in Latin *spiritus*) with a literal meaning of "wind" or "breath." The spiritual understanding is this: the very presence of the Holy Spirit, coeternal and coequal in the triune Godhead, lives in us!

It is important to note that instead of a dualistic view like that of the Greeks, where an immaterial, immortal soul lives separate from but within a material body, the Hebrews understood that the soul and spirit are a psycho-physical unity. These are but three familiar guideposts in Scripture:

- Then God said, "Let us make mankind in our image, in our likeness" . . . male and female he created them (Gen. 1:26a, 27b).
- Then the LORD formed a man from the dust of the ground and breathed into his nostrils the breath of life, and the man became a living thing (Gen. 2:7).
- What is mankind that you are mindful of them, human beings that you care for them? You have made them a little lower than the angels and crowned them with glory and honor (Ps. 8:4–5).

The original intent of God for creating a vast, innumerable host of spiritual beings (messengers—*angelos*) was to serve and worship Him. These spiritual beings, like everything in creation, have divine intention and purpose. We find reference to these types of angelic beings in Scripture:

- *Seraphim*—These are the highest-ranking angels in heaven, responsible for serving as the personal attendants of God and worshipping him. They have wings of fire and are incredibly beautiful (Isa. 6:2 ff).
- *Archangels*—In canonical Scripture four are named: Gabriel, Michael, Raphael, and the fallen one Samael who changed his

name to Lucifer, "the morning star." (Uriel is mentioned in the pseudepigrapha, in 2 Esdras, and the Book of Enoch identifies seven.) These powerful angels are responsible for protecting and interceding for major realms or territories and nations or large groups of people (1 Thess. 4:16, Jude 1:9).

- *Cherubim*—Depicted in Scripture as beautiful, youthful and responsible for protecting the entrance of heaven, cherubim also serve as messengers between God and humans (Gen. 3:24; Exod. 26:1, 31; 1 Kings 8:6–7, Ps 18:10; 80:1; Ezek. 10:14, 20; Heb. 9:5; et al.).
- *Guardian angels*—These are angels assigned to individuals—to you and me! They are assigned to protect and guide. They are forces of good helping people stay on the path toward God and to protect us from the minions of hell whose purpose is to kill, steal, and destroy (Ps 34:7; 91:11, Matt. 18:10; Acts 12:15; Heb. 1:14; Rev. 5:11; et al.).
- *Fallen angels*—Obviously these are not cherubim who are protecting heaven from humans, but rather the one-third of fallen angels who made the most tragic decision of their existence, within the free will that they were created with to follow the phony morning star (Rev. 12:4).

Besides these five categories of angels, the Bible also references spiritual beings who command or control thrones, dominions, powers, and principalities. Consider this, if every human being has at least one guardian angel (and some have more) then there are *billions* of these messengers, protectors, and worshippers of the Almighty creator of the universe and all that is in it!

Glory to God in the highest! His original intent is always good and full of love and mercy!

The numerology in God's grand design, when researched and discerned, is nothing short of astounding! Contrary to those who have attempted to postulate theories on the origin of the universe, the earth, and humankind based on happenstance, the Creator of all things (*El* or *Elohim*) did so with exact precision, intentional meaning, *and* a direct connection of the end with the beginning. The appropriate term is "harbinger," which means to foreshadow. This is a prophetic burden with a message received from a prophet about the future.

How important are format, order, sequence and numbers in Scripture? Let's start at the beginning—the beginning of the Word of God, the first word in Genesis 1:1, which is סדינים, *bereshet*. Note there are multiple spellings of this word in English. The word in Hebrew means "In [the] beginning." Isaiah 46:9-10 is known as the Bereshet Prophecy[6]: "Remember the former things of old, for I am God, and there is no other; I am God, and there is none like Me. Declaring the end from the beginning, and from ancient times things that are not yet done, saying, 'My counsel shall stand, and I will do all My pleasure'" (NKJV).

Where do we find the revelation of El's creation, purpose, and plans for mankind? Both Paleo and Classical Hebrew provides pictograms that contain the inner meaning of the Hebrew alphabet.

Again, the first word of Genesis 1:1 is *bereshet*—"in beginning." The first letter of *bereshet* is ב *bet*, meaning a house or tent; its numeric value is two; *bet* also means "in." So, the question is, who is inside the tent?

The second letter of *bereshet* is ר *resh*, meaning head, leader, or prince; its numeric value is two hundred, which indicates the all-sufficiency of El, and the complete insufficiency of man. *Resh* tells us who's in the house/tent. The combination of *bet* and *resh*—רב form the word *bar*, which means "son." Now we know who is in the tent: someone's son who is also the head, leader, or prince.

The third letter of *bereshet* is א *aleph*, the pictogram of El, Elohim depicted as an ox meaning strength, with a numeric value of one. God the Father is the strong leader who guides His family. The combination of *bet—resh—aleph*—ארב forms the *bara*, which means Creator or created. So, who is in the tent? The *bara*—the son; whose son is He; He is the son of El.

The fourth letter of bereshet is ש *shen*, pictured as teeth to crush and destroy, with a numeric value of three hundred. Three hundred is a signature letter to signify El's special ownership of something. *Resh* means the head person or prince inside the tent, but the prince in the house now comes out of the house. *Shen* is the prince coming out of the house to crush or to be crushed—or could it be both?

The fifth letter of *bereshet* is י *yod*, referring to something amazing that is going to unfold which will mark the end of one age and the beginning of a new age. Yod's numeric value is ten. Ten gives added spiritual significance of the hand doing a divine deed. There is no zero in Hebrew; therefore, the zero could indicate time. The prince is coming to earth to accomplish something His heavenly Father planned and purposed in heaven that will happen on the earth at an appointed time.

What is that something?

The sixth letter of *bereshet* is ת *tav*. *Tav* is pictured as a cross, the divine deed ordained in heaven that will fulfill a covenant and be revealed as a sign that is literally pictured as a cross. This sign is the center point for all human history from El's perspective. Everything that happened before this sign was sovereignly ordained, in order to set the stage for this one single event. From the sign of the cross it marks every epic event that El has planned for mankind for the future!

There are two prophetic details that are still to be revealed:

1. Where will it happen?
2. When will the event take place?

The first question is, where will the event take place? Why did the son come out of the house? The Son came out of heaven to come to the earth to accomplish His Father's plan and purpose to redeem mankind. This took place on (Paleo Hebrew *tav* ✝) a wooden cross/stake in which Messiah was lifted up on mount Calvary; this reversed the impact of man's death and destination of hell, and opened the door and fulfilled the covenant El had made with his Son to redeem man. *Bereshet* is all about new beginnings and going home.

The second question is when. *Has the Bereshet prophesy been completely revealed and fulfilled?* No; it has only been partially revealed, not completely fulfilled, even though the central view of the Bereshet Prophecy has been revealed.

Why has this prophesy been hidden for more than twenty-seven hundred years (from the timesd of Isaiah)? Ecclesiastes 3:1 (NKJV): "To everything there is a season, a time for every purpose under heaven." That time, that *kairos* time, is upon us!

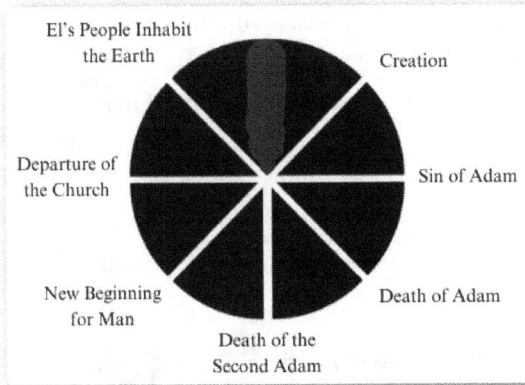

El's redemptive plan

There are *innumerable* other examples of the importance of numerology in God's grand design, emanating out of His original intent. What follows are just three examples of the important numeric symbolism in God's creation, as revealed in his holy Word. There are reams of other resources which describe biblical knowledge and revelation on this subject.

9 (nine)—Used forty-nine times in Scripture, the number 9 symbolizes divine completeness or finality: nine gifts of the Spirit and fruit of the Spirit; Hosea, the last king before the northern kingdom fell to the Assyrians in 723 BC, reigned for just nine years; the Day of Atonement (Yom Kippur) begins at sunset on the ninth day of Tishrei (Sep-Oct); Yeshua died on the ninth hour of the day, or 3 pm; the total destruction of Jerusalem's temple began on Ab (March) 9.

7 (seven)—Used more than seven hundred times in Scripture, the number 7 refers to completeness, a perfect number: the sevenfold Spirit of God; 777 as the threefold perfection of the Trinity; the seventy sets of sevens in Daniel 9:24–27 until the anointed one comes and we have seen the completion of sixty-nine sets of seven to date, with the US recognizing Jerusalem as the capital of Israel exactly seventy years to the day after its founding as a nation; seven days of creation: Day 1 light, Day 2 atmosphere (firmament), Day 3 dry ground and plants, Day 4 sun, moon, stars, Day 5 birds and sea creatures, Day 6 land animals and humans, Day 7 the Sabbath day of rest; and below, seven critical intersections of salvation history. Then there are seventy nations (Gen. 10); seventy of Jacob's clan who went to Egypt (Ex. 1:5); seventy palm trees that refreshed God's people at Elim (Ex. 15:27); seventy elders who served with Moses (Ex. 24:1); seventy princes in Judges 9:56; seventy men in the Sanhedrin; and Jesus sent out seventy apostles on mission.

40 (forty)—Used more than 150 times in Scripture, the number 40 seems to indicate a waiting or transition period for man, which God uses often: the great flood lasted for forty days/nights; Moses was forty years old when he killed the Egyptian, God called him to His divine task forty years later, and then Moses stayed on mount Sinai for forty days; the Israelites were led in the desert for forty years; Jesus fasted in the wilderness for forty days and forty nights; there were forty days between Jesus' resurrection and ascension.

Are these just a coincidental amalgamation of unrelated events that happen to use the same numbers? You can decide for yourself. But let us be reminded, since every thought and action will be recounted during our life review on the day of judgment: if God truly knows our thoughts before we ask or pray, knows the condition of our hearts, knows the number of hairs on our heads, knows when a sparrow falls in the field, created everything by the breath of his mouth, knows the end from the beginning . . . what then *should* we believe?

One final illustration of the exquisite precision and meaning within God's creation is the hidden code embedded in the "fall festivals." You might be thinking, "What do the ancient feasts of Israel have to do with me today?" First of all, they *are* the Lord's feasts, and as the "one new man" we are invited to celebrate these *moedim* or appointed times and remember He will be returning for His bride.

Spiritually, the former and latter rains correspond to the seven feast days given in Leviticus 23. The feasts are symbolic of God's redemptive plan. Pentecost concludes the spring feasts for Israel, just as it concludes the Lord's earthly ministry. It is believed that the period of time before the fall feasts begin is symbolic of the church age.

God tells us emphatically, "Three times you shall keep a feast to Me in the year" (Ex. 23:14, NKJV). These appointed times are rehearsals and windows of opportunities for God's people. Rejoice and thank Yahveh for revelation, revival, and intimate fellowship through Y'shua Messiah. Do not appear before Him empty-handed, bring an offering. (Note: The Jewish festivals are not based on our western Gregorian calendar, but rather the Jewish lunisolar calendar, regulated by the position of both the moon and sun.)

Rosh Hashanah

Rosh Hashanah means "head of the year" and is the civil Jewish New Year. This feast is identified with the awakening blast of the trumpet. In Leviticus 23:24–25 it is called the Feast of Trumpets. It is also called "The Day of the Great Sounding," including Yom Teruah, the day of the awakening blast referring to the "trump of God" shofar sounding in 1 Thessalonians 4:16–17. The details of the Feast of Trumpets encode many parallels of the anticipated catching-away of the saints to heaven (the rapture). The prophetic parallel is clear: no man would know the day or the hour (Mark 13:32), but we could know when it was "near, even at the doors" (Matt. 24:33).

Yom Kippur

This feast is translated into English as the "Day of Atonement." Our Father sent His Son Y'shua as the perfect atonement to take away the sins of all who trust in Him. The good news is we have a redeemer who exchanged His blood for ours and paid the debt we owe; all we have to do is accept His sacrifice on our behalf.

Y'shua is seated at the right hand of Yahveh and is the High Priest of the new covenant (Heb. 1:3; 7:25). Y'shua sitting indicates that his priestly atoning work has been accomplished. Prophetically the feast is identified as the tribulation, in which the future antichrist will form a final kingdom. Great judgments and distress will be upon the earth. This time is referred to by Jeremiah as the time of Jacob's trouble (Jer. 30:7). At the conclusion of the tribulation, Y'shua will deliver Israel from her enemies of destruction, and Israel's eyes will be opened to receive Y'shua as Messiah, bringing Israel to salvation.

Sukkot

Known as the Feast of Booths or Tabernacles, a time of joy and fellowship of recounting Yahveh's faithfulness to Israel. According to John 7:37-39, Yeshua attended this feast and connected the libation ceremony performed by the priest with the upcoming outpouring of the Spirit. We enter our new covenant of redemption through the blood of Yeshua and seal our public testimony of faith in baptism. Prophetically, the Feast of Tabernacles represents the thousand-year rule of Y'shua on earth from Jerusalem, known as the millennial reign. It is also an appointed season in which the Messiah will call all nations up to Jerusalem to celebrate the great feast (Zech. 14:16-21). Sukkot invites us to join in the rest and rejoicing that redemption brings when Y'shua will tabernacle with His people forever.

We will discuss the importance of God's promises to the nation of Israel and their central role during the end days in Chapter 5, "Religion." But here is one vital addition to the precise numerology of our Creator: The first jubilee—intended to be celebrated every fifty years— occurred during the reconstituted nation of Israel in 1917. The second jubilee was celebrated when Israel recaptured Jerusalem, after the Six-Day War in 1967. And the third jubilee occurred in 2017 when the United States, under President Trump, recognized Jerusalem as the capital of Israel. Nothing exists by happenstance!

God created everything with intent and purpose. His design was grand. His plan is immutable. The great deceiver wants us to believe our existence came from a big explosion from which some life form began and we evolved out of water then into land-based *homo sapiens.* How utterly ridiculous. All of this presupposes that these essential elements preexisted—but from what origin? Humankind may have discovered *some* scientific principles that explain portions of God's grand design, but science does not supplant the divine.

It is very important to understand the origin of all that opposes God, as well as the spiritual orientation of people who participate in this. We will begin to describe this in more detail in the following chapter.

CHAPTER 2

The Forever Loser and Liar

THIS CHAPTER IS an important anchor to the core message of the book. *Everything* that is happening around us now, or in the past, or which will happen in the future, is *directly* influenced by the spiritual battle between the light and darkness. Satan's hopeless effort to thwart God's creation, will, and purpose takes place both in the heavenly realm, but also for us who live within the confines of time and our mortal bodies. "For we wrestle not against flesh and blood, but against principalities, against powers, against the rulers of the darkness of this world, against spiritual wickedness in high places" (Eph. 6:12, KJV). The spiritually discerning understand the complex connectivity between the free will God gave us and the unfolding of human events. For others it *may* seem like an unfair scenario over which we have little control. And for those outside of the faith community, this assertion may seem like fanciful nonsense.

In my fourth book *All Who Wander: Rediscover God's Purpose on Your Journey*, I describe three different ways the enemy deceives us. The first tactic in Satan's strategy of deception is to cause as much of humankind as possible to believe that he does *not* exist. People see and experience evil everywhere. Yet, through lies and delusion, he convinces us not to recognize him as the source of evil, nor the dark angels from the spirit world which fell with him. These legions have other names such as demons, evil spirits, and unclean spirits. Nonbelief is most easily embraced by people in our postmodern, secular western societies who have removed or ignore any thought or concern for God. If any consideration at all is given to "the devil," they imagine him only as a mythical, comedic character with a red body, face, a goatee and tail, holding a pitchfork. Nonbelief is equally embraced by the majority of populations in communist and totalitarian countries that have been taught from birth, and therefore believe, that there is no God and certainly no devil. For the atheist, it is complete foolishness to entertain such a weak-minded position of superstition. There are billions of people in this category.

This is not the devil.

The second tactic in Satan's strategy of deception is directed toward those who do believe he exists. There are two broadly defined groups of people in this category. The first group is comprised of those who have yielded themselves to Satan's service and lordship. These human believers in Satan take on various roles of spiritual warfare against Christians and those who are still seeking to find God. They include witches and warlocks, spiritists and occultists, mediums and fortune tellers, voodooists and Satan-worshippers, to name some. The second group is large indeed, comprised of billions of people in every major world religion, including "nominal" individuals who attend Christian churches as well as those with no specific religious affiliation. These persons believe in a devil, but have no knowledge of his purpose or how to deal with him. They go about life on a wing and a prayer, just hoping that nothing bad happens to them. Most importantly, they have no clue about the activities of this enemy or how Scripture instructs us to deal with him.

The third tactic in Satan's strategy of deception is focused on believing Christians who have an understanding that he is the enemy and understand his purpose and devices. I put myself in this category, as perhaps you do. Nevertheless, this angel of darkness has the devious capacity to undermine our walk with God, and he always strikes at our most vulnerable places of access. As long as we follow the guidelines of Scripture; stay in close fellowship and communion with our Father, through His Son, empowered by the Holy Spirit; and exercise the authority given to us, we safely live under the covering of his wing. But Satan understands our proneness to wander. His three most effective areas of attack against believers are *fear, isolation,* and *doubt.* We must follow the exhortation, "Do not be anxious about anything, but in every situation, by prayer and petition, with thanksgiving, present your requests to God. And the peace of God, which transcends all understanding, will guard your hearts and your minds in Christ Jesus" (Phil. 4:6–7). When we wander, anxiety turns to fear. And fear is a sign that we are no longer living in faith trusting completely in the sovereignty of God.

Today we are experiencing a clear acceleration of evil and rejection of God's intended purposes. "Woe to those who call evil good and good evil, who put darkness for light and light for darkness" (Isa. 5:20). In Chapters 5–12 we will look at specific, documented ways that the enemy has infiltrated, in diabolical and hidden ways, our families, communities, countries, and the world.

> There was a time when Western society was very aware of the spirit world and its power. The church, too, believed in healing, deliverance and spiritual manifestations. We are told that Martin Luther was so aware of Satan's presence on one occasion that he threw an inkwell at him. . . . Then changes in philosophy turned our forebears from a God-centered approach concerning the interpretation of life to a human being-centered approach. And under the influence of the philosophical movements that culminated in what has been labeled the Enlightenment, we have become "Enlightenment Christians." We evangelicals followed our society in the worldview changes that led our people to secularism. The Reformation and the rise of universities played a major part in this movement, turning people toward interpreting advancements as purely human accomplishments and away from seeing God behind those accomplishments. This has led the majority of Western Christians, in keeping with the rest of society, to see spiritual beings and forces as either belonging to the realm of superstition or make-believe, not as real. And this in face of the fact that the Bible speaks a lot about satanic beings and shows how to handle them! The majority of Christians interpret life and even the Bible as if these beings and powers do not exist. For most Western Christians, spiritual power is a mystery and much of the Bible seems like fairy stories.[1]

The central objective of the enemy is to get us to supplant our relationship, love, worship, and dependence on God to one where we pridefully, just as he did, make ourselves the center of the universe. This is apostasy. Satan desperately wants us to worship "other gods," of which he is the puppet master. And his central strategy is to counterfeit everything God created. This evil being is unable himself to create *ex nihilo*, but he does deceive, tempt, lie, entrap, accuse, manipulate, disrupt, supplant, confuse, fight, steal, kill, destroy, and many other actions that affect our living years. Satan is not omnipresent, omniscient, omnipotent, or eternal. But because of our granting him "authority" by our disobedience to God starting in Eden, which affected all mankind, he does retain temporary dominion of this world. What follows are *short excerpts from* a sampling of longer Scripture passages involving the cunning and persona of the enemy:

> Did God really say, "You must not eat from any tree in the garden? . . . You will certainly not die," the serpent said to the woman. "For God knows that when you eat of it your eyes will be opened and you will be like God, knowing good and evil" (Gen. 3:1, 4–5).

> One day the angels came to present themselves before the Lord, and Satan also came with them. . . . "Does Job fear God for nothing?', Satan replied. . . . "But now stretch out your hand and strike everything he has, and he will surely curse you to your face" (Job 1:6, 9–11).

> Then he showed me Joshua the high priest standing before the angel of the Lord, and Satan standing at his right side to accuse him (Zech. 3:1).

> Then Jesus was led by the Spirit into the wilderness to be tempted by the devil. After fasting for forty days and forty nights, he was hungry. The tempter came to him and said, "If you are the Son of God, tell these stones to become bread. . . . If you are the Son of God . . . throw yourself down." . . . Jesus said to him, "Away from me, Satan!". . . Then the devil left him, and angels came and attended him (Matt. 4:1–3, 6, 10–11).

> Jesus said to them . . . "You belong to your father, the devil, and you want to carry out your father's desires. He was a murderer from the beginning, not holding to the truth, for there is no truth

in him. When he lies, he speaks his native language, for he is a liar and the father of lies" (John 8:42, 44).

The thief comes only to steal and kill and destroy (John 10:10).

Be self-controlled and alert. Your enemy the devil prowls around like a roaring lion looking for someone to devour (1 Peter 5:8–9, NIV84).

He who does what is sinful is of the devil, because the devil has been sinning from the beginning. The reason the Son of God appeared was to destroy the devil's work (1 John 3:8, NIV84).

And the angels who did not keep their positions of authority but abandoned their own home—these he has kept in darkness, bound with everlasting chains for judgement on the great Day (Jude 1:6, NIV84).

And there was war in heaven. Michael and his angels fought against the dragon, and the dragon and his angels fought back. But he was not strong enough, and they lost their place in heaven. The great dragon was hurled down—that ancient serpent called the devil, or Satan, who leads the whole world astray (Rev. 12:7–9, NIV84).

It is important to understand how Satan uses the *manipulation* of reason and logic to supplant our indwelling spiritual connection, which God breathed into us when we were created. First, we will reference the words of one specific proponent of the enemy, Karl Marx. He represents a multigenerational population of the deluded. Today, in our country and world, the 'religious' advocates of neo-Marxism spread widely, aggressively, and even violently their tear-it-down, anti-God falsehoods. Then, we will dig deeper into the Word of God on this matter.

The Inverted "Wisdom" of Karl Marx

I am using quotes from one source, because he represents millions of anti-God humanists.

- The foundation of irreligious criticism is: Man makes religion, religion does not make man. Religion is, indeed, the self-consciousness and self-esteem of man who has either not yet won through to himself, or has already lost himself again. But man is no abstract being squatting outside the world. Man is the world of man—state, society. This state and this society produce religion, which is an inverted consciousness of the world, because they are an inverted world. The struggle against religion is, therefore, indirectly the struggle against that world whose spiritual aroma is religion.[2]

- Religious suffering is, at one and the same time, the expression of real suffering and a protest against real suffering. Religion is the sigh of the oppressed creature, the heart of a heartless world, and the soul of soulless conditions. It is the opium of the people.[3]

- Religion is the impotence of the human mind to deal with occurrences it cannot understand. The democratic concept of man is false, because it is Christian. The democratic concept holds that . . . each man is a sovereign being. This is the illusion, dream, and postulate of Christianity. The social principles of Christianity preach cowardice, self-contempt, abasement, submission, humility, in a word all the qualities of the canaille [i.e. the common people, the masses—author's additional note]. [4]

The "religion" of reason and logic has, today, the largest number of adherents—greater than all the major world religions. As we read in the earlier list of Scripture references, the first "Age of Reason" was promoted in the garden of Eden by Satan. This process satisfied the desire of Eve's eyes, flesh, and pride by making her own decisions independent of God. Therefore, philosophy, "the study of the fundamental nature of knowledge, reality and existence"[5] was also first introduced in the garden.

The second Age of Reason, which occurred in the seventeenth century, added mathematics and science to philosophy in its removal of the divine. More will be said about this infiltration in Chapter 7, "Education."

From the beginning of human history this enemy has twisted, corrupted, and counterfeited. From the first Adam's fallen state, until the second Adam redeemed us, and until Jesus returns for us, we wrestle in this spiritual battle—but now, with the Holy Spirit living in us giving us power and authority. Jesus overcame "the mark of Cain." *And what is this?*

The Mark of Cain

Then the Lord said to Cain, "Where *is* Abel your brother?"

He said, "I do not know. Am I my brother's keeper?"

And He said, "What have you done? The voice of your brother's blood cries out to Me from the ground. So now you *are* cursed from the earth, which has opened its mouth to receive your brother's blood from your hand. When you till the ground, it shall no longer yield its strength to you. A fugitive and a vagabond you shall be on the earth."

And Cain said to the Lord, "My punishment *is* greater than I can bear! Surely You have driven me out this day from the face of the ground; I shall be hidden from Your face; I shall be a fugitive and a vagabond on the earth, and it will happen that anyone who finds me will kill me."

And the Lord said to him, "Therefore, whoever kills Cain, vengeance shall be taken on him sevenfold." And the Lord set a mark on Cain, lest anyone finding him should kill him (Gen. 4:9-15, NKJV).

What is Cain's punishment? To go up and down, and to and fro in the earth. Does that sound familiar? "And the LORD said to Satan, from where do you come? Satan answered the Lord and said, 'From going to and fro on the earth, and from walking back and forth on it'" (Job 2:2 NKJV).

Who's permitted the ungodly to rule in the kingdoms of this world? Does El care about these rulers? Yes, He gives them an opportunity to repent. "Therefore, I encourage first of all that supplication, prayers, intercessions, *and* giving of thanks be made for all men, for kings and all who are in authority, that we may lead a quiet and peaceful life in all godliness and reverence. For this *is* good and acceptable in the sight of God our Savior (1 Tim. 2:1, NKJV).

The line of Cain believes El is the enemy. If there is a godly person like Abel, Noah, Elijah, Daniel, Shadrach, Meshach, and Abednego, what will Cain do to them? Kill them!

> And Adam knew his wife again, and she bore a son and named him
> Seth, "For God [El] has appointed another seed for me instead of
> Abel [godly line], whom Cain killed" (Gen. 4:25, NKJV).

Therefore, indeed, I send you prophets, wise men, and scribes: *some* of them you will kill and crucify, and *some* of them you will scourge in your synagogues and persecute from city to city (Matt. 23:34, NKJV).

The Cain spirit wants to rule the world, and according to Scripture it has the authority to rule. "Whoever kills Cain, vengeance shall be taken on him sevenfold. And Yahweh set a mark on Cain, lest anyone finding him should kill him" (Gen. 4:15, NKJV).

Throughout history this warfare has continued, with varying results. Egypt had a probation period that ended for Pharaoh; his heart was hardened, but eventually let Israel go. Nineveh repented at the preaching of Jonah. With Rome, Pilate knew the Israelite leadership was corrupt. Herod died without repenting.

Cain and Abel represent two classes of people that will live in this world until the end of time. Abel represents the justice of an offended God, which could only be appeased by the death of His beloved Son. Cain represents those who carry out the works of Satan, in worshipping "god" in their own way, in partial obedience. Always pray that El gives the church wisdom to thwart the Cain spirit from corrupting God's plan and persecuting His people.

Every false religion has been based on the Cain principle. *What is the Cain principle?* Man can depend on his own merits and righteousness for salvation. "You are of your father the devil, and the desires of your father you want to do. He was a murderer from the beginning, and does not stand in the truth, because there is no truth in him. When he speaks a lie, he speaks from his own *resources,* for he is a liar and the father of it" (John 8:44, NKJV).

God could crush Satan like a bug, but He has chosen to work through us—refining, shaping, chastening, and forging our frailties into spiritual weapons! Those of us who make it through the gauntlet are becoming, in the fullest expression of God's intent, the ruling and reigning *ekklesia*. As in each generation from the beginning of man's existence on earth, today the Father is still raising up kingdom warriors for battle. Most are not known, and never will be. But some of the heroes of faith we do know. Moses stood against the false gods of Egypt. Elijah stood against the false gods of Canaan. Paul stood against the false gods of Rome. We now, in our time in salvation history, have just as many false gods, philosophies, and counterfeits to the truth to do battle with. But the central perpetrators are the same demonic forces that have created havoc since God chose the lineage of Abraham to be His own.

Consider these connected realities, as described by Messianic Jewish best-selling author and insightful prophet Rabbi Jonathan Cahn in his book *The Return of the Gods*. He refers to three of them as the "dark trinity" that led Israel into apostasy. These demonic powers are still—now—infecting America and all nations. Each of these demonic forces are found in Scripture. This is not myth.

The Possessor—Ba'al (*Baal, Baalim*) translation: lord and master—image of a bull calf

"He" was the chief god of the Canaanite pantheon. In late writings Baal was identified in the Syriac and Phoenician language as the Greek god Zeus, the head of the Greek pantheon. Behind these false gods which did not exist were demonic forces which *did* exist! Their purpose was to turn a nation away from God. These demonic forces are actively turning America away from Almighty God. We see it plainly today as it was in the days of old.

"The Israelites did evil in the eyes of the LORD; they forgot the LORD their God and served the Baals and the Asherahs" (Judg. 3:7); "these lying prophets, who prophesy the delusions of their own minds [and] make my people forget my name just as their fathers forgot my name through Baal worship" (Jer. 23:26b–27a).

There were many Ba'als; entire nations, regions, cities, even some individual families worshipped their own Ba'al. He was a god of fertility, lord of the rain, a warrior and the primary substitute conjured by the enemy against God. He/they were the god(s) of apostasy, of falling away and turning the people from worshipping the true God. Like Israel, America is a covenant nation. And also, like ancient Israel, we have removed Him from our institutions, government, schools, and from too many families. "Baal had turned Israel in upon itself. He caused the nation to war against its own foundations. The America where prayer and God's Word were imparted to its children, where Scripture was revered in its media and culture, and where the ways and precepts of God informed laws and national policies and were proclaimed in the public square—was no more."[6] "The spirit of Baal works toward the altering of perception.

Where there is one God, there is an ultimate and objective reality, a unifying reference point and a standard by which all can be discerned, measured, and judged. Where there is God, there is truth. But where there is more than one God, or many gods and Baals, the door is open for many truths, conflicting truths, and thus no truth."[7] America today has many Baals—humanism, "science," climate change, political dogmas, intransigent ideologies, money and materialism, intersectionality, critical theories, hedonism, and more. Most of these do not have graven images, nor do its adherents consider themselves worshippers. But where God is removed from the center of any pursuit or belief system, there is a demonic spirit involved.

The Enchantress—Ishtar (*Ashtara, Asherah*) translation: seductress, sexual deviant, transformer

"She" was the wife of Baal. In the Greek pantheon this was Aphrodite— once again gods of mythology, whom "modern man" reads of with humorous historical interest. This demon was responsible for unbridled sexual immorality and perversion. Is there sexual deviance and excess, human trafficking, gender confusion going on in America and much of the world today? Yes, indeed.

"Do not set up any wooden Asherah pole beside the altar you build to the Lord your God, and do not erect a sacred stone, for these the LORD your God hates (Deut. 16:21–22); "Judah did evil in the eyes of the LORD . . . They also set up for themselves high places, sacred stones and Asherah poles on every high hill and under every spreading tree. There were even male prostitutes in the land; the people engaged in all the detestable practices of the nations the LORD had driven out before the Israelites" (1 Kings 14:22a, 23–24).

This spirit causes humankind to trespass boundaries, break rules, engage in prostitution and pornography, destroy morality, marriage and faith, tolerate what is forbidden, and intoxicates and alters our minds. This demonic realm also has now accelerated the obliteration of all that differentiates the created order of male and female. This ancient spirit will:

- seek to alter the definitions of male and female.
- move to blur the lines and nullify the distinctions between the two.
- act to transform the nature of man and woman.
- seek to feminize all that is male and masculinize all that is female.
- war against the sanctity of sexuality and gender by confusing the two and merging the one into the other.

- appear at first on the fringes of society—but then come into the mainstream and permeate every part of culture.
- usher in the next stage of America's paganization.
- become the chief hammerhead to smash the biblical foundations of western civilization.[8]

The Destroyer—Molek (*Moloch, Molekh*) translation: the "king" the ultimate abomination to God—the sacrifice of children

In the Greek world Cronus (Kronos) is the related god. This demon is the dark arts controller of child sacrifice. Human and child sacrifice has been nearly universal at various points in history—Egypt, India, West Africa, Tibet, Aztecs, Celts, Druids, etc. The killing of unborn children began in the USSR in 1920s and in the USA in the 1960s, then was legalized by the Supreme Court in 1972. America has since murdered tens of millions of babies. God's judgment will be rendered!

Sacrificing children to Molech

"Do not give any of your children to be sacrificed to Molek, for you must not profane the name of your God, I am the Lord" (Lev. 18:21); "Say to the Israelites: 'Any Israelite or foreigner residing in Israel who sacrifices any of his children to Molek is to be put to death. The members of the community are to stone him. I myself will set my face against him and will cut him off from his people; for by sacrificing his children to Molek, he has defiled my sanctuary and profaned my holy name'" (Lev. 20:1–3).

To explain this reference further: Outside the walls of Jerusalem, southwest of the ancient city, lies a small valley. Since the seventh century BC, this valley was called Gei Ben-Hinnom; in Hebrew, meaning "Valley of the Son of Hinnom," and by the first century AD, was commonly known in the Aramaic language as Gēhannā. Today, the valley looks insignificant, unworthy of a second glance. In ancient times, however, this specific valley took on a different meaning, as Gehenna was the place of child sacrifice. In this valley, parents willingly offered their children to suffer a brutal killing, so that they would be a pleasing sacrifice to the Canaanite god, Moloch, who in turn would grant the people prosperity and favor.

Consider this disgusting historically documented event: the Greek philosopher Plutarch (46–119 AD) described the music that would accompany the sacrifices of children and its purpose: "And the whole area before the statue was filled with a loud noise of flutes and drums so that the cries of wailing should not reach the ears of the people."[9]

Didn't ritual sacrifice just exist in the dark past of human history? Hideous evil exists in each generation. Do an internet search of The Satanic Temple in Salem, Massachusetts to learn of their ritual abortions conducted today as a dark counterfeit expression of worship to the demonic realm! The existence of witches and other evil manifestations, then and now, are most certainly *not* a myth.

Another spiritual reality contributing to pervasive evil around the world, for which we have insufficient space to properly describe, are the Nephilim, offspring of the Watchers. Genesis 6 is a starting point. The book of Enoch, part of the apocryphal writings, offers expanded description.

We conclude this chapter with three sets of bullet-point summaries further describing Satan.

The creation and fall of the enemy (Ezek. 28:11–19):

- Lucifer was originally created in the service of El.

- Lucifer was originally created as a caretaker of El's throne.
- Lucifer is the first angel mentioned in the Bible.
- Lucifer is the first in whom was boasting found.
- Lucifer is the first in whom iniquity was found.
- Lucifer is the first in whom violence was found.
- Lucifer is the first in whom sin was found.
- Lucifer is the first in whom pride was found.
- Lucifer was the first in whom corruption was found.
- Lucifer was the first to defile worship.
- Lucifer was the first to lead mankind astray.
- Lucifer was the first to lie.
- Lucifer was the first to murder.
- Lucifer was the first to commit homosexual acts.
- Lucifer was the first to fall from heaven.

Some of the enemy's specific methods of attack:

- He uses surprise (descendants of Esau; Ex. 17:8).
- He attacks at the point of our weakness (1 John 2:16).
- He attacks at the point of our strengths (1 Chron. 21:1).
- He uses aggression (Isa. 5:29; Matt. 11:12; 1 Peter 5:8).
- He steals the good seed of the Word (Matt. 13:19).
- He sows tares—the children of evil (Matt. 13:38–39).
- He inflicts disease (Job 2:7; Luke 13:16).
- He initiates death and destruction (Job 1:12–19).
- He brings accusations against believers (Rev. 12:10).
- He induces mental and emotional disorders (Mark 5:1–6).

The enemy's list of counterfeits is endless:

- God is the center of everything—*versus*—man is the center of everything
- Our purpose is to worship God and enjoy Him forever—*versus*—do whatever pleases you
- Revelation—*versus*—astrology
- Jesus—*versus*—Santa

- God created us male and female—*versus*—an alphabet soup of gender confusion
- Traditional family—*versus*—alternative structures
- Monogamous, heterosexual relations within marriage—*versus*—polyamorous coitus
- Intentional design—*versus*—big bang happenstance
- Prophetic foretelling—*versus*—global warming apocalypse
- Ordained roles and order—*versus*—toxic masculinity and pronoun nonsense
- Our body is the temple of the Holy Spirit—*versus*—safe drug injection sites
- Normal childhood development—*versus*—gender-affirming care
- Freedom—*versus*—bondage

It is true that "For now we see through a glass darkly" (1 Cor. 13:12a, KJV); "For now we see but a poor reflection as in a mirror" (NIV); "For now we see but a faint reflection of riddles and mysteries as though reflected in a mirror (TPT). But until we are "face to face," the Lord has created multiple ways in which He communicates to his *ekklesia*—and we will give further evidence of this in chapter 4. In his gracious love for us, He has not left us in the dark!

Through my direct life experience as well as understanding of the Word, I have used a very simple framework for determining if a particular event, circumstance, person or institution aligns with God *or* the forever loser and liar:

◊ Satan always *pulls* us back to the past through guilt, shame, and fear.
◊ God always *draws* us into the future with forgiveness, healing, and restoration.

CHAPTER 3

Perversion, Corruption, Treason

WE NOW CITE some examples of perversion and corruption to emphasize their underlying spiritual origins. With regard to treason, this has *most certainly* been committed by key figures in our government! But since God has not *yet* publicly exposed this, and it has not been adjudicated in either our courts or the courts of heaven, I will only briefly comment. Scripture is our basis of understanding: "There is nothing concealed that will not be disclosed, or hidden that will not be made known. What you have said in the dark will be heard in the daylight, and what you have whispered in the ear in the inner rooms will be proclaimed from the roofs" (Luke 12:2–3).

Now, please read with discernment this prophetic message. The italics are mine to emphasize salient points.

> When I say all, I mean all. *I have promised you a complete exposure of the darkness currently ruling across all seven areas of society. All of them will be exposed, brought down and a judgement will be rendered against them.* I'm also moving across your nation to expose the darkness of the people who have aligned themselves with the lies and selfishness of the dark leaders. When I bring down the evil leaders there will be an eruption of violence from places where the enemy has raised up strongholds of darkness to support the evil one's agenda of power, lust and greed. I'm letting you know about these violent reactions ahead of time not to cause you to fear, but to instruct you how to combat this last kicking and screaming tantrum of a dethroned enemy. Do *not* tolerate the violence.
>
> Take authority over the punk's schemes and send my fire to burn up rebellion and violence as you release my backfire against their fires of violence. It will snuff out their flames and they

will find themselves coming face to face with my spirit of the fear of the Lord. Release my perfect love into these strongholds of fear and deception to pierce the hearts of the deceived and violent. When you send flaming arrows of my love into their hearts my perfect love will shatter their fears and deceptions. And my perfect love will transform them. Instead of freaking out over violence, realize I've painted a target on that area where you need to arise in authority and love to still the work of the violent ones and to see my Kingdom established in those places. *This is the thorough house cleaning that I'm doing in your nation. When I say all, I mean all.*

There is coming a triumphal return to your land. There will be a triumph of justice over bribed and corrupt judges and lawmakers. There will be a triumph of righteousness over those who call evil good and good evil. There will be a triumph of truth that will arrive over lies, propaganda and deception. *There will be a triumphal return of your rightful leader as he is exonerated, and those who accused him are proven to be the guilty ones.*

I am the God who sees. Nothing the wicked have done to your nation and to your life has escaped my notice. *I have seen every murder, every theft, every defilement. In every evil scheme they hatched, once I have seen it, it is forever recorded and it will demand judgment, justice and payback.* The only thing powerful enough to remove a dark deed from the record is the blood of my Son applied to that sin. I gave the wicked time to repent so that their sins could be blotted out, but they refused. Their pride and arrogance hardened their hearts to my love and my Spirit's voice of conviction. Now it is harvesting season and every seed sown has reached maturity.[1]

I am telling you that the answer to all the death schemes and agendas to steal identities, wealth and health are going to be found blowing in the wind. The wind is my spirit blowing away injustice and corruption and blowing in cleansing and freedom and great change. *My remnant army of Light are awakened to the deep darkness and they know that I am the only one who can rescue and bring lasting change.* You have been given eyes to see my Kingdom and you have been prepared to help bring my kingdom in all its glory and power to all areas of society. My Spirit wind will blow through you with Kingdom power to transform the world around you. *Every act of love, obedience and encouragement will release healing.* It will result in my Kingdom expanding. This is not a church activity. It is the way you live your life. The world is looking for answers and you have the answers and the power to bring change as you yield to my Spirit winds. Bribery and corruption will be exposed. Your justice system has been weaponized against those who would restore our republic to its rightful roots and foundations. The bribery and corruption going on behind the scenes is quite staggering and those still asleep can't imagine that it exists. *I am assuring you that nothing these perverted courts decide will stand.* I am telling you that massive bribery and corruption will be exposed. It will be laid bare before the world by linked audio tapes, hidden files, memos and secret video recordings. The arrogant controllers will find themselves before real courts of justice. I have receipts. I have the receipts of their bribery, extortion and greed. My hosts are guarding these receipts and at just the right moment they're going to be appear on the desks of those who are investigating the corrupt. *The landslide of fraud and corruption will be impossible for the lying media to bury.* And the truth will shake the nations awake. The corrupt will not win in the end because their bribery and corruption will be exposed.[2]

These two messages parallel a range of apostolic and prophetic sources who have expressed a similar framework for the immediate future. *The window of grace is closing for the wicked.* These words also have direct implication for the outcome of the 2024 presidential election, but most certainly for the unknown number of complex and contentious years to follow. It will be interesting to look back in time to see what actually occurred!

This is their central message, as I discern it: Much of our U.S. government and leaders are thoroughly corrupt, some rising to the level of treason. All will be exposed and God's judgment will be rendered. There *seems* to be a clear indication of who will become the forty-seventh president of the United States. However, oppositional mayhem and violence will both precede and follow the election and inauguration. Certain voices have spoken of a "cataclysmic event" that will take place. Take special note of what will occur from October 2024 through June 2025. The Kingdom will prevail in the face of unrest and evil. We are not to be afraid, but we *must be* strategically active in intercessory prayer and other elements of spiritual warfare.

What is a lie and what is the truth? Who determines what is perverse, corrupt or treasonous? It is both my observation *and* life experience that absolutely *everyone* sees, hears, and understands words, messages . . . life through their own lens. That means each of us, by innate behavior, is self-focused, self-interested, and biased. Does that mean all truth is relative or that absolute truth does not exist? Not at all. We must step out of a temporal definition as the starting point to answer these questions.

Perversion

What follows are a few present-day applications of the work of this *dark trinity* described in Chapter 2. Perversion is broadly defined as "the alteration of something from its original course or meaning leading to a distortion or state of corruption of what was first intended."[3]

The innocently unaware and the incredulously disinterested have no true understanding of how pervasive this abhorrent evil is. Both our government and our media have intentional purpose in minimizing, obfuscating, or outright not communicating the truth. Why have we heard so little about Jeffrey Epstein's Little Saint James Island participants? I'm going out on a limb here to suggest that there were not many saints on this island—big or little. Why have the details of his alleged (but who believes this) suicide in prison not been released? Why is Ghislaine Maxwell *so* inaccessible, in a low-security federal prison in Tallahassee, Florida? It is reported that the FBI has Epstein's "Little Black Book." All these matters of secrecy need to be released when a truly trustworthy administration controls the White House.

Let's give equal opportunity to Sean Combs, the Puff Daddy to P Diddy mogul. He has been indicted and is in jail awaiting adjudication of allegations of sex trafficking and racketeering. One can only hope he does not "expire" like Epstein. Hollywood and all those fine folks. *Somebody knows sumptin'!* Many caught up in these activities are, for now, still unexposed. Not for long. If you believe, as I do, the prophetic word that opened this chapter, we are in the midst of a significant time of shaking! The perverse will try to run from the light. Ultimately, they will be exposed.

And what about the horror of child trafficking—globally, for sure, but also exploding in America. Our Judeo-Christian–founded country is now the largest consumer of the child sex trade in the world. As someone who has traveled extensively and seen, first hand, particular countries historically known for sex trafficking, it is an unbelievable abomination that we are now number one in the consumption and proliferation of this evil. Ishtar has seduced America!

The transgender agenda (and a ream of other prefixes before the word gender) is yet another category of perversion which has this demonic origin. There is extraordinary effort to infiltrate our social structure with an intentional inversion of truth. This includes the confusion and mutilation of our children, originating from the same dark center of evil.

And for decades now, we listen to the political "left", which pushes to protect the "right to choose" abortion. This is a central platform of the Democrat party. We must fight against this evil from the bowels of hell, and continue to oppose it—spiritually and prayerfully, yes, but also politically, and at every level of our society.

Corruption

Factors contributing to the fall of the Roman Empire, in very simplistic terms, were caused by: 1) corruption, 2) internal divisions, and 3) the invasion of hordes from outside their political boundaries. Give some thought to America today based just on these three criteria. You can decide for yourself if there are vital lessons to be learned from history, and actions which we must take!

This author believes that the United States government, *more than any time in our history*, is infested with corruption at virtually all levels. Washington DC is a cesspool of sycophants and dirty money. If this is true, then we are in the throes of an enveloping dystopian tyranny. One definition is, "cruel, unreasonable and arbitrary use of power and control."[4] Americans now see more clearly the collusion of compromised public, private, and social sector leaders *and* the tentacles of our massive seventeen-agency intelligence apparatus joining forces to control and invert our justice system. They are blatantly out in the open, doing anything to retain power and control *over that portion of the population they deem necessary*. It is the bicoastal elites versus the "fly-over" states, with some exceptions of course. This happens in tandem with and is supported by an also *thoroughly* corrupt corporately owned and controlled media. In lockstep coordination they keep the echo chambers of information filled with untruths, diversions, and disinformation while at the same time doxing, shadow-banning, and censoring all opposition.

Again, this perspective relates to the human condition which affects the people who control human institutions. Almighty God will bring ultimate judgment. But it is *very important* to remember that in partnership with the effectual fervent prayers of the righteous (James 5:16), He will hold back the demise of our nation for a season—*if*, in fact, we do continue to pray with fervency and urgency!

Let us examine one example of corruption, understanding that there are many interrelated elements and participants: the rabid persecution and prosecution of Donald Trump.

This chronological list gives a good visual snapshot of the continuous pursuit to literally destroy this man, first by attempting to thwart his election, then to remove him from his term of office following his election, then to ensure that he does not return to the White House, including two assassination attempts, the first at his political rally in Butler, PA on July 13, 2024. An all-out, *yes*, coordinated assault!

- Intelligence agencies spying on Trump campaign and transition team (2015–2016)
- The necessary (to the deep state) elimination of General Michael Flynn (2016-2017)
- Russia collusion hoax funded by the Democratic National Committee (2017–2019)
- Pelosi led House Impeachment #1 (2019–2020)
- Pelosi led House Impeachment #2 (2021)

- January 6 "insurrection" hoax (2021–2023)
- Biden administration (DoJ) coordination of ninety-one felony counts in two state courts and two federal districts (2023–2024)
  - Alvin Bragg / Juan Merchan—*Alleged* falsified business records case (New York)
  - Letitia James / Arthur Engoron—Nondisclosure matter (New York)
  - Dept. of Justice / Jack Smith—Mar-a-Lago documents case (Florida) *Dismissed*
  - Fani Willis / Scott McAfee—*Alleged* election subversion (Georgia)
- Assassination attempt (July 13, 2024) by a 20-year-old "working alone" *Does anyone believe this?*

We will construct a short narrative for just four of these bullet points (Russia/Flynn, Bragg case, January 6, assassination attempt) and two "honorable mentions" to conclude. For starters, a highly classified binder assembled in 2016 on alleged Russian election interference went "missing" during Trump's last days in the White House. Supposedly the CIA is still searching for this file that somehow *vanished* from a safe!

> *The Federalist* reported on the Substack publication *Public and Racket*, indicating that the Obama-era CIA worked with international spy agencies to fabricate the Russian collusion hoax. The US intelligence agency asked the "Five Eyes" (i.e., global intelligence apparatus from the US, Canada, Australia, New Zealand, and the United Kingdom) to participate. Obama's CIA director, John Brennan identified twenty-six Trump associates for the Five Eyes to "bump," or contact and manipulate them. Unknown details about the FBI's investigation of the Trump campaign and raw intelligence related to the intelligence community's surveillance of the Trump campaign are in a ten-inch binder that Trump ordered to be declassified at the very end of his term.[5]

> Also, Susan Rice, Obama's National Security Advisor, later "unmasked" 300 persons on the Trump transition team.

The Democratic National Committee accelerated this hoax with money laundered through the law firm of Perkins Coie LLP on behalf of the Hillary Clinton presidential campaign. The now infamous "(Christopher) Steele Dossier" is a thirty-five-page compilation of unverified (*translation: false*) intelligence reports written between June and December 2016. They included various salacious allegations and suggestion that Russia was involved in getting Trump elected, or, as Clinton has continuously whined, about stopping her from getting elected. The report of special counsel (and former FBI director) Robert Mueller took twenty-two months to investigate, cost US taxpayers $32 million, and "ultimately found no collusion" between the Trump campaign and Russia.[6]

With regard to patriot and highly accomplished Lieutenant General Michael Flynn he represented a clear and present threat to the deep state. Under the newly forming Trump administration he was appointed National Security Advisor. (Previously he had served as intelligence chief of the JSOC in Iraq and director of the Defense Intelligence Agency.) His knowledge, experience, patriotic commitment and hutzpah would certainly expose the complicity of the cabal and especially high-ranking members of the previous administration(s). "They" (and they still must be fully revealed in the days ahead) concocted a bogus accusation related to a phone call he had with Russian ambassador Sergey Kislyak. It was a coordinated, swift public "assignation by narrative". He understandably pleaded guilty when the "blob" threatened to imprison his son in an "off the record" squeeze play. I highly recommend you watch his 2024 release of the movie, *Flynn: Deliver the truth, whatever the cost*. These are a few excerpts. "Understanding the government corruption of the General Michael Flynn story, if you understand what happened to him you start to peel back the curtain on everything. The General Flynn story is actually the foundational story that America needs to understand the truth of what has occurred in our government and the mounting corruption since then. The Flynn's pulled together, the American people can pull together because if we pull together and we drive this darkness out, then we can help the whole world."

With regard to the Bragg/Merchan case, these are excerpts from a report from the House Judiciary Committee released on April 25, 2024. The title of this report is as telling as the content: *An Anatomy of a Political Prosecution: The Manhattan District Attorney's Office Vendetta against President Donald J. Trump.*

> The New York County District Attorney's Office's (DANY) multi-year investigation into former President Donald J. Trump is unprecedented. As revealed in former Special Assistant District Attorney Mark F. Pomerantz's self-serving book, *People vs. Trump: An Insider's Account.* Since at least 2018, the DANY has weaponized the criminal justice system, scouring every aspect of President Trump's personal life and business affairs, going back decades, in the hopes of finding some legal basis—however far-fetched, novel or convoluted—to bring charges against him. When one legal theory would not pan out, instead of discontinuing its politically motivated investigation, the DANY simply pivoted to a new theory, constantly searching for a crime—any crime— to prosecute President Trump. . . . Pomerantz's book described as a 300-page exercise in score settling and scorn, revealed the extent to which the DANY (and District Attorney Alvin Bragg) investigation of President Trump was politically motivated. Pomerantz described his eagerness to investigate President Trump, writing that he was delighted to join an unpaid group of lawyers advising on the Trump investigation, and joking that salary negotiations had gone great because he would have paid to join the investigation.[7]

This author has a unique personal perspective, since Mark Pomerantz and I graduated, three years apart, from Wolcott (CT) High School. Known for his cleverness, among other traits, his nickname then was "Sharky," which now holds greater significance.

In this sham case, along with the engineered verdict on May 30, 2024 under conflicted Judge Juan Merchan, who should have recused himself, it was no surprise to many of us watching. Why have members of this prosecuting team had multiple visits to the White House? Why is a #3 Department of Justice official brought into a civil case at a state level court to directly assist this case? Why was "acting judge" Juan Merchan, *clearly conflicted*, chosen for this case instead of one of the twenty-four permanent judges in the Southern District of New York? As Ralph Reed, chairman of the Faith and Freedom Coalition, was quoted in the article "10 Evangelical Reactions to Trump's Guilty Verdict: A Very Sad Day":

"Today's verdict is as shameful as it was predictable. The entire process was nakedly partisan from the start, with New York's leftist prosecutor campaigning on taking down President Trump. The deck only continued to be stacked as the judge permitted prejudicial testimony, prohibited the defense from offering evidence to counter the prosecution's bogus charges, especially on federal campaign law, and then instructed the jury in a way that all but guaranteed a guilty verdict. No honest observer believes this trial was based on justice or fairness—it was based on hatred for Donald Trump, revenge for his successful conservative presidency, and a desperate desire to derail his campaign."[8]

Specific to the "deep state" and January 6 - America needs more bold patriots like Kash Patel and Julie Kelly. I commend to your reading Patel's *Government Gangsters: The Deep State, the Truth, and the Battle for Our Democracy*, and Kelly's *January 6: How Democrats Used the Capital Protest to Launch a War on Terror against the Political Right*.

> What exactly is this Deep State? Some are elected leaders. Others are yellow journalists in the media who serve as peddlers of propaganda and disinformation at the behest of the ruling elites. Still others are Big Tech tycoons and actors affiliated with non-governmental organizations who carry water for the Democrat Party and the radical left (and) members of the unelected federal bureaucracy who think they have the right to rule America, not Congress or the president. . . . At first glance, they can seem to be everywhere and nowhere all at the same time. . . . The Deep State is the politicization of core American institutions and the federal governmental apparatus who acting through networks of networks, disregard objectivity, weaponize the law, spread disinformation, spurn fairness, or even violate their oaths of office for political and personal gain, all at the expense of equal justice and American national security.[9]

Regarding the January 6 insurrection hoax let me encourage you to locate the *Epoch Times* original documentary *The Real Story of Jan. 6*. I previously referenced the Julie Kelly book and the still emerging evidence, that when fully exposed, will paint a completely different picture. The outcome will be in juxtaposition to Impeachment #2.

> January 6th was not an insurrection. It was not a coup. It was not an assault by domestic terrorists on our democracy. January 6 was a completely avoidable tragedy and anyone who broke the law that day should face the consequences for their actions after an impartial investigation and fair trial. But what we're witnessing now are sham investigations in a two-tiered system of justice, lying to our faces with one purpose: to destroy the truth. The unholy trinity of the Deep State, Big Tech and the Fake News Mafia have gone into overdrive to spread falsehoods and suppress the truth about what happened that day. [10]

There are some important facts about January 6 that readers should be aware of:

- FBI whistleblowers testify that there were at least two dozen undercover agents in the crowd, involved in exacerbating agitation. I refer you to an online article by Marcus Allen, FBI staff operations specialist, titled, "Total Vindication for FBI Whistleblower Who Questioned [FBI Director Christopher] Wray's Narrative of January 6."[11]
- Days before January 6, Trump had requested the presence of the National Guard. His request was denied by both the Speaker of the House and the mayor of Washington DC.
- There is video evidence that some being prosecuted by the Department of Justice actually tried to stop violence and urge peacefulness among the crowd that day. And there is new information indicating that a fake "bomb" was planted outside of the vice president's residence as an additional act of violence, on hold, in case it was needed.
- Despite countless media reports that a police officer was bludgeoned to death with a fire extinguisher, this is false.
- The cleverly populated January 6 Committee hid exculpatory evidence—i.e., evidence exonerating Trump—and after their sham hearings were over, they destroyed evidence. Including taped interviews with most of the prosecutors of the various Trump indictments.

- Liz Cheney and her committee falsely claimed they had "no evidence" to support Trump officials' request that the White House had asked for 10,000 National Guard troops. In fact, an earlier transcribed interview conducted by the committee included precisely that evidence from a key source. The interview, which Cheney attended and personally participated in, was suppressed from public release until March 2024. Cheney frequently points skeptics of her investigation to the Government Publishing Office website that posted, she said, "transcripts, documents, exhibits and our meticulously sourced 800-plus-page final report." However, transcripts of fewer than half of the one thousand interviews the committee claims it conducted are posted on that site. It is unclear how many of the hidden transcripts include exonerating information suppressed by the committee. [12]

Here are a few questions to ponder regarding the assassination attempt on the 45th president of the United States, and leading contender for #47 which took place in Butler, PA on July 13, 2024. Why have all the denied requests for additional secret service protection on Trump events or at Mara Lago not been publicly released? Why was the building on which the shooter fired, not manned by appropriate personnel and with inadequate lines of communication between the secret service and local law enforcement? Why was the shooting site, now covered with the blood of the deceased shooter, scrubbed so quickly and his body cremated before autopsies and other information was properly disseminated? Why after 1,000 FBI interviews has no motive been determined? Why did this "apparent" loner, 20-year-old have three encrypted foreign bank accounts? Of course, there is no government collusion? Another media hyped conspiracy theory!

Now for two "honorable mentions" (impeachment/assassination attempt). One must give Nancy Pelosi credit for shrewd and devious political acumen. The first impeachment of President Donald Trump occurred on December 18, 2019. On that date, the House of Representatives adopted two articles of impeachment against Trump: abuse of power and obstruction of Congress. On February 5, 2020, the Senate voted to acquit Trump on both articles of impeachment. Contributing issues included that Trump purportedly threatened to withhold military aid to Ukraine and extended an invitation to the White House for Ukrainian president Volodymyr Zelenskyy in order to influence him to investigate Joe Biden. This author anticipates that Joseph Robinette Biden still has some 'splainin' to do, relative to his own involvement in Ukraine (and a few other countries)! The second impeachment of President Donald Trump occurred on January 13, 2021. The House of Representatives adopted one article of impeachment against Trump for "incitement of insurrection," stating that he had incited the January 6 attack of the US Capitol, an alleged insurrection.

Finally, we briefly consider some of the extracurricular business dealings of Joe Biden and the larger involvement of his family members. Whatever corrupt practices Joe Biden did or did not do—are still a matter of investigation. *Again, God's judgment will be rendered at a time still to be determined, but presumably after the publishing of this book.* The following excerpts are the April 2, 2024 transcript from the press conference by James Comer, Chairman of the House Oversight Committee.

> The investigation reveals a family that engaged with some of America's most powerful adversaries planning to sell one of the largest sources of cobalt for electric vehicles in the world to the Chinese. For example, the Bidens flourished and became millionaires by simply offering access to the family among dozens of shell companies that Biden set up.

> There were millions of dollars of wire transfers, flights on Air Force 2 to conduct personal business meetings with heads of state, all the while Joe Biden was aware of what was happening, while he turned a blind eye. Many transactions related to these businesses have raised red flags and U.S. banks. A Suspicious Activity Report or SAR is a document a bank must file with the Treasure Department when a transaction is suspected to be related to money laundering or fraud or other types of criminal activity. According to media reports the Biden family accumulated over 150 SARS. One SAR generated by an American bank to the Treasury Department connects Hunter Biden and his business associates to international human trafficking, among other illegal activities [minutes 2:00–3:07].

The SARs and bank records in the new Congress as part of our investigation have evidence that the finances, credit cards and bank accounts of Hunter Biden and Joe Biden were co-mingled if not share. And on some accounts at least red flags were raised by banks to the account owner or owners indicating suspicious or illegal activity. One of Hunter's closest associates, Eric Sherwin, was accessing Joe Biden's money and writing checks to reimburse Hunter. Sherwin arranged the Biden's international deals around the world at the same time he was a frequent visitor to the White House and Joe Biden during the Obama Administration visiting close to 30 times and sometimes with international business partners and Hunter. According to Hunter's calendar Sherwin was also the president of Hunter's company and was appointed by President Obama to a position in the administration after an apparent falling out with Sherwin. Hunter began coordinating business himself and increasingly the deals brought in Joe Biden as a direct equity holder. One of these deals involves a sale of American natural gas to China. Evidence suggests Joe Biden had a 10% equity stake through his son [minutes 3:56–5:03].[13]

These are further *allegations and investigations* in process by the House Oversight Committee and other entities—with results to be determined:

- Joe Biden was "the big guy" with a 10% stake in various dealings that Hunter Biden was involved in and paid handsomely for. Records indicated money was generated from deals in China—BHR, China—CEFC, Russia, Kazakhstan, Romania, and Ukraine. Tax evasion, anyone?
- Following subpoenas to obtain Biden family associates' bank records, Chairman Comer issued subpoenas for Hunter and James Biden's personal and business bank records. The House Oversight Committee has identified more than twenty shell companies and uncovered how the Bidens and their associates raked in more than $24 million dollars between 2015–2019 by selling Joe Biden as "the brand." Financial records obtained show Hunter Biden's business account, Owasco PC, received payments from Chinese-state linked companies and other foreign nationals and companies.

- The Biden family members who received foreign money as a result of these activities included Hunter Biden, James Biden (Joe's brother), Sara Biden (sister-in-law), Hallie Biden (daughter-in-law), Kathleen Biden (daughter-in-law), Melissa Biden (daughter-in-law), two nieces or nephews, and one grandchild.
- The Hunter Biden laptop was originally purported not to be his. *Then* the contents were alleged to have been created (somehow) by Russians disinformation. A letter from fifty-one former intelligence officials was published just days leading up to the 2020 presidential election, warning that reporting about the laptop's contents "has all the classic earmarks of a Russian information operation." And today there is no question that the laptop is, in fact, Hunter's because it was used in his felony gun case as evidence by the defense.
- The DNC, in close coordination with the lying media, continues to loudly proclaim that there is no connection between Joe Biden and his son's activities. Oh, really? There is a news clip of Joe bragging about getting the Ukraine prosecutor fired who was investigating Hunter's Burisma holdings dealings, by withholding aid to Ukraine—the very "crime" Trump was alleged to have engaged in. Why was Moscow's former first lady Yelena Baturina and fellow oligarch Vladimir Yevtushenkov left off the US sanctions list? Why was one of Biden's first acts as president to cancel the FBI task force investigating China? Why are most of Hunter's business partners in jail: two Americans, one Chinese (one has "disappeared"), one Romanian and Ukrainian? The House Oversight Committee has records from four out of twelve banks related to the twenty shell companies the Bidens created. The investigations continue.

With the synchronous howling of the corporate media, the Democratic party, and of course the Biden/Harris administration proclaim that there is *no evidence* of wrong doing. Once again, time will tell.

Treason

This author believes that actionable evidence of treason *will be* identified, documented, and adjudicated sometime in the near future against multiple senior elected officials in our government, senior military officers, senior directors of the intelligence agencies—and especially, the hidden collusion between the three. Treason is most fundamentally understood as betraying one's own country. Treason begins with an obligation of allegiance followed by wrongful intent and action to violate that obligation. This is a very short section—because I am not attempting to build a case or bring evidence in a public forum like a book. Nor am I suggesting anyone in particular will be exposed for treason. My belief is grounded in the prophetic warnings you have already read. And in this regard, the courts of heaven will be the determining jurisdiction from which civil exposure and judgment will follow.

But there is one additional caution I submit—which we have been warned about by our own intelligence agencies. Some very bad people have crossed our border, and America will experience multiple cataclysmic events. People will be killed. Our slumbering populous will finally awaken to the premeditated and pervasive perversion, corruption, and treason that has occurred! One specific scenario *which is likely* is an EMP or other type of coordinated attack on America's electrical grid or other infrastructures. The outcome of our national elections will result in conflict and times of great stress. God will bring us through this tumultuous time!

CHAPTER 4

For Those Who Discern

WHILE FLYING INTO Ninoy Aquino International Airport in Manila, Philippines to attend a hospital and college foundation board I served on, I was working on the research notes for this chapter. This was my last journal entry as we landed: *Prophecy, validated and consistent with Scripture, is the foretelling—after all of the enemy's lies, deception, schemes and opposition to everything the Creator has established—which confirms that Satan is defeated for all time and eternity. God wins!*

In this chapter we will briefly reference four groupings of information regarding the prophetic:

1. The centrality of the people and nation of Israel to salvation history
2. Basic definitions
3. The Lord Jesus return, and events foretold in Revelation for the end of the age
4. Declarations from four contemporary prophetic voices

§   §   §   §   §

In the midst of the perilous times in which we live—a time of false Christs, wars and rumors of wars, ethnic tensions, famines, pestilences, and earthquakes all increasing in a labor-pain-like progression—we need to remember that we are living during a very privileged season of church history. In Daniel 12:4, the prophet was told to seal up the book until the time of the end. And today, we live in that time, during which what Daniel— and other prophets like Ezekiel, Jeremiah, and Isaiah—wrote is no longer sealed or shut up from our understanding. . . . We are living in an era of unprecedented prophetic activity and clarity.[1]

At the very core of biblical prophecy is the importance of understanding the lineage of Abraham, Isaac, and Jacob whose name God changed to Israel

(Gen. 35:9b–10) The *ethnos,* from the Greek root (*ethne,* i.e., the people or nation) of Israel is central to salvation history.[2] God chose this people and therefore promised He would preserve them according to His will and for a divine purpose. After the Roman Empire sent armies to wipe out Israel and its temple, dedicated to the worship of the only true God, the people were scattered among many *ethnos* until May 14, 1948, the establishment of the modern political state of Israel. When the first prime minister, David Ben-Gurion, read their new Declaration of Independence, those who discern biblical prophecy understood the enormous magnitude of this moment, as proclaimed in Ezekiel 36:8–10 affirming, "My people Israel . . . for indeed I am for you."

The *ethnos* of Israel began to be referred to as "Jews" during the Babylonian captivity, because the majority in those difficult days were from the tribe of Judah. As identified in Chapter 1 God declares, by the word of his mouth, the existence of all things with exact precision. The progression of the (now) state of Israel, the eventual return of the lost tribes of Israel, and the *relatively* soon (we believe) rebuilding of the third temple on the present-day Temple Mount, over which the current Dome of the Rock exists, is central to biblical prophecy. You cannot understand the last days if you do not realize that the regathering of the Jews back into their national homeland is paramount foretelling in Scripture. And seventy years to the day, space between May 14, 2018, the United States under the Trump administration, followed by other Western allies, recognized Jerusalem as the capital of Israel, another important prophetic marker!

What is prophecy? A nonsectarian definition is, "a claim of what the future will be like, which is not based on any ordinary source of information."[3] A simple, but fundamentally sound understanding of prophecy from a biblical perspective is, 'a message from God' and a prophet as 'someone who gives declarations from God'. The Hebrew word for prophet is *nabi,* derived form an action verb which means to 'bubble forth" like a fountain. Our English word prophet comes from the Greek *prophetes,* which means 'to speak for another, especially one who speaks for God.[4]

There are eighty-eight prophets mentioned in the Bible. Of these, sixty-three are in the Old Testament and twenty-five are in the New Testament. The first reference in the Bible of the existence and purpose of a prophet is found in Deuteronomy 18:18–19: "I will raise up for them a prophet like you from among their fellow Israelites, and I will put my words in his mouth. He will tell them everything I commanded him. I myself will call to account anyone who does not listen to my words that the prophet speaks in my name."

There are five major prophetic books in the Bible referred to as the Major Prophets: Isaiah, Jeremiah, Lamentations (also authored by Jeremiah), Ezekiel and Daniel. "Christianity counts the Twelve Prophets as twelve individual prophetic books, and refers to them as the *dodekapropheton*, Greek for twelve prophets, or simply as The Minor Prophets, indicating their relative length when compared to the Major Prophets." These are Hosea, Joel, Amos, Obadiah, Jonah, Micah, Nahum, Habakkuk, Zephaniah, Haggai, Zechariah, and Malachi.[5]

Forgive this elementary level of explanation. There are libraries full of erudite sources with extensive details, and various positions of apologetics. Again, we are surveying a complex area of scholarship specifically for the purpose of establishing an integrated context to understand these perilous times and how we can embrace freedom.

There are approximately 2,500 prophecies in the Bible, of which about two thousand have been fulfilled *to the letter*, with no errors or even minor percentages not coming to pass. The remaining five hundred are unfolding rapidly as the days go by.[6] Those who are spiritually discerning can *feel* that the fulfillment of what was foretold is all around us. In the middle eight chapters we will describe these "mountains of trouble" in our communities, our nation, and in the world, which is also direct evidence of prophetic foretelling. Evil, in these end days, is abundantly present, as predicated.

> God is not the only one, however, who uses forecasts of future events to get people's attention. Satan does too. Through clairvoyants (like Jeanne Dixon and Edgar Cayce), mediums, spiritists, and others, come remarkable predictions, though rarely with more than 60 percent accuracy, never with total accuracy. . . . The acid test for identifying a prophet of God is recorded in Moses in Deuteronomy 18:21–22. God's prophets, as distinct from Satan's spokesmen, are 100 percent accurate in their predictions. There is no room for error.[7]

Biblical prophecy began after the split of a unified Israel under Davidic rule in the ninth century BCE. The northern kingdom remained as Israel and the southern kingdom was called Judah. In broad terms the majority of prophecy in this period did not focus on predicting the future. Rather, much of Old Testament prophecy addressed social and political issues of that day such as social justice, public morality, human sexuality, religious idolatry (such as Baal worship), and judgment for violating the laws of God. But embedded in them also were expressions of mercy and encouragement to turn back to God. The most critical corpus of prophetic expression was the foretelling of the (first) coming of the Messiah. There is, and had to be, explicit descriptions of his lineage and the covenants and promises that accompanied his coming.

The next core grouping of prophecies addresses the return or second coming of the Lord Jesus as both King and Judge. In this rapidly approaching event, he returns for his "bride"—those whose names are written in the book of life—and exercises righteous judgment upon those who rejected him. There are eighty-nine chapters in the Bible which foretell or describe the birth of Jesus, and 150 chapters where the primary topic is the return or second coming of the Lord.

The remaining prophecies, from the Revelation, have clear connectivity to key messages given through Old Testament prophets, and focus on these categories of foretelling: the church, the rapture, the tribulation, the millennium, the day of judgment, and heaven. In talking with a friend who did not have a solid understanding of Scripture, I asked if he had read the book of Revelation recently. "No," he said, "it's too scary. I just try to avoid it."

Some other common responses, from people with a similar level of Biblical knowledge, include:

> Yes, I read it, but it's just too confusing.

> I know the seven churches mentioned in Revelation were actual churches in literal cities in Asia Minor, but how does this apply and to whom is it addressing today in our diverse global Christian church?

All the symbolism—seven golden lampstands, seven stars, a being having the appearance of jasper and ruby with a rainbow that shines like an emerald; a sea of glass, living creatures with strange appearances, twenty-four elders, a lamb with seven horns and seven eyes; a white horse and a black horse, white robes, and seven trumpets and locusts and scorpions and a dragon and some creature with ten horns and seven heads . . . and *so much* death and destruction. What does it all mean?

I often respond with some attempted explanation, but it is a challenge. "Whoever has ears, let them hear" (Rev. 2:17). Many reading this book will most assuredly have more knowledge of the prophetic. You also understand that the assortment of friends above represents, frankly and unfortunately, a majority of Christians unfamiliar with the importance of prophecy.

What follows are five (arbitrary) selections from biblical prophecy.

- 2 Kings 2:3–11—A group of fifty prophets provided eyewitness account of what had been foretold about the day of Elijah's supernatural departure from earth.
- Jeremiah 31:38–40—2,600 years ago the exact location and construction of Jerusalem's nine suburbs was predicted for "the last days"—that is, in the time period of Israel's rebirth as a nation which took place in 1948—and that construction took place precisely as predicted.
- Micah 5:2—In approximately 700 BC, the tiny village of Bethlehem was identified as the birthplace of Israel's Messiah.
- Zechariah 11:12—In the fifth century BC it was foretold that the Messiah would be betrayed for thirty pieces of silver (the price of a slave) and that this money would be used to purchase the "potter's field."
- Malachi 4:5—This describes "the great and dreadful day of the Lord." Like the understanding of the "week" mentioned earlier, it is definitely not a twenty-four-hour period. Rather, it predicts seven years of tribulation.

How Then Shall We Live?

For those "cessationists" who believe that prophetic messages from God ended in the time of the book of Acts, you may wish to skip the last portion of this chapter, for you will automatically reject its validity. For those who embrace contemporary words of prophecy—*yes,* we must test the spirits to see that they are of God. *Yes,* there will be false prophets among us who must be discerned. *But also yes,* there are prophetic voices today through whom God speaks for our edification and instruction.

Four prophetic sources are quoted here. These messages are deeply valuable and germane for our time, but again due to space limitation, I reference shorter sections from longer prophetic messages each have given.

Apostolic Council of Prophetic Elders - Cindy Jacobs, Generals International, Red Oak, TX[8]

This encouraging but sobering communication was sent electronically on January 1, 2024: "We are excited to send you the compilation of the Word of the Lord for 2024 from the Apostolic Council of Prophetic Elders and Global Prophetic Consultation. 200 prophets from 32 nations met together and the following is a compilation of the words that we had consensus on for the new year."[9] A selection of excerpts follows.

- 2024: The Year of Shakings and Open Doors
- The ancient Prince of Persia is now flexing his muscles and wants to align the powers of darkness over the nations of Russia (the Bear) and China (the Dragon). We see Iran, Russia, China, and North Korea in alliances to redraw the map of the world territorially.
- We are issuing a worldwide call for "wartime" watchmen and women to fast and pray and be on the wall of the nations. Through the fervent prayers of many around the world, World War 3 has been averted for now—although it is tenuous.
- Many times, we ask ourselves as prophets, "What time is it?" It is time for the bridegroom to come out of the bridal chamber. And brides must wear combat boots (Joel 2:16). We see this literally happening in the war season today.

- Future wars will be on a technological level with not only drones, but robotic soldiers. War technology is going to seemingly advance with lightning speed.
- "For nation will rise against nation, and kingdom against kingdom. And there will be famines, pestilence, and earthquakes in various places" (Matthew 24:7). Matthew 24 is the roadmap for this season beginning in 2024.
- Lawlessness will become particularly rampant in the nations and will begin to turn into anarchy if not carefully prayed over by watchmen and women.
- As we are in the digital age, currencies will one day largely go digital. We are not to fear this as God will show us what to do in every economic season.
- "Mama bears," known for their fierceness against anyone who tries to hurt their children . . . now large and small gatherings of women are forming . . . to fight against their children being indoctrinated with nonbiblical truths and being taken over by government.
- God is cleaning house (requiring holiness and a clean heart) to make way for His glory to be released so that He can see a people walking in great resurrection power.
- The Lord spoke to us a theme of "Come Up Higher" in 2024. This is a season where God is calling us to build. Doors of influence, doors of opportunity, and doors to obtain wisdom are being opened . . . we must recognize and go through them.

Tim Sheets, Oasis Church, Middletown, OH[9]

Jeremiah 1:9-10 tells us that prophetic words that God puts in our mouth are empowered to uproot, pull down, destroy, and also plant and build up. . . . God's Word is alive. It is powerful. It accomplishes what He sent it forth to do. There are assignments in these words, as Isaiah 55 describes. These words are going to activate mighty angels. Thousands and thousands of saints are decreeing together for the purpose of God to be established and done. Wrap your faith in these words that God has given to me for about five years now.

I will now deal with the oppression of my people. I've heard their cry and I will break the hold of the task master's rule. Though they bow their necks in stubborn resistance I will harness them with nose rings and lead them to their place of destruction. Like oxen to the slaughter, I will pull them to their place of defeat. The words of their Pharoah will be as chaff in the winds as my angels of breakthrough scatter and shatter their influence in the land. For the King says, I am breaking open doors to freedom. I am revealing paths of liberty. I am breaking through with my power and I am ending the task master's rule. For you have seen the fireworks of your adversaries, now you will see the Spirit's fireworks. You will see the fire power of the *ekklesia*. It will not be fireworks of grandeur in the sky streaking and falling to the earth for show. No, it will be fireworks of explosive power, raining down upon thrones of iniquity. My fireworks will explode against demon princes. My fire power will explode preparing the way for my Kingdom's invasion of the earth. My power will explode against rulers of darkness. They can scatter, they can run but they can't hide. My warriors will find them. I'm coming to explode against and destroy the works of hell. This is not something I wish for. This is something I planned for.

Holy Spirit has now released weapons of war I have reserved for your time. New weapons are going off in the spirit realm. Hear the sound of air raid sirens. I will now move in great strength, positioning and aligning myself for aggressive movement upon the earth, says the Lord, for you will see the strong arm of your God as you have never seen before in your generation. Indeed, I am rising in my aggressive nature and I will show that I am the great one. I will show that from my throne is true and ultimate authority. I will show the weakness of those who rise to disdain me and disdain my people. For now, I will, says the Lord, release strategies upon the earth that indeed block the adversary's strategies.

Great revival fire will burn throughout the world as my greatest awakening now begins Regions and entire nations will become affected in my increasing Glory. My shaking will come. Walls, strongholds, obstacles of hell's fortification are going to be shaken down even as you, the people of God, are shaken free. My shakings will also open ancient wells of revival. I will shake open the capped wells of evangelism. I will shake open the ancient wells of healings, miracles and mighty deliverance. I will shake down the barricades to new roads. I declare, says the Lord, new roads, new inroads, new mantles, new vision, new harvest. Behold I do new things and you will see it spring forth. For the battle lines are drawn. The strategies are in place. Preparations have been made. And I will now gather my angel armies with my *ekklesia* armies in a unified coalition. The coalition of my willing, says the Lord. Those who run to battle not run from it. My earth and heaven armies will attack thrones of iniquity, thrones of idolatry, thrones of rebellion, thrones of witchcraft, thrones of humanism and anti-Christ demons. But I am releasing entire divisions of angel armies to go along and assist the decrees of my heirs. My greatest campaign, says the Lord, is now due and will come forth from the shaking. It will accelerate an alignment with my purpose and thrones of dominion of Washington, DC will come down.

Arise and roar *ekklesia*. Arise and roar *ekklesia*. Arise and fight. Arise and shine, indeed your light has come. Arise with great hope and display a heart that is not shaken. For I will perform my Word with zealous passion. Look not at the shaking, look at me, says the Lord and you will see the aggression of the Lord of Hosts. You will see the strong arm of the Lord. You will experience the aggression of heavens warriors, moving in unrelenting purpose on your behalf. And you will experience the presence of my Glory that advances my mightiness to protect, to save, to strengthen and change this nation . . . Millions of prodigals are about to come home. I am convinced some of the greatest apostles, pastors and ministers (are) in this new era.

Remember what God has said in difficult times like we are facing now in America, Non-sensical times, crazy times, ignorant times, doctrines of demons times, blasphemous times, unfair justice times, wickedness times, woke religious times. Never doubt in the dark what God has shown you in the light. Remember what God has promised. Remember his prophetic words. Remember those scriptures before darkness surrounds and before the enemy's attack. God is now bringing it to pass in very unique ways. However long it takes, our job is to arise and preside in the name of Jesus. The Word of God breaks that darkness up like a sledgehammer does to rocks according to Jeremiah 29:11. The Word of God is like a fire that burns things up. Arise and shine as the glory comes over us in greater measure. We are to arise and reflect the glorious power and the authority that we have been given by our King. We are not to stumble our way through the darkness. We are to stay focused on what God has said. His promises, His prophetic words will prepare us in advance for what is coming. His prophetic promises will warn us concerning inherent consequences when a nation turns away from God. They will prepare us to shelter from storms that wicked leaders cause. They provide understanding to uproot evil and to tear it down. They instruct us how to pray. Christ has promised I will anoint my *ekklesia* to prevail. The prevailing anointing will come. It requires us to stand in faith, to persevere. It requires a remnant standing in God's Word.

Diana Larkin, A Watchman's Journal, Jamestown, NC[10]

Resurrection Day is coming! As empires tumble, leaders fall and systems fail it is very important that you overcome fear of the future or fear of defeat by speaking my promise—Resurrection Day is coming. Keep rehearsing examples of death to life I've laid out for you in my Word. There is the opening and closing of the Red Sea, the calling forth to life of Lazarus, and the ultimate resurrection from death to life forever more of my Son. I can do it again. Are you afraid of lack? Remember how I fed the nation of Israel in the wilderness; Elijah at the stream when he was hiding from Jezebel, widows supernaturally provide for through Elijah and Elisha, and the feeding of the multitudes through my Son's hands. Am I able to protect and provide for my children when my judgements fall? Well, think about Noah and his family in the ark, Israel protected from my judgements in the land of Goshen, and Israel protected from Egypt and other surrounding enemies all the time they were in the wilderness. My son kept and protected as the enemy sought to take his life many times. When my son died it was because he gave his life away as a ransom for many. As the shakings come keep these words in your mouth, Resurrection Day is coming.

Rebellion against the most-high God has grown among the arrogant elite to a showdown between their gross evil and the light and goodness of my heart. Their darkness and rebellion have multiplied until they are flaunting it before the world and inviting open rebellion against Me. The weight of this gross evil is bearing down on my creation and the earth is groaning under the gross darkness. I have told you this season of rescue, judgement and justice will be like the Red Sea deliverance. The earth will shake as the children of light call forth my judgments and justice. You will see the earth respond by opening its mouth and swallowing up the wicked. And you will see them no more. My fire will break out and consume the wicked and their platforms. The evil foolishly called for this showdown because they were deceived into believing they could win. I have commissioned you, my army of light, to join me in this showdown. Come with your swords of truth, the high praises of God on your lips and demand as my sons and daughters that darkness and rebellion bow their knee and come under my judgement and justice. Declare light and life to arise over hearts and over your nation. The earth will respond to your warfare and it will swallow up the gross darkness at My command and release the clean and enduring fear of the Lord and an era of peace and plenty.

In the Courts of Heaven, I have rested my case against the empire of darkness. I have seen all their secret meetings and all the blueprints for bringing destruction death, and chaos. . . . These plans drip with hatred, greed and ruthlessness. Your cries for deliverance and for freedom were the grounds for bringing a case against the deep darkness. My special forces angels were assigned to uncover and expose hidden agendas. . . . Remember I have rested my case in Heaven, and its verdicts will be upheld on the earth. You will see dark to light—guaranteed.

Wanda Alger, Ways of Wisdom, Crossroads Community Church, Winchester, VA[11]

The way things have been done need to change. You can no longer walk as in days past. Are you paying attention to the lessons I am trying to teach you? Are you making the adjustments needed in the massive transformations about to occur? New systems are being created. Are you adjusting to the upgrades? New wine skins are being formed. Are you allowing me to stretch you? New leadership is emerging. Are you recognizing my anointing? New alignments are being created. Are you leaving the familiar and embracing the new? That which lies ahead has never been done before, has never been seen before. Do not limit my workings to a presidential election or a judgement on witchcraft in high places. Do not limit my power to overturning corruption or vindicating the accused. Though these will be necessary components in my dealings, my gaze is fixed beyond these markers. What I have purposed to do will be ground-breaking, mind-blowing, life-altering. Until now you have not had the capacity to imagine or even believe for the things about to take place. You have been hypnotized and immobilized by the enemy for decades. It has taken the past several years to break the spell and get your attention. At times I've put you in stealth mode in order to secretly lead you past the enemy's camp to give you a glimpse of the promised territory ahead. Much of what I have been accomplishing has been undetected on purpose.

We are moving into a period of collective intelligence and prayer. The Lord is taking the spotlight off of celebrity ministers and giving the platform to His people. He is doing a sovereign work in the collective. The Holy Spirit is taking center stage and ministering deeply among those who are pure of heart and hungry for His presence.

For those who discern, these words will resonate with your spirit. My sheep listen to my voice; I know them, and they follow me. (John 10:25).

Now we will investigate and document the manifold ways in which the enemy has deviously infiltrated every domain of our society. For those readers who may not know the origin of the term "seven mountains of societal influence," here is a brief summary. The term originated in 1975 when Bill Bright, founder of Campus Crusade for Christ (now CRU); and Loren Cunningham, founder of Youth with a Mission (YWAM) (and by some accounts, Francis Schaeffer, cofounder of the L'Abri community in Switzerland) *each* received a dream or impression from the Lord in approximately the same timeframe. The "take-away" is this - to truly transform any nation the gospel of Jesus Christ must permeate each of these seven major centers of influence—and the ekklesia must retake the domains that the enemy has stolen! We, the people of faith, *must* participate in and effectuate this change by focused, continuous intercessory prayer, in conjunction with discernment and strategy that has military precision.

Many people in America and other Western democratically governed countries are asking, "How did we get here? How did everything get turned upside down, and who is responsible?" The following chapters will shed some light on these questions!

TIMES OF PERIL—
Seven Mountains of Trouble (plus one)

CHAPTER 5

Mountain of Trouble—Religion (of Abrahamic origin)

Satan's intention is always diabolical, but until recently was mostly achieved in a stealthy manner. The gloves are off now! Anyone who is not catatonic or spiritually blinded is fully aware of the compromised and dangerous world in which we live. Yet, in keeping with God's plan, grace, and mercy, a final great outpouring of the Holy Spirit in our generation is being offered for repentance and revival. It comes in tandem with the acceleration of evil as the culmination of this age comes to its *designed* fulfillment.

We will begin each "mountain of trouble" in Chapters 5–11 with three poignant thoughts for "consideration" and end with three prayer points. As you read about many topics and current affairs remain attentive to the involvement of the spiritual realm. Satan has greater opportunity to create division and strife among us, unless we stay centered on the spiritual battle. May the Holy Spirit grant us increased discernment!

Consider this:

- Christians, especially new believers in countries hostile to Christianity, face more extreme persecution and death for their faith than in any other time in history.
- It is estimated that 95% of Christians in historically "Christian countries" have never shared their faith which led another person to a relationship with Jesus Christ.[1]
- Only 4% of Gen Z (15–25 years old) hold a biblical worldview and have the highest recorded affirmation for identifying as LGBT or other "queer identity," transgender, or non-binary.[2]

A term like "religion" encompasses a universe of different pathways. We can only briefly address a few points of comparison between the three Abrahamic religions: Judaism, Christianity, and Islam. Each anchors their origins on the life and faith journey of Abraham from Ur Kasdim (about two hundred miles southeast of present-day Baghdad). *Two of these faiths are connected and interdependent; one is a counterfeit.*

Nearly all cultures of the world retain "moral" laws identified from the beginning of recorded history. These were expressed first with Sumerian cuneiform symbols, and eventually words, during the period 2900–3400 BC in Mesopotamia, now modern-day Iraq, Iran, Kuwait, Turkey, and Syria. In close historical proximity, the hieroglyphics of the Egyptians also identified common moral laws. Subsequently, each major people group in every area of the world developed similar moral laws. Romans 2:15 reminds us that God's laws are written on our hearts, and that our conscience also bear witness regardless of time in history or location on the planet. This is further evidence of the grand design and original intent of our Creator!

It is actually uncanny how similar moral laws are across cultures—in ancient China, Babylon, Egypt, Greece, and Rome; across Anglo-Saxon and American Indian culture; through Buddhist, Hindu, Christian, and Muslim sacred writings. All basically agree in this area. Oxford scholar and professor C. S. Lewis gives evidence of this common moral law summarized below:

1. Don't do harm to another human being by what you do or say (The Golden Rule).
2. Honor your father and mother.
3. Be kind toward brothers and sisters, children and the elderly.
4. Do not have sex with another person's spouse.
5. Be honest in all your dealings (don't steal).
6. Do not lie.
7. Care for those weaker or less fortunate.
8. Dying to self is the path to life.[3]

Keep this in mind as you read individual examples in the following chapters of how the enemy has controverted God's intent and has incrementally moved people into deeper and deeper ignorance of God's immutable truth, resulting in an increasing willingness to ignore His laws. The Father desires for us to live in freedom and in intimate relationship with Him.

Jews and Muslims

We have already established the centrality, the divinely appointed covenantal relationship, of the Jewish *ethnos* to God and therefore to salvation history. We Christians are grafted into the root of Jesse (Isa. 11:10; Rom. 11:11 ff) *because of* them. The political nation of Israel also has a definitive role in the fulfillment of what has been foretold. There has not been any other people group on the planet that has been the focus of so much death and destruction over centuries. Why? Because Satan kills, steals, and destroys in a futile attempt to thwart God's plan. Therefore, those who seek to destroy the Jewish people do so under the dominion of this same enemy. What follows are various declarations made by adherents of Islam:

- "It will be a war of annihilation. It will be a momentous massacre in history that will be talked about like the massacres of the Mongols or the Crusades."—Azzam Pasha, Secretary-General of the Arab League, in 1948 after the UN recognized the newly established nation of Israel. They were attacked simultaneously by Egypt, Transjordan, Iraq, Syria, Lebanon, Saudi Arabia and Yemen . . . and were defeated.

- "Our battle with the Jews is long and dangerous, requiring all dedicated efforts until the enemy is overcome and the victory of Allah descends. The complete destruction of Israel is an essential condition for the liberation of Palestine and the establishment of a theocratic state on Islamic Sharia law. Jihad is the methodology, and death for the sake of Allah is its most coveted desire"—from the thirty-six Articles of the Charter of Harakat al-Muqawama al-Islamiyya (Hamas) aka The Resistance Movement, closely affiliated with the Society of the Muslim Brotherhood (translated by Muhammad Maqdsi, 1990). Remember, Islam is responsible for 9/11 and 10/7!

- Every published photo in Iranian media and its proxies, after the death of one of its leaders, includes the gold Dome of the Rock in the background, signaling "on the way to Jerusalem"—the complete destruction of Israel.

- "We cannot, in exchange for money or projects, give up Palestine and our weapons. We will not give up the resistance. We will not recognize Israel. Palestine must stretch from the [Jordan] river to the [Mediterranean] sea."—Ismail Haniyeh, political leader of Hamas, 2020.

In 1939, amid rising international tensions, Führer and Reich Chancellor Adolf Hitler told the German public and the world vis-a-vis his Reichstag speech that the outbreak of war would mean "the annihilation of the Jewish race in Europe." He did his best to make good on this promise.

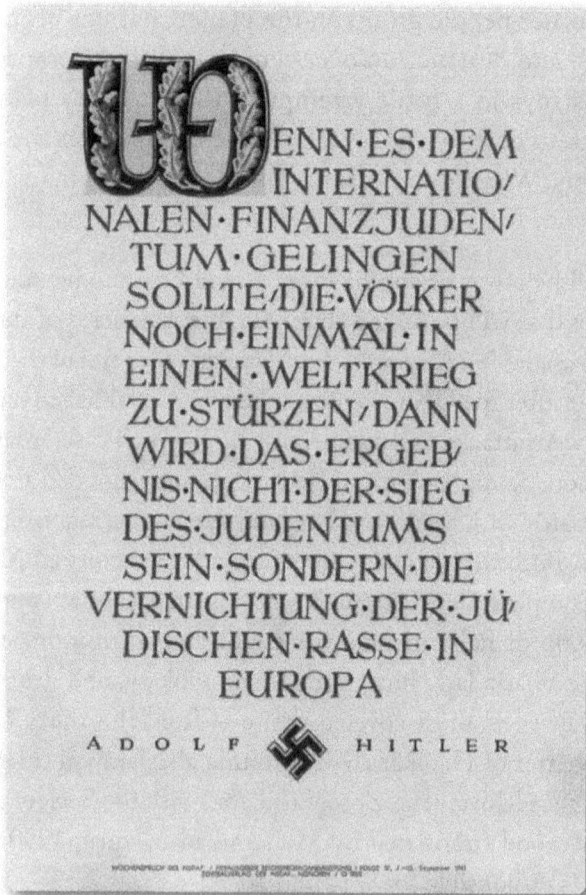

WENN·ES·DEM INTERNATIO/ NALEN·FINANZJUDEN/ TUM·GELINGEN SOLLTE/DIE·VÖLKER NOCH·EINMAL·IN EINEN·WELTKRIEG ZU·STÜRZEN/DANN WIRD·DAS·ERGEB/ NIS·NICHT·DER·SIEG DES·JUDENTUMS SEIN·SONDERN·DIE VERNICHTUNG·DER·JÜ/ DISCHEN·RASSE·IN EUROPA

ADOLF HITLER

Nazi Poster

Antisemitism, also called "the longest hatred," has persisted in many forms for more than two thousand years. The Bible chronicles persecution and scattering among the nations of the Jews. What persona perpetrated this, and for what reason has this existed? It is clear that *the* enemy, is responsible. Examples are well documented throughout history and the *reason* has been identified. This is why "the two-state solution" will never be the solution, because particular followers of Allah want to destroy Israel!

UN Resolution 181 on November 29, 1947, recognizing Israel as a sovereign nation, is a seminal moment in salvation history. It brings to pass the prophetic words of Isaiah 66:8, 10: "Who has ever heard of such things? . . . Can a country be born in a day or a nation brought forth in a moment? Yet no sooner is Zion in labor than she gives birth to her children. . . . Rejoice with Jerusalem and be glad for her." And Genesis 12:3 clearly indicates, "I will bless those who bless you, and whoever curses you I will curse; and all peoples on earth will be blessed through you."

This is a story about two brothers, whose destinies have now affected billions of people. Firstborn Esau settled in Petra with the Edomites, of whom the lineage of Palestinians today belongs and the larger Islamic world is fixated. Second born Jacob, whose lineage is the Israelites, settled in Jerusalem, to which the greater Judeo-Christian world is conjoined. Genesis 27:39-41 paints the sobering picture of the providence of this story: "His father Isaac answered him [Esau], 'Your dwelling will be away from the earth's richness, away from the dew of heaven above. You will live by the sword and you will serve your brother. But when you grow restless, you will throw his yoke from off your neck.' Esau held a grudge against Jacob because of the blessing his father had given him." Malachi 1:1-5 adds salt to the wound, which still festers in the twenty-first century, "A prophecy: The word of the LORD to Israel through Malachi. I have loved you, says the LORD. But you ask, 'How have you loved us?' 'Was not Esau Jacob's brother?' declares the LORD, 'Yet I have loved Jacob, but Esau I have hated, and I have turned his hill country into a wasteland and left his inheritance to the desert jackals.'" And so, this intractable enmity remains to this day.

Psalm 83:3-5 speaks of the ongoing hatred of people who openly oppose the Jewish people: "With cunning they conspire against your people; they plot against those you cherish. 'Come,' they say, 'let us destroy them as a nation, so that Israel's name is remembered no more.'" Verses 6–8 continue with a listing of these people groups (now nations): Edom and Moab (Jordan), Hagrites (Syria and Egypt), Byblos and Tyre (Lebanon), Assyria (Turkey), Ammon (Iraq), Amalek and Philistia (Gaza and Palestinians), and the Ishmaelites (the larger Arab, now Muslim, world). And while this particular scripture does not mention Persia (Iran), they lead the active and aggressive demonstrations of vehement hatred for the Jews and the nation of Israel.

One of these perpetual haters is Hamas and they are in the Bible! The Hebrew word for Hamas is *chamac*. It means sinful violence, evil. Hamas, used as both a noun and verb, appears sixty-seven times in the Bible. More specifically, the word *ḥāmās* in the Old Testament is used almost always in connection with sinful violence. It does not refer to the violence of natural catastrophes; it is often a descriptor for extreme wickedness. Here are just three Scripture references. In the days of Noah, God saw the earth was filled with violence (*ḥāmās*), so he sent a flood, "for the earth is filled with violence (*ḥāmās*) through them. Behold, I will destroy them and the earth" (Gen. 6:13); "But Egypt will be desolate, Edom a desert waste, because of violence (*ḥāmās*) done to the people of Judah, in whose land they shed innocent blood" (Joel 3:19); "Because of the violence against your brother Jacob, you will be covered with shame; you will be destroyed forever" (Obad. 10).

This is also a story of a fraudulent imitation, a grand deception of El's original intent. There are today fifty-seven majority Muslim countries. The largest branch is the Sunni at 1.5 billion people. The Shia are comprised of 240–340 million people. And there are fifty sects within Islam, with a smaller total representation. Like the adherents in every major religion, they fully believe in what they believe.

It is important, also, to understand *why* no Islamic countries are willing to extend a welcome to their Palestinian brothers suffering for decades in Gaza.

> The purpose of Islamic migration, known as *hijrah*, is the expansion of Islam through emigration . . . to immigrate in the cause of Allah is considered in Islam to be a highly meritorious

act. "I charge you with five of what Allah has charged me with to assemble, to listen, to obey, to immigrate and to wage Jihad for the sake of Allah" [quote from the Haddith—al-Kāfi, Vol 1, Book 4]. Learn from the crisis in Europe, where Islamic supremacists who have settled there have a clear objective: to uphold their loyalty to Islam while simultaneously enhancing their influence and control and undermining Western laws and values. Some of these demands include ensuring the availability of Halal foods, advocating for courts to operate based on Islamic Sharia law rather than local statutes, avoiding the recognition of Christian holidays, eliminating Holocaust education, permitting Muslim women to wear the niqab, covering their faces in public, requesting permission for child brides and the sexual mutilation of young girls, polygamy (and more). Muslim migrants do not want to assimilate into Western host countries; their aim is to transform those nations into Islamic entities. They don't need to use force to achieve this; and they are content with a gradual process, as the Quran encourages patience. Muammar Qaddafi, the former Libyan president, once remarked, "We Muslims don't need to use force against Europe because our emigration and high birth rates will accomplish our objective."[4]

Let me emphasize this point: lies, counterfeits, delusions, fraudulent imitations, falsehoods, all originate from *the enemy*, Satan. It is important that we love people of other faiths and pray for them. We must do this also with people of other political parties, with woke corporate heads, with compromised government officials—actually, everyone who does not understand or follow a biblical belief system. They are not the enemy. But *the enemy* knows this divides us!

For my primarily Christian readership, understanding what you know of Scripture—see how amazing is the lying lair of this forever loser. These are a few bullet-point of Islamic eschatology which originates from two predominant sources: the Quran, and the Sunnah as documented in the Hadith.

- Judgment Day will be preceded by apocalyptic signs including: 1} immorality, homosexuality, satanic music, alcohol abuse, tyrannical rulers, lying, cheating and violence including murder; 2) unnatural phenomenon like earthquakes, famine, the sun rising in the west, deluges of rain.

- The appearance of satanic evils including the Antichrist (called the Dajjal), Gog, and Magog. This supreme evil being is blind in one eye and will deceive the starving masses, *especially the Jews.*

- The arrival of two messianic saviors: the Mahdi (the Guided One) and Jesus (the Prophet). The Mahdi will defeat the Dajjal, reestablish Islamic law, fill the world with justice, and put an end to Christians' misconceptions about Jesus being the Son of God. Jesus returns to *help* the Mahdi kill the Dajjal, and they rule and reign together for a time until the Judgment Day.

- Oh yes, and there is a final battle—but this one is between those faithful Muslims and the infidels of the west. Hmm . . . the infidels of "the west" didn't exist when this was written.

I end this section with a true story. Before the Taliban retook control of Kabul and the remainder of Afghanistan, I called an Afghan friend of mine (and will keep his name anonymous) to ask if he felt endangered and whether would he like me to help him get out of the country. His answers were yes and yes, particularly since he had worked for multiple western NGOs. I contacted another US-based friend, a retired special operations military veteran, and he agreed to assemble a team. It was a truly cloak-and-dagger extraction. With his wife and three young children, they left their home, car, documents, and virtually all belongings. They took only a throwaway phone and some extra clothing and toiletries, as if they were visiting relatives. We had them board a public bus for a grueling ten-hour ride, through three checkpoints, to Kandahar. Some creative activity got them across the border to Pakistan, where a waiting transition team got this party of five to a safe house then moved them carefully to Islamabad. I raised funds for all of this and personally submitted their complex SIV (special immigrant visa) application.

We next got them to Germany and on April 2, 2024—after receiving approval from the Chief of Mission, US Embassy in Kabul, and logistics details through the National Visa Center in New Hampshire—*they have now started their life in what his compatriots call The Great Satan!* Ironically, it was the same week that *some* news media picked up pro-Palestinian demonstrators in Dearborn, Michigan shouting "death to America"—now students at nearly every secular university are doing the same. Every single one of the wonderful people who prayed, funded, and risked their lives for this family were Christians. One of them, a Christian convert from Islam, still has to this day three "fatwas" over his head with the threat of death. My friend is a devout Muslim.

So, what is my role now? I am *telling* him about Jesus' love for him and his family, but I am doing so after *exhibiting* love. We *must* remember who the true enemy is—and fight with spiritual weapons!

Christians

The word "Christian" and its true essence are understood by the faith community. The "world," however, is replete with misconceptions and misrepresentations.

There is no point in attempting to define a "Christian," the "church," or people of "faith." It's vitally important, of course, but that could not possibly be accomplished here. We assume most readers are part of the body of believers in the risen Savior. Our purpose is to identify some of the markers of infiltration of the enemy in juxtaposition to the will and purposes of God.

We start with two people who could not be more diametrically opposite in their faith orientation and the results of their life's work. "You will know them by their fruits" (Matt. 7:16, NKJV). Only God knows our hearts, and He is the ultimate judge. Every person who has ever lived, past or present, will fall into one of two categories. *There isn't a third option.* Based on the choices and decisions we make in life, we will either live with Him for eternity or be banished from His presence for eternity. Of course, He will deal mercifully with those who did not have the capacity in life to choose, born or preborn. God said, "Before I formed you in the womb I knew you" (Jer. 1:5a, NKJV).

Reinhard Bonnke, until his death in 2019, was a German evangelist and extraordinary kingdom ambassador in Africa, ministering in the power of the Holy Spirit with his team from Christ for All Nations through gospel crusades and healing ministry. He embodied the application of absolute truth based on the Word of God.

Paul, faced the agnostics and Stoics of Athens and said, "*Truly,*
these times of ignorance God overlooked, but now commands all men
everywhere to repent" (Acts 17:30). Therefore, he wrote to Timothy,
"Our Savior Jesus Christ . . . has abolished death and brought life and
immortality to light through the gospel." In Romans 1:22, Paul also
talks about those who *"professing to be wise . . . became fools."* We
may live without knowing the distance to the nearest star or the
secrets of the atom. But there is no real life at all without the secret
of God. We are lost before we start. Agnosticism is total disaster.
We either live by faith or we do not live at all. Jesus said, *"He who*
believes in the Son has everlasting life; and he who does not believe
the Son shall not see life, but the wrath of God abides in him" (John
3:36). Faithless life is lifeless life.[5]

Saul D. Alinsky died in 1972 in his upscale beach community of Carmel,
California three months after his published *Playboy* interview. His magnum
opus was the book *Rules for Radicals: A Pragmatic Primer for Realistic
Radicals*. From his own words, "Lest we forget at least an over-the-shoulder
acknowledgement to the very first radical: from all our legends, mythology,
and history (and who is to know where mythology leaves off and history
begins—or which is which). *The first radical* known to man who rebelled
against the establishment and did it so effectively that he at least won his
own kingdom—*Lucifer*" (emphasis mine).[6] In his prologue he continues to
expose his allegiance: "The revolutionary force today has two targets, moral
as well as material. Its young protagonists are one moment reminiscent of
the idealistic early Christians, yet they also urge violence and cry, burn the
system down." The *Chicago Sun-Times* extols, "Alinsky impressed a young
[Hillary] Clinton, who was growing up in Park Ridge at the time Alinsky
was the director of the Industrial Areas Foundation in Chicago." *The Nation*
(magazine) proclaimed that Alinsky was "This country's leading hell-raiser .
. .". Advocate of hell and demonic influencer indeed. You will know them by
their fruits, *and* those who follow them.

What has become of the institutional Christian "church" and
individual "Christians" now in our third decade of the twenty-first
century? In a snapshot: the Christian church in the global north is in
trouble. When you stop to consider how far *we* have strayed, collectively

and individually, from knowledge of and obedience to God's Word it really is quite stunning! But the growth and vibrancy of Christians in the global south is exploding, a testimony of God's faithfulness to those who humble themselves and repent.

We will consider three categories, again in simple summary format:

1. *The attacked:* Christians living out their faith genuinely under great persecution
2. *The apathetic:* Timid, sit-on-the-sidelines Christians trying to stay safe and keep their disinterested heads down
3. *The apostate:* Those who have embraced false positions contrary to the gospel for whom it is written, "Not everyone who says to me, 'Lord, Lord,' will enter the kingdom of heaven, but only the one who does the will of my Father who is in heaven" (Matt. 7:21).

First, let us consider where Christians exhibit the most selfless and sacrificial expression of their faith—where believers are multiplying, without the benefit of accessible teaching tools and abundance of materials. It is most certainly those who live in countries of severe persecution and imminent death—the suffering church. Similar to the early church under Roman domination and brutality, people who must face physical abuse and death for adhering to their faith in Jesus hold a special place in God's heart.

One of the ministries which keeps track of the global persecution of the followers of Christ is Open Doors, founded by Brother Andrew. They publish an annual World Watch List, for the top fifty countries where being a Christian is not easy! Most are either Islamic or communist/totalitarian regimes, with the one addition of India, which today under Prime Minister Narendra Modi has instigated a decidedly militant Hindu environment. I have many personal Indian Christian friends, pastors, and educators who chafe under the persecution of his government.

From this Open Doors World Watch List these are the top twenty, ranked by a point system that tracks multiple factors including oppression, persecution, injustice . . . and death:

1. North Korea—communist/atheist
2. Somalia—Islamic
3. Yemen—Islamic

4. Eritrea—Islamic
5. Libya—Islamic
6. Nigeria—Islamic insurgency in the north
7. Pakistan—Islamic
8. Iran—Islamic
9. Afghanistan—Islamic
10. Sudan—Islamic
11. India—Hindu nationalism and persecution
12. Syria—dictatorship
13. Saudi Arabia—Islamic
14. Myanmar—Buddhist and military persecution
15. Maldives—Islamic
16. China—communist/atheist (CCP government)—but with many believers!
17. Mali—Islamic
18. Iraq—Islamic
19. Algeria—Islamic
20. Mauritania—Islamic

I commend to you the book *When Faith Is Forbidden: 40 Days on the Front Lines with Persecuted Christians* by Todd Nettleton. As a ministry partner of The Voice of the Martyrs (founded by Richard Wurmbrand), Todd brings to life the sobering reality of one of the ways Satan is hammering people of faith. Of course, there are many true believers in Christ who face ridicule, ostracizing, humiliation, cancellation, doxing, and other nonterminal forms of persecution. Second Timothy 3:12 assures us, "In fact, everyone who wants to live a godly life in Christ Jesus will be persecuted." This will most assuredly increase in the evil and challenging days ahead until the culmination of this age.

It would be remiss not to mention areas of the world where outpourings of the Holy Spirit *are* penetrating people groups with the light of truth as never before. One of the most incredible movements is among those of Islamic faith. Despite the severe penalties for converting to Christianity, as well as the pervasive and often violent cultural reaction to Christian converts, more Muslims are becoming followers of Christ than any time in history. Another must read is *Dreams and Visions: Is Jesus Awakening the Muslim*

World? by Tom Doyle. Under the threat of fatwas, Sharia law, secret police, and more, a man in radiant white, revealing Himself as Jesus, has appeared to multiple thousands in dreams, infiltrating the sleeping in Iran, Saudi Arabia, Egypt, Jordan, Syria, Iraq, Gaza, the West Bank, and most assuredly immigrant Muslims to Europe and other nations. "There is good reason to think there are more than one million believers in the Islamic Republic of Iran, and you can be certain that none of them are nominal!"[7] I have direct contact with ministries serving in evangelism and outreach to Muslims, and they are seeing amazing results!

Other locations of revival globally include Nigeria, Thailand, India, and Myanmar, to name a few—always in places of great persecution. Americans are waking up to the sobering reality that our nation has driven God out of our public square, public K-12 schools, universities, corporations, government, and many churches. Adversity is intended to lead to repentance *while* the window of opportunity to do so is available. Statistics from the Pew Research Center for the Study of Global Christianity reflects a growth rate of Christianity in Africa at 2.77% and Asia at 1.5% (compared with 1.17% in the global north), resulting in 61% of Christians now living in the global south![8]

Now we turn to the equally tragic but self-initiated effect among those of the Christian community—those suffering from apathy, by definition people with "lack of interest, enthusiasm or concern."[9] In Chapter 2 I also referenced a distinct strategy of the enemy toward believers, using *fear, isolation,* and *doubt.* Encompassing each of these methods, the enemy has infiltrated the faith community in devious ways. C. S. Lewis understood this strategy: "Indeed the safest road to Hell is the gradual one, the gentle slope, soft underfoot, without sudden turnings, without milestones, without signposts."[10] Fear, isolation, or doubt, at various times, encumbers most Christians at some vulnerable point(s) in our life. But Revelation 3:16 has a sobering warning about staying in this state of mind, this condition of the soul, indefinitely: "So, because you are lukewarm—neither hot or cold—I am about to spit you out of my mouth."

"The Pew Research Center revealed that in 2021, the percentage of Americans who self-designated as atheist, agnostic or of no particular faith rose to 29% of all U.S. adults. Even more stunning is . . . those who are between the ages of 18–29 . . . the self-designation marks 39%. The number of professing Christians dropped to 63% in 2021. The conclusion of the Pew researchers was fitting: 'The secularizing shifts evident in American society so far in the 21st century show no signs of slowing.'"[11] Today these percentages are even more sobering.

These realities contribute to the accelerating road to apostasy in much of the Christian church in the global north. The battle for the hearts and minds of people is fierce, and Satan is throwing everything possible into the effort. A central platform for this battleground is the cultural dissonance surrounding race, gender, abortion, the control of speech, and related issues. This can be encapsulated in a centralized theme: biblical justice versus social justice. "Biblical Christianity and ideological social justice are distinct and incompatible world views. They are opposed in their understanding of ultimate reality, power, authority, human nature, morality, epistemology, and much more. . . . The hour is late, but I believe there is still time. We, the Bible-believing church, must humble ourselves, cry out to God, and courageously defend the truth against the greatest worldview threat of a generation."[12]

During Jesus' day the Sanhedrin was composed of seventy leaders. Only Nicodemus (John 3) and Gamaliel (Acts 5) had even a hint of the *full* gospel that Jesus lived and proclaimed—word, deed, and power. We don't know how many were aggressively trying to deny, stop, or kill Jesus but presume many were silent. They were silenced by the angry, howling mob— first-century cancel culture. Today some of our Christian leaders embrace false teaching, denying what Holy Scripture proclaims. But *many more* are silent in the face of pressure. The silence from God's people must end! Dietrich Bonhoeffer declared, shortly before being convicted in a sham court proceeding then hung at dawn in Flossenbürg Concentration Camp, "Silence in the face of evil is evil itself."

One of the preeminent gods of our present age is the satanically motivated "religion" of so-called social justice which exists to deconstruct the traditional systems and structures of our western Judeo-Christian culture. Proponents aggressively promote a victim class, an oppressor class (usually white), and the need to redistribute power and resources in pursuit of *equity* (now coupled with *diversity* and *inclusion*). God's plan and purpose is quite different. Biblical justice involves obedience to His moral standards. But just as in the garden of Eden, the enemy is masterful at twisting words into subtle subversion.

"Words matter . . . All cultural change begins with language change . . . The Bible is far more than a message of salvation, as absolutely vital as that is. It is a comprehensive worldview that defines and shapes all aspects of reality and human existence.". . . So, when the evangelical church intentionally or unintentionally exchanges the biblical definition of a word as important as justice with a counterfeit, it is no small matter . . . The counterfeit is sourced in hollow and deceptive philosophies (Colossians 2:8) that emerged in Europe in the 1700s (and following centuries) with lineage back to famous philosophers and activists including Immanuel Kant, Friedrich Nietzsche, Karl Marx, Antonio Gramsci, and Michel Foucault. Over time they mutated and merged into a school of thought that contemporary academics call critical social justice. . . . Other names include identity politics, intersectionality, or cultural Marxism. Then there is the add-on or hyphenated alleged forms of justice like reproductive-justice, climate-justice, or trans-justice. Tragically, this false worldview is making deep inroads into the evangelical church, which is in grave danger of abandoning true justice for an imposter.[13]

Like nearly every concept in this book, there is only sufficient opportunity to paint a picture, create a framework, and move forward. I highly encourage you to read the book *Why Social Justice Is Not Biblical Justice* by Scott David Allen, from which *some* of this chapter's content is derived, including the chart which follows. Our very simplistic but accurate conclusion: *the core struggle of humankind is not class, race, or gender, victim versus oppressor; it is rebellion against God and disobedience of those precepts that He established for our well-being.*

	Social Justice	Biblical Worldview
What is ultimately real?	The *human mind* defines what is ultimately real.	The God of Genesis 1:1 defines ultimate reality: "In the beginning, God created the heavens and the earth."
Who are we?	Creatures whose identity is *wholly* socially determined. We are products of our race, sex, and gender identity.	Creations and image-bearers of a good, holy, and loving God with inherent dignity and immeasurable worth.

	Social Justice	Biblical Worldview
What is our fundamental problem as human beings?	Oppression: White, heteronormative males have established and maintain hegemonic power structures to oppress and subjugate women, people of color, and sexual minorities (LGBTQ+) and others.	Rebellion: *All have sinned*, and fallen short of the glory of God. Our rebellion against God has resulted in *broken relationships*-between God and man, between man and his fellow man, and between man and creation.
What is the solution to our problem?	Revolution: Oppressed victims and their allies must unite to unmask, deconstruct, and overthrow these oppressive power structures, systems, and institutions.	The gospel: On the cross, God incarnate bore the punishment we deserved for sinful rebellion in order to show us a mercy we could never deserve. His death on the cross and His resurrection opened the way for the reconciliation of all of our broken relationships.
How can we be saved?	Victims are morally innocent and do not require salvation. Oppressors can never be fully pardoned, but partial salvation is available if they confess their complicity in oppression and support the revolution.	"If you declare with your mouth, 'Jesus is Lord,' and believe in your heart that God raised him from the dead, you will be saved. ...Everyone who calls on the name of the Lord will be saved." (Romans 10:9, 13)
What is our primary moral duty?	To stand in solidarity with, protect, and defend the oppressed: women, people of color, sexual minorities (LGBTQ+), etc.	To *love* God with all our heart, soul, mind, and strength (which involves living in obedience to all that Christ commanded) and to love our neighbors as ourselves.
How do we know what is true?	The notions of objective truth, reason, logic, evidence, and argument are discredited tools that oppressors employ to maintain their hegemony. We gain knowledge of "truth" through victim, who, based on their experience of oppression, have greater insight than oppressors.	Divine revelation: (1) God's written Word (2 Timothy 3:13); (2) The "law written on our heart," or human conscience (Romans 2:15); and God's revelation in creation (Romans 1:20). To this we apply our God-given capacity for reason, logic, discussion, and debate to assemble and weigh evidence in pursuit of truth.
Who has ultimate authority?	*Victims are the final authority.* The claims of victims based on their subjective, lived experience must be believed without question.	God (and His revealed Word in Scripture) is the final authority.

	Social Justice	Biblical Worldview
Is there a future, final judgement?	No. There is no god who will return to punish the wicked and reward the upright. Rather, injustice must be rooted out here and now by those with the power to do so.	Yes. Jesus will return and accomplish perfect justice. He will preserve all that is good and rid the world of all that is evil. Until then, He extends mercy and forgiveness to sinful people.

It is necessary here to identify a few of the many ways in which the enemy has infiltrated institutional "Christian" churches. It would be impossible to describe this, in any meaningful way, for the fifteen self-governing churches among the Eastern Orthodox community or the Oriental Orthodox community which includes Copts, Armenians, Ethiopians, and Assyrians. It would also be equally impossible to describe this evil infiltration in the roughly 45,000 Protestant denominations and subgroups. *Yikes, are you kidding me?* This suggests 44,999 ways to disagree with the Christian next to you! These sheer numbers confirm that Satan's minions have been extraordinarily effective in dividing and neutralizing us all. *The Holy Spirit, today more than ever, is calling us to unity—not grievance or disassociation.*

In the remaining reflection, then, we briefly address the Roman Catholic Church, diverse in its own right but the most ecclesiastically homogenous group, including adherents from both the diocesan communities and Catholic "orders."

In the 1960s a very important shift occurred, as a result of the Second Vatican Council. In layman's terms, the church began migrating from a traditional ecclesiastical body to a globalist body. Starting in 2013 under current Pope Francis, it is now following (not leading) the larger cultural metamorphosis toward leftist, woke globalism. He has made clear that he stands with the liberal traditions. Examples include working to marginalize and remove "conservative" priests and bishops, such as outspoken pro-life bishop Joseph Strickland of Tyler, Texas. He has joined to ban fossil fuels, as demanded by climate crisis devotees. He is embracing the streams of sexual deviance and tolerance under the banner of inclusion. Scripture requires acceptance of the individual, not the sin. He is a critic of capitalism—some would say a Marxist view, in light of his outreach to liberationist, anarchist, communist, socialist, and liberal movements particularly in Latin America.

Others have ascribed the term "Black Pope"—not because of race, of course, but because he is the first Jesuit (Society of Jesus) pope to be installed—and this term has a long historicity.

Most Christian catechisms and confessions proclaim, "We believe in the holy catholic church." The word "catholic" (Latin *catholicus*, from the Greek adjective (*katholikos*) means "universal" and comes from the Greek (*katholou*) "according to the whole," and is a combination of the Greek words (kata), "about" and (*holos*), "whole." In simple terms, Christians believe in the totality of the universal expressions of faith in Jesus Christ within doctrinal orthodoxy, not including cults and heresies. This is another important topic of consideration, but not possible to develop sufficiently here.

Whether it relates to the origins of the Christian "church," the covenant extended to the seed of Abraham, the founding of America, or anything that God had a divine intent and purpose for—the enemy has expended every ounce of energy, and soon his final breath, to undermine, infiltrate, subjugate, confuse, destroy what cannot be destroyed. God wins. The forever loser—loses!

Pray for . . .

- protection, grace, and favor multiplied on the persecuted church.
- a spirit of humility and repentance to grip every true believer.
- the Holy Spirit to place a hedge of protection around Israel and for the peace of Jerusalem, as His ordained will is brought to completion

CHAPTER 6

Mountain of Trouble—Family

A CENTRAL ELEMENT of God's original intent and grand design is *the family*. Historically, from the dawn of time and across *every* culture on planet earth, the "traditional" or "nuclear" family is essential to our Father's purposes.

Today, our families are undergoing severe attack and disruption. This deterioration is happening, now at an accelerating rate. On all levels of human relationship, the enemy has woven a sticky web of deception to foster disobedience and entrapment in our spiritual journey.

God *only* created two genders: male and female. The family begins with the joining of these two persons. In the representative Scriptures to follow are guidelines for living within the boundaries that our loving Father knows are best for us. He has ordained the monogamous, heterosexual union between a male husband and a female wife within the bond of marriage, forming a divinely ordained family unit into which children are born and raised. They in turn become a blessing both to their parents and Creator, so that each may achieve *their* highest created purpose. Scripture clearly speaks to God's good, pleasing, and perfect will (Rom. 12:2) in these matters.

There are many dynamics which define, undermine, press in on, and subvert the family. We will briefly comment on the five topics below:

- Gender identity (and the war on children)
- Traditional family
- Pornography and trafficking
- Abortion
- Race

Consider this:

- The percentage of children living without their biological fathers:
    - Black children—64%
    - Hispanic children—42%
    - White children—24%
    - Asian children—16%[1]
- "We're here, we're queer, we're coming for your children."[2]
- "The education of all children, from the moment that they can get along without a mother's care, shall be in state institutions."—Karl Marx[3]

Dear reader—it is *all* about the children! The gift of procreation for us to bear offspring in the image of God, and His heart of love for these most cherished and special creations, is at the center of the Father's purpose for humankind. It is also the very bull's-eye, the central focus of Satan's vicious attacks on our families at multiple levels in each community and society at large. On a temporal level every revolution starts with the indoctrination of children, separating them from their parents so that the state can control their development. Events today validate that our vulnerable, beautiful children are in the highest danger. We who are citizens of heaven, servants of the Most High, *must* protect them! First . . . the Word of God (emphasis added):

> So, God created man in his own image, in the image of God he created them; *male and female* (Gen. 1:27; Matt. 19:4).

> Therefore, *a man shall* leave his father and mother and *hold fast to his wife*, and the two shall become one flesh (Gen. 2:24; Eph. 5:31).

> Because of the temptation to sexual immorality, each man should have his own *wife* and each woman her own *husband* (1 Cor. 7:2).

> *Wives*, submit to your husbands *as to the Lord* . . . *husbands*, love your wives, *just as Christ loved the church* and gave himself up for her (Eph. 5:22, 25).

Each one of you also must love his wife as he loves himself, and the *wife* must respect her *husband* (Eph. 5:33).

Children, obey your parents in the Lord, for this is right. Honor your father and mother (Ex. 20:12; Deut. 5:16; Eph.6:1–2a).

Children are a gift from the Lord; they are a reward from him (Ps. 127:3).

You shall not lie with a male as one lies with a woman; it is an abomination (Lev. 18:22).

God gave them over to shameful lusts. Even their *women exchanged natural relations for unnatural one* (Rom. 1:26).

Cursed is the man who has *sexual relations with any animal* (Deut. 27:21).

Do not be deceived: neither the sexually immoral nor idolators nor adulterers nor *male prostitutes* nor *homosexual offenders* . . . will inherit the kingdom of God. . . . Flee from sexual immorality (1 Cor. 6:9b, 23).

For you created my inmost being, *you knit me together in my mother's womb.* . . . My frame was not hidden from you when I was made in the secret place (Ps. 139:13, 15a).

I made a covenant with my eyes not to look *lustfully* at a young woman (Job 31:1).

. . . anyone who looks at a woman *lustfully* has already committed adultery with her in his heart (Matt. 5:28).

How can a *young person* stay on the path of purity? By living according to your word (Ps. 119:9).

A woman must not wear men's clothing, nor a man wear women's clothing, for the Lord your *God detests anyone who does this* (Deut. 22:5).

. . . to loose the *bonds of wickedness* and undo the straps of the yoke, to let the oppressed go free and to break every yoke (Isa. 58:6b, ESV).

. . . the Lord hates . . . hands that shed *innocent blood.* . . . Your Father in Heaven is not willing that any of these *little ones* should perish (Prov. 6:6a, 17a; Matt. 18:14).

Gender Identity

Building any durable structure requires laying a solid foundation. This applies to understanding gender. We have referenced selected passages of Scripture which describe the creation (not evolution) of humans, male and female, both formed in the imagine of God. Science has developed an XY sex-determination system used to classify certain species of mammals, including humans, reptiles, fish, insects, plants, etc. The majority of male humans have XY chromosomes (called heterogametic) and the majority of female humans have XX chromosomes (called homogametic). The presence of the Y chromosome is responsible for triggering male development. In the absence of a Y chromosome, the baby will develop as a female. There are various exceptions to this norm, though percentagewise they are very rare. For example, the developing fetus with Klinefelter Syndrome will have XXY chromosomes. For those with Swyer Syndrome, women will have XY chromosomes and males will have XX chromosomes.

What is *neither* acceptable science *nor* supported in Scripture is the myth that gender is a social construct. Do an internet search using this phrase "gender is a social construct," or any derivative, and you will find reams of nouveau "authoritative" definitions and explanations. In fact, one of the corrupted "professional" institutions which contributes to this, the American Psychiatric Association, has removed gender dysphoria from the DSM-5 (Diagnostic and Statistical Manual of Mental Disorders). Poof – it no longer exists. But it does!

Why is this demonically centered perversion burgeoning in our present day? The answer to this question, as it relates to "family", applies equally to each of the other six mountains of societal influence. The source is the same—*the enemy, Satan.* Knowing his time is short, until he and his minions are thrown into the abyss, he has disseminated in our present context this most aberrant twist on human sexuality. This challenge is more than an academic one for this author. I have family members who have been drawn into this delusion. And as someone who is speaking out strongly in this manner, it does not surprise me that our true enemy has chosen this avenue of attack. Your prayers are coveted!

Here is a sampling of our societal dysphoria which contributes directly to the gender dysphoria of our present era:

- "Cambridge Dictionary modified definitions of 'man' and 'woman' . . . to include people who identify as a gender other than their biological sex. The definition of a woman, which previously represented the longstanding view on sex, now states that a woman is 'an adult who lives and identifies as female though they may have been said to have a different sex at birth. Similarly, a man . . .'"[4]
- "UN report castigates religion for stymieing the sexual orientation—gender identity agenda . . . the 67 countries that prohibit sexual acts between same-sex adults . . . are dogmatic interpretations of scripture and colonial-era legislation . . . (and) the denial of reproductive rights (ergo, abortion) is a form of state sponsored violence"[5]
- "Pride is a time to recall the trials the Lesbian, Gay, Bisexual, Transexual, and Queer (LGBTQ+) community has endured and to rejoice in the triumphs of trailblazing individuals who have bravely fought—and continue to fight—for full equality. . . . Now, therefore, I Joseph R. Biden, Jr., President of the United States of America . . . do hereby proclaim June (starting in 2021) as Lesbian, Gay, Bisexual, Transgender, and Queer Pride Month."[6]
- The California Department of General Services will begin collecting voluntary data "to allow the state to gain a better understanding of registered and certified business owner(s) demographics related to ethnicity, race, gender identity, and sexual orientation."[7] Furthermore, California is at the forefront of leading the nation to transform minor consent and confidentiality laws with parental rights severely limited. California is now a "sanctuary state for transgenders."
- A Texas father, Jeff Y., lost custody of his son James, whose mother Anne G. influenced her son in the direction of choosing to become

transgendered. She relocated to California, a sanctuary state for gender transition. "That means that Younger's rights to protect his son from chemical or surgical castration have essentially been terminated."[8]

- For 2024's Transgender Visibility Day (March 31) the Cartoon Network (with an audience demographic of 3.9 million 6–12 years old viewers) proclaimed the following: "Addressing someone using their pronouns and names shows that you respect them as their authentic self! We celebrate the journey of our trans and gender-non-conforming friends."[9]

- Calm discussions of transgender medicine are rare. There are few other areas of health care where professionals are so afraid to openly discuss their views, argues Hilary Cass, a British doctor. On April 9, 2024 she published a 388-page report, commissioned by England's National Health Service, assessing the evidence for and against treatment for children who identify as transgender. The treatments at issue include puberty blockers, cross-sex hormones and surgery. "There is not a reliable evidence base to show that the benefits of offering such treatments to children outweigh the harms. Many studies have been published, but they are often of poor quality so that outcomes for patients receiving treatment are not compared with outcomes for those who do not . . . some draw conclusions from tiny samples . . .some lack control groups. Far too little effort has been made to observe long-term effects. Some clinics even resist attempts to gather such data. It is unusual for us to give a potentially life-changing treatment to young people and not know what happens to them in adulthood. America should follow England's lead on transgender care for kids."[10]

- According to a National Institutes of Health study, gender-affirming treatment remains a topic of controversy. The literature to date reveals concerning trends regarding suicidality in transgender individuals. Gender-affirming surgery has a 12.12-fold higher suicide attempt risk than those who did not. Transgender US military veterans have more than 20 times higher rates.[11]

- The application for medical services at the Lyon-Martin Community Health Services in San Francisco with "The Transgender District," embedded in the stationery header includes five gender (trans) categories and 146 sub-entry options:

- ○ Trans Status (5 entries)
- ○ Pronouns (18 entries)
- ○ Gender Identity (97 entries)
- ○ Sex Assigned at Birth (6 entries)
- ○ Sexual Orientation (20 entries)

In a Tucker Carlson interview with Vivek Ramaswamy (2024 former Republican candidate for president) his cogent argument was made: "The gay rights position holds that the sex of the person you are attracted to is 'hard wired' (biologically predetermined) on the day you were born—even though there is no 'gay gene.' Conversely, the LGBT position holds that your sex is completely fluid over the course of your life, even though there is a definitive sex chromosome. You cannot believe the two positions at the same time; they are fundamentally contradictory." Vivek postulated that both of these positions are nonsensical, and actually represent a cultlike belief system. "The worst religions are those who fail to recognize themselves as a religion. The most dangerous religions of all are those who claim to be secular in nature, but are actually religious in their conviction. It's the same thing you see in the climate movement—actually."[12]

Is this just a matter of communication; of understanding the other side? Shouldn't we be tolerant of people? No, it is *not* just a matter of words, or understanding better. *What we have here* is a deliberate, diabolical, and destructive effort by the demonic realm to thwart and supplant the will and purpose of the Creator. So therefore, ruling and reigning *ekklesia*, as well as awakening believers in Christ who heretofore didn't want to "make waves", be offensive, or be persecuted or doxed . . . *it is time to stand up and push back.* We don't advocate physical altercation, but a prayer-centered, faith-enduring, quiet determination to engage wherever the Holy Spirit leads you to be engaged!

Among the most pernicious evils that aggressively attack our children are those which expose them to perversion at a young age. Drag Queen Story Hour in our public libraries and other facilities, even at some churches, represent this unacceptable practice. Every totalitarian from of government has openly declared that controlling children at the youngest possible age is the most effective way to indoctrinate them into their belief system. The neo-Marxists in America today, who push critical theory, in all its forms, have learned this tactic well.

Drag Queen Story Hour

One individual who has taken on a redemptive campaign of opposition to this demonic realm is Kirk Cameron, founder of Sky Tree Book Fairs. They brand themselves as 'book fairs for soaring imaginations, rooted in truth.' Their website proclaims their goal to 'celebrate literacy while ensuring books are wholesome and trustworthy.'[13]

Another abomination is the infiltration of this demonic perversion into some elements of the Christian church. I will say, without hesitation, that where there are true believers in Jesus Christ who may attend such a church, in alignment with Scripture, *they should leave that church* and join another truly worshipping community.

It is encouraging to see tangible and passionate challenges arise through various campaigns and initiatives. Many prophetic and apostolic leaders have spoken on this topic. Two among many, Lou Engle and Cindy Jacobs, have proclaimed that a new movement of the Holy Spirit has been birthed. God is raising up women, mothers, "mama bears" to protect our children and grandchildren. This important, formidable force of called, gifted and empowered women is now on the move! Here are some valuable resources:

Family Research Council - https://ftc.org

Focus on the Family – https://focusonthefamily.com

Moms for America – https://momsforamerica.us

A Million Voices Washington DC – https://louengle.com

Don't Mess with our Kids – https://dontmesswithourkids.us

Protect Kids California – (found on Facebook)

This is not just a "project" for these organizations. This is truly a global movement of the Holy Spirit! Pray and discern specific ways you can be involved personally. Protecting God's children will require entire divisions of kingdom warriors. *It's that serious!*

Traditional Family

It is now clearly obvious, and out in the open, that an all-out attack on the family is underway. The "deep state" is moving rapidly to pass legislation in as many US states as possible to remove the heretofore exclusive right of parents to guide and protect their children. Even the most basic parental responsibility for decision-making and life choices of the child are being blocked. We have already quoted Karl Marx. Let us remember *also* that a central ploy of the Maoist Chinese communists was for the state to supersede parents in all matters of their children's lives, rights and education. Examples include the one-child policy (controlling how many children a couple can have); purging the country of the four "olds" (removing allegedly old ideas, old culture, old customs, and old habits); turning children against their parents during the Cultural Revolution (fostering suspicion and betrayal); and taking over the complete education (cradle-to-grave indoctrination) of the child from the youngest age. I have more to say about China in Chapter 12.

In the US, parents are fighting back with school boards of education, and centralized union policies that mandate many initiatives against the gospel. The will and purpose of God will prevail if we prayerfully and forcefully engage. The right to choose the health care and vaccinations your own child receives has devolved into mandates and punitive measures for disobedience. "My body, my choice" only applies when it fits the leftist narrative

Finally, we must comment on one key piece of legislation undermining traditional marriage, euphemistically titled The Respect for Marriage Act (H.R. 8404) and passed by Congress on December 8, 2022. Tony Perkins aptly noted, "As you all know, 47 Republicans violated the GOP platform—and, not to mention, God—and voted to define marriage as that for which God destroyed Sodom. . . . How appalling."[14]

Franklin Graham called it a deceptive smokescreen and expounded further, cautioning that it "could impact you, your family, your church, and our nation." He compared it to the so-called Inflation Reduction Act that "did nothing but increase inflation and further hurt our economy." He further warned that this new legislation is "designed to provide strong protections for same-sex marriage—but fails to protect those of us who believe marriage is between a man and a woman. It is dangerous legislation that would be used against individuals, churches and organizations who honor traditional marriage."[15]

It is encouraging to see an unexpected understanding between the "leftist" world view and those on the "right" regarding one damaging outcome from a diminished nuclear family. Note the New York Times article, by Nicholas Kristof, with the heading, *Destruction of the Nuclear Family Leads to Poverty for Children.*" He states, "We are often reluctant to acknowledge one of the significant drivers of child poverty – the widespread breakdown of family – for fear that to do so would be patronizing and racist. But just as you can't have a serious conversation about poverty without discussing race, you also can't engage unless you consider single-parent households. The racial situation has actually changed a great deal, and it's gotten worse for many children in minority communities, but it's also gotten spectacularly worse for may white children." [16]

Tangible data presents some uncomfortable realities. Two parent families are beneficial for children. Places that have more two parent families have higher rates of upward mobility. Another NY Times article by Albert Mohler Briefing is worth reading also. It's title: *Creation Order Rings Out Loud: Even the Most Determined Secular Society Cannot Escape God's Design for Marriage and Family!*[17]

Pornography and Trafficking

What summary statement can effectively underscore the pervasive infiltration and destructive outcomes of sexual promiscuity enhanced by pornography and often tied to the sexual abuse of children? We've already stated it: these willful acts are *pervasive and destructive* to the individual, to the family, to the community, and to society. Statistics lack a name and a face but here are a few related to pornography:

- The global pornography industry is worth around $97 billion.
- Approximately 35% of all internet downloads are related to pornography.
- An estimated 40 million Americans regularly visit porn sites, including 70% of men aged 18–24.
- There are 4.2 million adult websites, making up 12% of all websites.
- Around 1.7% of adult women have worked in the porn industry at some point in their life.
- *9% of porn users are children under 12 years old.*[18]

Other than names written in the book of life and records kept in the courts of heaven, I cannot fathom that there is available empirical data on sexual promiscuity. But just look around; it's everywhere. Here are a few glimpses into this world:

- Recommend that you consult *The Journal of Psychology: Interdisciplinary and Applied*, Volume 135, Issue 1, "A Meta Analysis of the Published Research on the Effects of Child Sexual Abuse, undertaken for six outcomes—PTSD, depression, suicide, sexual promiscuity, victim-perpetrator cycle and academic performance.
- "Studies show that by age 44, the average man has had about seven sexual partners and the average woman has had four. About 33 percent of men and 9 percent of women report having more than 10 sexual partners."[19]

What is perverse or illicit is in the eye of the beholder—is it not? *Absolutely no*, but that is what Satan wants you to think. Man is the master of his own fate. *Don't tell me what I can and cannot do!* God's Word is clear. One of the most telling indicators of how far humankind has fallen in this area of sin is the proliferation of organizations and legislative initiatives to make legal or *de facto* acceptable (but not moral) what has, since the creation of humankind, *not* been acceptable or moral. These are just a few examples out of multiple hundreds:

- The UN report *The 8 March Principles for a Human Rights-based Approach to Criminal Law Proscribing Conduct Associated with Sex, Reproduction, Drug Use, HIV, Homelessness and Poverty* calls to legalize sex with minors and pushes toward normalization of pedophilia. The UNAIDS website offers no legal guidance for these matters for children under 18, but advises lawyers, judges, and law enforcement to consider "the rights and capacity of persons under 18 years of age to make decisions."[20]
- NAMBLA—North American Man/Boy Love Association; a pedophilia and pederasty advocacy organization
- ACT UP—AIDS Coalition to Unleash Power; international political group
- BiNet USA—The Bisexual Network of the USA Inc.; promotes bisexual visibility and distributes educational information
- BoB—Boys of Bangladesh; primary dating site for Bangladeshi gay men
- Gay and Lesbian Coalition of Kenya; promoting the growth of intersectionality
- GLAAD—Gay & Lesbian Alliance Against Defamation; media monitoring and messaging
- IGLYO—Int'l Lesbian, Gay, Bisexual, Transgender, Queer & Intersec Youth and Student Organization; based in Brussels, Belgium, with forty-five countries as members
- Intersex South Africa—member OII (Organization Intersex Int'l); the largest global intersex organization
- MOVILH—Movimiento de Integración y Liberación Homosexual (Chile)
- NCTE—National Center for Transgender Equality; policy advocacy and media activism
- Pink Dot SG—annual pride event in Singapore, supporting diversity and inclusion
- Queer Nation—confrontational tactics, slogans, and the practice of outing

Abortion

The battle in America over the rights of the unborn child is as virulent and protracted as any war we have fought. What else can be said *here* about abortion that for decades hasn't already been expressed by a myriad of people? More than 63 million children in the US, *alive at conception*, have been terminated since 1973. I can only offer the basics here—in the context of the United States—on this most complex topic.

The landmark US Supreme Court decision in 1973 *Jane Roe* (a pseudonym) *versus Henry Wade* (410 U.S. 113) using the due process clause of the 14th Amendment in a 7–2 ruling granted a woman the fundamental right to privacy, therefore protecting her right to an abortion. The June 24, 2022 landmark US Supreme Court decision (No. 19–1392, 597) *Dobbs versus Jackson Women's Health*, in a 6–3 ruling, upheld Mississippi's abortion law, and in a 5–4 ruling held that the Constitution does *not* confer a right to abortion. The effective result was to return decisions regarding abortion to the states. The political "right" overcame what was long considered an original ruling on specious grounds. The political "left" has been screeching ever since about overturning fifty years of precedent and, subsequently, acting out in hostile and violent ways. This includes harassing certain Supreme Court justices outside of their homes; calling them out in the press to intimidate future rulings; creating so-called reproductive health bills which pay for abortions, travel to abortion friendly states, and making abortions available to unaccompanied pregnant minors; setting fire to or defacing pregnancy and right-to-life centers; and blocking, cancelling, or doxing pro-life figures in the public square, just to name a few.

Judaism was the original pro-life faith community. They stood in juxtaposition to the child-sacrificing cultures that surrounded them. The Judeo-Christian community of our present day carries this mantle: "Before I was born the Lord called me; from my birth he has made mention of my name" (Isa. 49:1, NIV84). The gestating child is *not* just an incorporeal fetus. From conception it retains a soul and spirit, breathed into it by the Lord. *This matter cannot be viewed as a political one; it is a moral one.* It is stunning to realize that out of 195 (currently recognized) countries in the world, only seven allow abortions past the twenty-four-month mark—and the US, China, and North Korea are three of them!

Another stunning development, certainly underreported, is the number of Democratic states that are reacting to the 2022 landmark Supreme Court decision and codifying further draconian legislation, usually with monikers like "Reproductive Rights" or "Freedom of Reproductive Choice." One case in point is the state of New Jersey, one of fifteen states (currently) that uses Medicaid payments to cover abortions and other "reproductive health care." Watch how many now grant rights of pregnancy termination up to the time of birth. The US government channeled nearly $2 billion to Planned Parenthood and four other abortion businesses in 2019–2021. The statistics in 2022–2023 are even higher! There is also a *huge* industry in the harvesting/sale of fetal tissue and parts of the baby's body. You will not *see* this reported in the legacy media. In fact, the two undercover journalists who exposed Planned Parenthood selling aborted baby parts (a felony) were themselves prosecuted by the California attorney general—Kamala Harris! All of this is evil!

These research findings are worth pondering; the reasons for women seeking abortions in the US (as identified during intake) are:

- 0.3%   risk to the woman's life or a major bodily function
- 0.4%   rape and incest
- 1.2%   abnormality in the unborn baby
- 2.2%   other physical health concerns
- 95.9% elective (i.e., birth control) and other unspecified reasons[21]

Finally, consider the "lawfare," the intentional pressure applied by the current US Department of Justice on those who "oppose" abortion. One example of many is pro-life activist Lauren Handy's May 2024 indictment and sentence for five years in prison for her advocacy in Washington DC against abortion facilities.[22] Many others who have simply prayed outside of abortion facilities have been arrested. And we must remember the public threat made by Senate Majority Leader Chuck Schumer (prior to the Dobbs decision), against Supreme Court justices Gorsuch and Kavanaugh, "I want to tell you . . . you have released a whirlwind and you will pay the price. You won't know what hit you . . ."

Human Trafficking

The amazing movie *The Sound of Freedom*, directed by Alejandro Gómez Monteverde and released by Angel Studios, exposes in a most compelling way the travesty, the agony, the horror, the sin of human trafficking, much of it with children even in the single digits of age. Why did this film sit in the can, languish on the shelf for five years? A temporal answer is that after Disney bought Twentieth Century Fox, and since the film has a strong religious and conservative message, it did not appeal to the decision-makers at Disney. Frankly, early Disney executives would be aghast at the garbage that their corporation is putting out today. Human trafficking now exceeds the multiple billions of dollars in profit generated by almost all other dark money industries. A huge percentage of the victims are children. But the real reason, again, is not a temporal one. Remember *who* has declared an all-out war on children!

Consider this sobering reality: the United States is the #1 consumer of human trafficking victims. According to the International Justice Mission, "The number of children trafficked and abused *daily* could fill Glendale, AZ State Farm Stadium (63,400 seat site of Super Bowl LVII) 189 times. Currently there are almost 50 million children, women and men being trafficked or trapped in modern slavery, making it one of the largest and fastest growing criminal industries in the world."[23]

In addition, "Victims of exploitation and trafficking are to be found all over the world. Many have been exploited while escaping religious or ethnic persecution, of fleeing war, like refugees from Ukraine, writes Marion Carson, who has encountered many such victims through her role as chaplain of Glasgow City Mission. She challenges Christians and the church to first examine ourselves as we tackle the causes of human trafficking . . . and to be a prophetic voice against the values and norms of the world in which slavery is able to flourish."[24]

Our last entry in this section touches briefly on the hidden but symbiotic relationship between the porn, abortion, and trafficking industries.

> At least one of my six abortions was from Planned Parenthood because they didn't ask any questions. Those are the words of a sex trafficking survivor who took part in the study, *The Health Consequences of Sex Trafficking and Their Implications*

for Identifying Victims in Healthcare Facilities, which found that 55% of sex trafficking victims in the study had obtained abortions. Thirty percent had undergone more than one abortion. These three unethical and horrific industries (porn, abortion, trafficking), each thrive off of the others. DKT International, which sells the abortion pill and owns the worldwide rights to sell manual vacuum aspiration kits, fought against the 2003 law requiring organizations funded by the U.S. to take an official position against sex trafficking. To do so could have hurt DKT's business. DKT International was founded by Philip Harvey, who has made millions of dollars selling pornographic films and sex toys through his company Adam and Eve. Those films, according to a report by National Review, likely contain footage of sex trafficking victims forced to participate in pornography. . . . Harvey sits on the board of the UK-based Marie Stopes International, one of the largest abortion chains in the world. Meanwhile, sex trafficking victims are frequently forced to undergo multiple abortions to be able to continue "working." Abortionists are, therefore, making money off of sex trafficking. . . . The abortion industry is profiting tremendously financially [from sex trafficking]. It's a cruel, inhumane, brutal circle in which Planned Parenthood can often be found at the center."[25]

There are many organizations that concerned people wanting to fight trafficking can be involved with: Operation Underground Railroad, International Justice Mission, The Exodus Road, The A21 Campaign, Faith Alliance Against Slavery and Trafficking, The Medaille Trust, Agape International Mission, and many more. And, when needed, the National Human Trafficking Hotline is 888-373-7888.

Race

For years my friend and brother from another mother, George Bell, taught and preached on the dual nature of the kingdom of God—it is both present and still to come. Since race and racial tensions have been (intentionally) exacerbated in our present culture, his views are especially valuable. Marxist and socialist-led movements divide everyone into oppressor and oppressed groups, pit whites against BIPOCs, and unquestionably add new tensions to families. George shared these thoughts:

> My experience growing up in a multi-ethnic community in South Los Angeles gave me insight into the human fabric of blacks, whites, browns, yellows, and reds. Though different, yet I felt they were the same. It is essential that our basic needs, security, belongingness, love, and true identity are actualized in the Creator, and not our own image. Therefore, we are all one. Without the characteristics mentioned above we are not human. It is so important to understand that we are all created in God's image. No matter what ethnicity we are as hyphenated people groups, at some point we all emerged from social injustice and economic disparities. We are all different shades of hue dealing with the same addictive structures that bind us to society preventing us from being fully healthy. This obscures reality.

In George's childhood neighborhood, he felt "they were all the same—Asian, Black, Latino, and Caucasian." He further shared:

> In today's Western culture, there is a tremendous need for truth seekers to peel back layers of interpolation which promote historical bias. We need to make known an accurate account of biblical history through the present from a Christo-centric perspective. In the 21st century our hyphenated identities—Anglo-American, African-American, Mexican-American, Asian-American, have blurred God's truth and the biblical account of our common humanity. Today, each people group fashions God in their own image. Humankind's lust for power, prestige, and wealth has blinded the masses to the fact we are nations of immigrants, we are a world of immigrants all a long way from Eden! We have departed from the absoluteness of Scripture and contrived our own image of God, the color of His children, and His purpose for mankind. Advancements in technology provide accessibility

through a global infrastructure to spread the Gospel of Yeshua, thankfully weakening these draconian beliefs and opinions. With His help people are seeking anew the truth of God Almighty. We believers are called to a Spirit-empowered life, mobilizing other Christ-followers to seize this opportunity to make disciples in our community and the world.

Note the following list of the ten largest cities in America with metro populations, their mayors, and ethnicity (time-sensitive to the third quarter of 2024):

10 Largest US Metro Areas—Population, Mayor, and Ethnicity

1. New York, New York—18,937,000—Eric Adams,—African American
2. Los Angeles, California—12,534,000—Karen Bass—African American
3. Chicago, Illinois—8,937,000—Brandon Johnson—African American
4. Houston, Texas—6,707,000—Sylvester Turner—African American
5. Dallas-Fort Worth, Texas—6,574,000—Eric Johnson—African American
6. Miami, Florida—6,265,000—Francis Suarez—Cuban American
7. Atlanta, Georgia—6,106,000—Andre Dickens—African American
8. Philadelphia, Pennsylvania—5,785,000—Cherell Parker—African American
9. Washington DC—5,490,000—Muriel Bowser—African American
10. Phoenix, Arizona—4,717,000—Kate Gallego—Caucasian American [26]

In the last quarter of the twentieth century and the first two decades of the twenty-first, African Americans increasingly became involved at all levels of local government. Today more than one-third of America's top one hundred cities are governed by African Americans, with many female mayors. The vast majority of African American mayors belong to the Democratic Party (fifty out of fifty-five largest US cities), four were independent, and only one was Republican.[27]

God's original intent and design was for the family to be the bedrock of humankind on earth *so that* children would be nurtured in a wholesome environment to grow to maturity—physically, emotionally, and spiritually. Marx, Lenin, Hitler, and Mao all focused on separating children from parents and indoctrinating them early. Sadly, our own Judeo-Christian societies have added a whole lot of adjectives before the word "family." From God's original starting point we now have "broken," "blended," "dysfunctional," "fatherless," "single parent," "extended," "nuclear," "step-," and more. Is there any wonder *why* Satan has thrown so much at the family? More than anything we need to repent—to change direction *or at least move* in some direction! We can no longer sit by the sidelines watching our country and our families disintegrate. We *must* pray and then specifically ask God what *we* need to do to join this movement to reclaim the territory which has been lost to the enemy. May He strengthen us on this journey.

Pray for . . .

- this global movement of the Holy Spirit, raising up "Esthers" for such a time as this in the life of our nation(s) with a specific commission to protect our children.
- resources to thwart the demonic realm, which controls so much of this earthly domain, to be penetrated by the penetrating light and authority of Jesus Christ and defeated.
- a revival of the traditional family, and that men and women will understand their vital role and follow the admonition of Scripture in raising of our children.

CHAPTER 7
Mountain of Trouble—Education

ONE EVENING I was watching a local news channel as they featured university students protesting the celebration of Columbus Day. Without forethought, I muttered loud enough for my fifteen-year-old, who attended tenth grade in a public high school *at the time*, to hear me say, "It's perfectly fine to add an Indigenous People's Day to our holiday calendar, but let's keep them *both*." The quick response surprised me: "Oh no, we can't do that because of all the bad things Columbus did." Huh? Who teaches our children this?

> For decades we have known about the lunacy of college campuses, which are . . . indoctrination camps. North Korea has concentration camps. America prefers cancellation, marginalization, and labeling—but the reality is the same: America's elites are hell-bent on changing the landscape in America, one incoming freshman class at a time—and they are succeeding. In America today, private thoughts are not allowed to translate into public speech, provoking the question, 'Are we really free?' Many parents have remarked, 'We sent a patriotic, faith-filled conservative off to college and soon had an America-hating socialist on our hands.[1]

In many school board meetings across the nation, parents who have exercised their right to speak on behalf of *their* child's education have been reprimanded, shut down, removed from the meeting, surveilled by some element of our intelligence apparatus, and even jailed!

How did we get here—and most importantly, how must we respond?

Consider this:

- "Give me four years to teach the children and the seed I have sown will never be uprooted."—Vladimir Lenin
- "The largest union in the United States supports not steel workers or the teamsters, but school teachers. Public schools in the United States are the largest state-owned monopoly in the world, outside China."[2]
- "Train up a child in the way he should go and when he is old, he will not depart from it" (Prov. 22:6, KJV).

Let's review a brief history of the takeover of our educational system— and that is what has truly happened: a bloodless coup, while we were lulled into a slumber. In this section I consulted a book I highly recommend you read, *Battle for the American Mind: Uprooting a Century of Miseducation* by Pete Hegseth with David Goodwin. There are other valuable books in the Recommended Resources section on this topic.

American educational "reformer" John Dewey lectured often in the 1890s on the theme "The School and Social Progress." He viewed classical Christian education as being dominated by medieval concepts of learning that were narrow and one-sided. He began the drumbeat, sounded increasingly today, that schools should not serve the rights and preferences of parents. Dewey mirrored the vocabulary of V.I. Lenin, who in a 1922 speech had spoken of the state controlling the "commanding heights" of government and society—in other words, centralized control of education and virtually all other centers of influence in society. There is an entire genre of reading that describes the birth, metamorphosis, rise, and complete infiltration of "progressives," aka Marxists, into the American educational system. Again, this book can only scratch the surface of these deeply complex issues.

This progressive philosophical framework was fashioned into a Hundred Years' War—albeit a hidden one, at least to the parents, not the perpetrators. The first Hundred Years' War occurred from the mid-fourteenth to mid-fifteenth century between England and France over succession to the French throne. In Chapter 12 we will address another Hundred Years' War *in progress*—China's planned ascension to world domination. The important reason to mention all three here is to emphasize that:

1. Systemic disruption and eventual disintegration of a system or a country is always planned, and usually takes place over a long period of time.

2. As this is happening, most people naturally and understandably view these matters through a political, economic, or social lens—in other words, a temporal one. But there is a spiritual enemy and purpose involved in *all* of these matters, which is not immediately recognizable to most . . . but understood by those who discern.

3. It may seem simplistic, but the "fruit" or the manifestation of any movement or philosophy, with whatever name is used for it, will always result in one of two outcomes: freedom or bondage, light or darkness, good or evil.

During this same time frame another attack (of the enemy) was manifested through the work of Marxist law professor Max Horkheimer, who founded the Frankfurt School of Critical Theory in 1923. Critical theory critiques society to identify and reject oppressive power structures. It also is dismissive of evident objective reality. Thus, a young person today can justify saying, "Why should my biology dictate my sex or gender?" or, "The rules of math or science, if they are deemed oppressive must be rejected." This turns everything that was stable upside-down.

Critical theory postulates the question (and the answer), "If there is no God, how shall we live?" But the Marxist Frankfurt School accelerated this trajectory further by saying, "Since we know there is no God, what is the ultimate good in society?" Critical theory rejects all belief in God, sin, rights endowed by the Creator, redemption, the ability and necessity to forgive, and more.

The Frankfurt atheist Marxists looked at western society and its western Christian ideals, saw that everything important was ordered vertically, and said the answer was to be critical of everything and tear it down! "The Frankfurt School decided the answer was to be 'critical' of every social construct so they could 'deconstruct' our culture and flatten it. If you wonder why George Soros is hell-bent on deconstructing our legal system, this is why. Domain after domain of social construct comes under critical theory: critical pedagogy (deconstructing education); critical gender theory (deconstructing biological sex); critical social theory (deconstructing politics); critical language theory (deconstructing language), and, of course, critical race theory. Each domain needed to be torn down so that it could be rebuilt on the new determinant of 'equity.' We are finding out, now, where the new god of equity will take us."[3]

Horkheimer's like-minded colleague Herbert Marcuse published his treatise "Repressive Tolerance," which advanced the now accepted concept of postmodernism. Like critical theory, it offers an alternative to morality. This system redefined everyone into "oppressor" and "oppressed" categories. Their main tenet is that tolerance serves to protect and preserve a repressive society. Therefore, the leftists in America today aggressively advocate that one cannot tolerate intolerance. This is why politically protected groups like Antifa and Black Lives Matter are allowed to rage. Their violence is justified because the norm of tolerance to be opposed by any means are represented by the oppressors—capitalists, whites, and ultimately Christians.

Critical theory and postmodernism, therefore, form the nucleus around which our current aggressive movements find their origin, promoting transgenderism, i.e., men "identifying" as women who push their way into women's sports and locker rooms, queer studies, drag shows for children, the non-science-based LGBTQIA+ world, and all the other add-ons to these multi-letter subgroups which the legacy media hyperventilates over.

The heart of this takeover of our education system most certainly also includes rewriting the books and curricula thought to be unacceptable. But it goes deeper than just written or digital materials. More importantly, it involves a fundamental shift in the pedagogy. From the Greek word *paidagōgía* or *paidagogos, it is* a combination of *paidos* (child) and *agogos* (leader), and describes the art and science of teaching students. In classical teaching systems (eastern or western) the teacher walked with and built a relationship with the student, and taught not only academics but also manners and virtue. In the United States our pedagogy was a distinctly Judeo-Christian one. It no longer is!

During the majority of America's history, parents actually expected public schools to teach Christianity and the Bible, with prayer as a part of the daily experience. "The Progressives realized that classical Christian education did something much more powerful than just teach virtues—it cultivated a Western Christian Paideia with a foundation in divine Truth. .

. . This type of paideia was a feared and powerful tool because it anchored, not in the "progress" of human institutions, but in an unchanging, divinely inspired set of assumptions."[4]

By the 1930s progressivism had embraced this neo-Marxist façade fully. It was further strengthened by the rise of humanism and their Humanist Manifesto I. The product of "many minds," here are a few excerpts from their 1933 document, and three bullet points from it:

> The time has come for widespread recognition of the radical changes in religious beliefs throughout the modern world. The time is past for mere revisions of traditional attitudes. Science and economic change have disrupted the old beliefs. Religions the world over are under the necessity of coming to terms with new conditions created by vastly increased knowledge and experience . . . There is a great danger of a final, and we believe fatal, identification of the word religion with doctrines and methods which have lost their significance and which are powerless to solve the problem of human living in the Twentieth Century.
>
> **First**, Humanists regard the universe as self-existing and not created. . . .
>
> **Third**, Holding an organic view of life, humanists find that the traditional dualism of mind and body must be rejected. . . .
>
> **Fifth**, Humanism asserts that the nature of the universe depicted by modern science makes unacceptable any supernatural or cosmic guarantees of human values.

There have been revisions (i.e., further rejection of God's original design and intent) in Humanist Manifesto II (1973) and Humanist Manifesto III (2003). A few adherents of this belief system include Eleanor Roosevelt (first lady, diplomat, and activist); Margaret Sanger (founder of American Birth Control League, which became Planned Parenthood Federation of America); Upton Sinclair (prolific author and 1934 Democratic Party nominee for governor of California), among many others.

The death knell for our God-honoring educational system occurred in the 1960s under the (Earl) Warren Court, with God's formal eviction from the classroom. This court approved multiple cases which have now become the accepted norm. One ruling in 1962 affirmed that having students start their school day with a nondenominational prayer *was unconstitutional.* In 1963, the court ruled that devotional Bible reading in public schools *was unconstitutional.* In 1965 the Supreme Court ruled that students praying aloud over lunch *was unconstitutional.* Now, sixty-plus years later, with these restrictions in place, public education and the teachers who promulgate it are integral to the system which has not only forgotten God but insist that God has no place in our public schools at all. It's the "separation of church and state," after all, right? No, it's the counterfeit of the enemy, once again moving humankind away from our created purpose!

> Without realizing it, today's American students absorb a deep affection for scientism (science is the only way to find truth), equity / equality (there is nothing better or worse, just different), individualism (identity politics), neo-Marxism (the government can and should solve all inequalities) along with a host of other modern and postmodern affections that lead to servitude.[5]

Our last section will offer some recommendations that parents and grandparents can do to overcome this tyranny. There *is* hope and God *is* in control! But first, in this complex ocean of topics, we will now jump into a much more limited wading pool of information, which I will provide in three related subtopics:

- The effects and policies of the NEA and AFT unions
- A basic look at our school funding and global comparisons
- Specific examples of the leftist infiltration of public education

"Teachers" Unions

The quotation marks around the word "teachers" in the title of this section are intentional. Who wouldn't support the dedicated women and men who invest critical hours five days a week (and more) for our children? We should, and most of us do, support our teachers on an individual, interpersonal basis. But public-school teachers and the greater public school system are subject to both soft and hard control.

The forerunner to the NEA was the National Teachers Association, founded in 1857. It was not a union but an association of teachers who collectively desired to create methods and develop tools to better educate our children. In 1900 the name was changed to the National Education Association, and in 1906 the NEA was "chartered" by Congress. A congressional charter essentially gives legal recognition to an existing organization for the purpose of affirming and endorsing it. Virtually no one in today's public school system, teachers or administrators, understand that up to the disastrous Supreme Court decisions of the 1960s the NEA was publishing and promoting material that contained Bible verses, prayers, and writings about kindness and other elements of moral character. In fact, multiple publications were printed in massive quantities and distributed to the majority of schools nationwide so each had access to them every school year. One example is the "Selections for Memorization" booklet. Within this *de facto* culture of public-school education, at this time, was promotion of the education triangle which encouraged students, teachers, and parents to work together toward a common goal! What is most important to understand is that the policies and practices of this era reflected the predominant culture of America—faith-oriented, family-centric and patriotically inclined.

The current president of the NEA is Rebecca Pringle.

An equally subversive union is the American Federation of Teachers (AFT) led by Randi Weingarten. We cannot do justice, nor have the space in this chapter, to fully describe the intractable damage caused by these two unions and the persons who lead them. Eliminating the federal Department of Education and returning the authority to the states is the ultimate objective and the only way to begin to undo their centralized destruction of our public school system.

We have shown the chronology of how Marxist ideology and goals infiltrated our originally decent, commendable public education system. Obviously, more people who believe in this system were needed to make permanent change happen. The conduit for providing personnel for this new religion (i.e., belief system) involved the Frankfurt School slowly, and inextricably like a boa constrictor, embedding itself in the premier school training teachers at all levels, the Columbia University Teachers' College based in New York City. (I would suggest that this is no longer the premier teaching school.) Today, almost all universities train indoctrinated teachers for K-12 and throughout the university level. They have now created and sent out corrected thinking "apostles" into the harvest for more than sixty years. Despite the verbiage of their various campaigns, the Marxist left was not so much interested in equality, racism, justice, or gender. Their real target was, *and still is today*, control of thought and behavior after dismantling all vestiges of our western Judeo-Christian heritage as established in our American foundations of faith and family.

This happened in direct correlation to the NEA being taken over by the unions. Once centralized control was secured, the symbiotic interdependence between government and the unionized school system was codified. (We will document this same dangerous symbiosis between government and corporations in Chapters 8–9.) Read the Core Values of the NEA off their website with the themes of Equal Opportunity, A Just Society, Democracy, Professionalism, Partnership, and Collective Action and you may envision a passing marching band during a 4th of July parade. But keep scrolling, friends, and there are links for "White Supremacy Culture Resources," "LGBTQ+ Resources," "Supporting Transgender, Non-binary, and Gender Non-conforming Students," and more. Their 3 million members in 14,000 communities with "State Aspiring Educators" in their affiliate organizations in all 50 states—coupled with the history just described— pretty well documents how we got here! Today teachers in public schools are not allowed to teach creation, to pray openly, or refer to God, and as a matter of rote fall back on the misconstrued phrase "separation of church and state." Game over? Not yet!

Since we haven't yet addressed government, this quote is one chapter premature—but here it is: "So, there is no Department of Education without the NEA. There is no Common Core curriculum without the Department of Education. There is no Common Core without Democratic presidents. And there are no Democratic presidents without the NEA."[6]

Comparatives

In this short section we will look at two primary areas: 1) US financial investment in our public education, as well as some newly reported foreign "donations"; 2) one student academic proficiency chart for this investment in the "top 10" countries.

These are a few statistics—and remember, all statistics are relevant to a specific timeframe:

The top ten states which spend the most money per student (annually):

1. New York ($25,359)
2. Connecticut ($20,744)
3. New Jersey ($20,247)
4. Alaska ($19,924)
5. New Hampshire ($18,632)
6. Rhode Island ($17,231)
7. Massachusetts ($17,136)
8. Wyoming ($17,018)
9. Hawaii ($16,284)
10. Delaware ($15,406)[7]

Total expenditures by academic level:

Early childhood—In 2019, 49% of three-to-four-year-olds and 86% of five-year-olds were already enrolled in school. However, to date, the US government still has not presented any expenditure report on early childhood education.

Elementary and secondary schools—The total revenue from these levels of institution amounted to $761 billion—$59 billion of which is from federal sources, $357 billion from state sources, and $345 billion from local sources. Learn more about Title 1 schools and funding for young learners.

Postsecondary and beyond—Total expenditure and revenue for public postsecondary institutions amounted to $386,707,398 and $408,931,242 consecutively for fiscal year 2017–2018, and $401,128,627 and $415,887,527 for fiscal year 2018–2019 (NCES, 2021). Title IV institutions are part of postsecondary schools. As illustrated below, state governments provide the largest percentage of the revenue of public-degree granting institutions.[8]

Universities, until recently, significantly "unreported" donations from numerous foreign actors, each of which had an agenda to influence. The Associated Press reported, "Feds say U.S. colleges 'massively' underreported foreign funding. According to early findings in the report, most of the 12 schools have had financial dealings with Huawei, the Chinese tech giant that some U.S. officials say is a threat to national security."[9] Or, this 2023 headline, "U.S. Universities including Cornell, Harvard and MIT Raked in $13B in 'Undocumented Contributions' from Foreign Donors."[10] Notably, countries in the Middle East, China, and Russia were included in these undisclosed donations. It brings some clarity to the pro-Palestinian demonstrations and intense anti-Semitism which appeared to come out of nowhere in 2024 on universities across America. In fact, dark money has been seeded across America's educational system for years.

Top ten countries with the "best" education:

	Country	Education Index	Literacy Rate
1	Germany	0.94	99%
2	Finland	0.93	100%
3	Iceland	0.93	99%
4	New Zealand	0.93	99%
5	Norway	0.93	100%
6	United Kingdom	0.93	99%
7	Australia	0.92	99%
8	Denmark	0.92	99%
9	Ireland	0.92	99%
10	Singapore	0.92	96.77%[11]

You can make statistics "do" almost anything with positioning, criteria selection, and interpretation. Our purpose here is just to paint a picture. The US spends more per student than any other country, so why do our student's proficiency scores continue to decline, and have done so for years? U. S. students' math skills have remained stagnant for decades. And, consider this sobering statistic: "The national average reading/language arts proficiency is 46%, based on state averages that range from 25% to 85%."[12] Contributing factors are much deeper.

The United States isn't investing as much in *human* capital as other developed countries. And our teaching philosophy has been radicalized. Merit-based criteria, personal responsibility, the validity of testing, and other traditional methods now give way to DEI-based infiltrations. Our country is falling behind many others which have greatly improved in the same time period. Who is to blame? Why is this happening?

A few of the contributing factors to these questions are identified in the next section. Whether or not they serve as an "answer" *for you* is up to you. I prefer to see these as symptoms—with the originator of all this chaos already identified.

Infiltrations of Education

For illustration I offer these bulleted representations of our current educational environment:

- California Senate Bill 107 (Jan 5, 2022): "This bill would prohibit a provider of health care, a health care service or a contractor from releasing medical information related to a person or identity allowing a child to receive gender-affirming health care. . . . This bill additionally would prohibit law enforcement agencies from knowingly making or participating in the arrest or extradition of an individual pursuant to an out-of-state arrest warrant."[13]
- United Teachers Los Angeles position paper on opening schools (July 2020): "The COVID-19 pandemic in the United States underscores the deep equity and justice challenges arising from our profoundly racist, intensely unequal society. . . .When politicians exhort educators and other workers to 'reignite the economy,' UTLA educators ask, '*who are you planning to use as kindling?*' As it stands, the only people guaranteed to benefit from the premature physical reopening of schools amidst a rapidly accelerating pandemic are billionaires and the politicians they've purchased."[14]

- The California Community College administration has just adopted a rule that will require faculty to take a loyalty oath to use diversity, equity, inclusion, and accessibility (DEIA) principles and anti-racism in their teaching.[15]

- The Los Angeles Unified School District (LAUSD) created a guide to organizing "Rainbow Clubs" for elementary students, which included lessons on "LGBTQ+ liberation, activism, and protest art. . . . This is a space for celebrating many types of identities, including Lesbian, Gay, Bisexual, Transgender, Nonbinary, Queer, Questioning, Intersex, Ace and Two Spirit identities! This is called fighting for social justice."[16]

- According to Parents Defending Education, at least 1,040 US school districts have adopted policies instructing or encouraging faculty and staff to keep students' gender identities a secret from parents. Those districts include more than 18,000 schools responsible for 11 million students. The vast majority of those school districts (593) are in California.[17]

- "Only the student," the NYESD declares, "knows whether it is safe to share their identity with a caregiver." The baseline assumption, then, is that "un-affirming" parents are dangerous to their children. If Kevin wants to be and go by Kimi but doesn't want his parents to know, the best practice, according to the NYESD, is as follows: "The teachers call her Kimi and use she/her pronouns at school. When calling home for any reason, teachers use the name Kevin and he/him pronouns. . . . The National Sex Education Standards also recommend introducing children to the concept of 'gender identity' starting in kindergarten."[18]

- Parents in Portland, Oregon can now send their kids to a free social justice summer camp founded by anarchists. A group called Budding Roses, which was founded as a project of the Black Rose / Rosa Negra Anarchist Foundation, holds a free two-week summer camp. A registration portal proclaims, "We believe that empowering youth to become critically engage with social justice issues lays the groundwork for transformational social change tomorrow and today. Budding Roses teaches children the chant, *Cops and borders; We don't need them.*"[19]

- SB 818 was signed into law by Governor Pritzker (of Illinois) which "creates personal health and safety standards for grades K-5 and updates and expands comprehensive sexual health education standards in grades 6–12. . . . The bill also ensures that comprehensive personal health and safety and sexual health education in Illinois is affirming of identities included in those who historically have been stigmatized or excluded including LGBTQIA and pregnant or parenting youth."[20]

- The Centers for Disease Control and Prevention (CDC; headquartered in Atlanta) has posted a document to its youth website, entitled "LGBTQ Inclusivity in Schools: A Self-Assessment Tool." The pages include several dropdown menus with resources for "professional development," "tools for supporting LGBT youth," and "health considerations for LGBT youth." Each includes a list of documents and guidance pertaining to pro-LGBT materials.[21]

- One of the most serious, cancerous infiltrations of atheist, Marxist indoctrination involves most of our public universities and a frightening percentage of our private ones. Besides the influence of foreign funding previously cited, the core of this orientation comes from the broader myth of intersectionality. In plain language, this is the theory that everyone has their own unique experiences of discrimination and oppression and that we must consider everything and anything which marginalizes people—gender, race, class, sexual orientation, physical ability, etc. This constant drumbeat pits a finite grouping of oppressors against seemingly endless classes of victims—always division, never conciliation!

Actionable Recommendations

It's time to radically change our approach. Do we attack or retreat? "It's not enough to yell at the school board when they erase the names of holidays, change the gender designations on bathrooms, force our young, healthy kids into masks, and advance critical race theory curricular—*you need to become the school board, or a mayor or state legislator* . . . [because] the teacher unions still control the classroom, the curricular is still poisoned, and the gains that are made . . . are almost always soon overwhelmed." [22]

From kindergarten through twelfth grade, we are giving the majority of our children attending public schools 16,000 hours of access to educators and administrators. And who are our kids being taught by? Well . . . still by many dedicated, wonderful, patriotic, decent people. Increasingly, however, *many* others are fully indoctrinated. Then consider who has the classroom freedom to even teach wholesome traits and curriculum? The system is closed and controlled. Just look around, and you will see the results of decades of intentional, calculated, "progressive" (understand: Marxist), union-controlled transformation. Critical theory (whether queer- or race-focused), 1619 replacing 1776 as the founding of our country, a radical trans agenda being legislated with parental rights removed, represent just the tip of the iceberg. As I have now heard many saying publicly, DEI, in truth, should be defined as Discrimination, Exclusion and Indoctrination, a transliteration of this concept closer to reality.

So, given this state of affairs, *what do we do?* A good military strategist will breakdown the battlefield into actionable parts. And what is the battlefield? The hearts and minds, the well-being of our children, families, and society! Unfortunately, one of the central contributing factors of our lethargy has been the anemic position of the church in society. We have "careful" pastors who don't want to offend anyone. Others put out "seeker-sensitive" mush that no longer proclaims the gospel. Worse yet, some pastors and priests believe this stuff!

> Empty church pews, combined with secular classrooms, have *intentionally* bred a sheer anti-American, anti-Western, and anti-Christian culture that is just now revealing itself. Not only do we not have our Christian faith, but we now don't even have faith in America. Fighting for the former, without fortifying the latter, is a losing proposition, because cultures like classrooms and politics always believe in something.[23]

These are just a few points of engagement in the battle plan to salvage our kids in pre-K through high school, our future leaders:

1. *Become knowledgeable and fully informed* about all the types of available schooling options in your state—homeschooling, charter schools, faith-based schools, learning pods, micro-schools, and more.
2. For those who have the will and capacity, i.e., who discern that a viable

alternative is feasible and affordable, *get your kids out of the secular public school system.*

3. At all levels of our community, state, and nation, *advocate for universal school choice* and be a strong voice of rational thought to counter the NEA and AFT nonsense.

4. Learn about ESAs, *education savings accounts,* and become an activist in your state to make these funds portable and transferable to whatever *your* school of choice is.

5. Every church or group of influencers *that can* should *establish a new Christian school.*

6. Volunteer to set up a *Take Back Education Prayer and Advocacy group* in your church or community. Identify a leadership team and develop a plan.

7. *Take back the rainbow!* It belongs to God and his promises in Scripture. Identify the LGBTQIA+ campaigns, books, and thought leaders. Then support groups like Sky Tree Book Fairs, founded by Kirk Cameron, and other wholesome organizations.

8. Don't just criticize or wait for leadership to add this to their responsibilities. *Take the initiative—it's your child or grandchild!*

Postscript on Universities

There is no possible way, within the limitations of this chapter, that we could adequately cover the infiltration of evil and subversion at the university level. To properly counterbalance their negative effect on our society at large requires an entirely different set of actionable recommendations. For those who are prayerfully called to focus on this area of spiritual warfare I encourage you to research widely, network extensively, and begin to formulate a strategy.

One excellent source as a starting point is Campus Reform, a project of the Leadership Institute (www.campusreform.org). They identify themselves as a conservative watchdog to the nation's higher education system. Founded in 1979 by Morton C. Blackwell, they work alongside student activists and student journalists to report on the conduct and misconduct of campus administrators, faculty and students—striving to report with accuracy, objectivity, and public accountability. One of their many excellent associates is Nicholas Giordano. Among many resources they have developed, the very useful "Campus Profile" scores universities from coast to coast. Criteria includes the names of both conservative and liberal organizations, required student fees, whether SAT/ACT tests are required, "Open Secrets" data, a Foundation for Individual Rights and Expression rating, university policies flagged that are inconsistent with free speech principles, the existence of any bias reporting system-residual COVID-19 mandates, and more.

The last cursory point we will make on universities is their destructive anti-western ideologies and complete intolerance to free, open speech and debate. One specific example is *The Hamas Network in America: A Short History* (https://extremeism.gwu/hamas-network). The civil disruption, tent encampments, the unquestionable hate speech, blocking of public access on bridges and highways—the sheer level of vehemence occurring during the timeframe this manuscript was being written—is stunning, *but not surprising.*

> Hamas supporters have long operated in the United States. Internal Hamas documents and FBI wiretaps introduced as evidence in various federal criminal cases clearly show the existence of a nationwide Hamas network engaged in fundraising, lobbying, education and propaganda dissemination dating back to the 1980s. The network formalized its existence in 1988, when it created the Palestine Committee in the U.S. the Committee's goals include "increasing the financial and moral support for Hamas," "fighting surrendering solutions," and "publicizing the savagery of the Jews."[24]

The antisemitic, pro-Hamas demonstrators at Columbia University include outside paid agitators, from this network. *The Wall Street Journal* (and other media) have reported that student organizers were consulting with veterans of former campus protests for months before launching their campaign. Ironically, some of the major funders of this anarchy are top donors to Biden/Harris and now the 2024 Harris/Walz campaign including Soros, Rockefeller, and Pritzker. Consider also that 14,000 out of Columbia's total student body of 40,000 are foreign visa holders. Authorities need to arrest, expel, then deport these arsonists, anarchists, and terrorists! Imagine if a mob calling for the death of people from the black or transgender community were engaged in this type of activity. Why is the response so completely different?

Again, *who* is truly behind the hatred of Jews and the destruction of Israel, the covenant people through whose lineage God chose for Jesus to be born? Once again, we know the answer and, therefore, need to pray accordingly.

Pray for . . .

- the Holy Spirit to give you specific guidance on what your role *will be* (not might be, can be, or we'll see) in returning spiritual authority over this massive domain of enemy control in your community, county, and state—prayer, organizing, networking, funding, joining, running for office, etc.
- the wisdom, energy and focus to become a fully informed and radically engaged activist tracking the legislation, movements, events, and people who are facilitating the dark agenda of the enemy against our children.
- *all* the children in your family and sphere of influence, in whatever level or type of educational institution they are enrolled in. There is a massive push by the enemy to subvert, subjugate, and ultimately destroy these precious creations of God.

CHAPTER 8

Mountain of Trouble—Government

GOVERNING SPANS MULTIPLE levels of jurisdiction and control. We will briefly address intergovernmental entities, including that "great temple of useless-ness" the United Nations and the World Health Organization, in Chapter 12. The American government is our focus and the infiltration of evil in this leviathan entity will include our military.

We make no attempt to remain politely neutral or nonpartisan. You are completely free to disagree. My foundational belief is that since *every* human institution is made up of people, *their spiritual orientation* is a trustworthy indicator of what they produce—good or evil. All of humanity will be judged on our life choices. Every person in every position of governmental authority (or any authority) is either God-honoring/God-seeking *or*, those who foolishly choose the liar and loser and his oppositional agenda.

Let me offer full disclosure as to my orientation. I have spent over half of my life, and currently live, in the People's Republic of California, described by some as "Cal-Unicornia." We are a one-party, absolute majority, locked-down-and-throw-away-the-key leftist juggernaut. On the other hand, California was blessed by the Creator as a beautiful and bountiful land. As of this writing there are 46.9% registered Democrats and 43.1% registered Independents, Republicans, and "Other" in this state.[1] So there is some hope! Now more than ever we must not only be vigilant, but active.

One Breitbart News Daily broadcast by host Mike Slater offered some insightful commentary on the political makeup of America. He referred to one of the 2,500-year-old Aesop's fables, comparing the country mouse to the city mouse. After leaving the country and experiencing the life of the city the country mouse returned home, preferring the simplicity and safety (and lower income) of the country to the glitz and danger of the city. Extrapolating this, Slater said that American cities comprise 4% of the land but 62% of the population. He postulated that every state is actually a "red" state, but that most cities are "blue." He noted that rural California has as many conservative patriots as Nebraska (though Omaha and Lincoln diminish that equation—again, city versus country).[2] This makes clear why Democrats want to eliminate the Electoral College and determine election outcomes on the popular vote. The urban population in the United States is now 81%. This pattern is consistent with global urbanization statistics as well. Our founding fathers had great wisdom!

We will now address these five subsets:

- The founding of America
- US government tyranny (with some Canadian references)
- US military depletion and degradation
- The Democrat Party

Consider this:

- Look at the platform of the Democratic Socialists of America and ask yourself which major political party has successfully aligned their policy demands.
- One of the most evil and despicable realities of our present open-border situation is the trafficking of children and young women (some men) in the commercial sex trade.
- The tentacles of various branches of the US government and our seventeen intelligence agencies are increasingly limiting our God-given *and* constitutional freedoms.

The Founding of America

Among our earliest settlers, America was predominantly birthed by people who sought the free worship of God outside of the tyranny of government oppression. We are the second nation to have an established covenant with the Creator. *Israel was chosen by God* to be His people. In what was to become America, believing *Christians committed* that our founding would also be based on a covenant with this same Sovereign. These are a few stones of remembrance:

In 1620, while still sailing on the English ship the Mayflower, the Pilgrims created the first founding document in America. Called the Mayflower Compact, this two-hundred-word document created by William Bradford and William Brewster bound the signatories into agreement to pledge their intention to abide by the future laws and regulations for the general good of the colony. It was signed by the forty-one adult males out of a total of 102 passengers, and was fashioned as an adaptation of a Puritan church covenant. This is a selection from this document: "In the name of God, Amen.... Having undertaken for the glory of God, and advancement of the Christian faith . . . a voyage to plant the first colony in the northern parts of Virginia; do by these presents solemnly and mutually, in the presence of God and one another, covenant and combine ourselves . . .(to) enact, constitute and frame such just and equal laws." This document, signed on Cape Cod on November 11, 1620, clearly links their covenantal commitment with their Christian faith, and the anticipated Christian faith of subsequent pilgrims and sojourners.

In his sermon of 1630 (later titled "Dreams of a City on a Hill") John Winthrop's declaration and warning included these words, spoken in the colloquialism of the period (emphasis added):

> *Thus stands the cause between God and us.* We are entered into covenant with Him for this work. We have taken out a commission. *The Lord hath given us leave* to draw our own articles. We have professed to enterprise these and those accounts, upon these and those ends. *We have hereupon besought Him of favor and blessing. Now if the Lord shall please to hear us, and bring us in peace to the place we desire, then hath He ratified this covenant and sealed our commission,* and will expect a strict performance of the articles contained in it; but if we shall neglect the observation of these articles which are the ends we have propounded, and dissembling with our God, shall fall to embrace this present world and prosecute our carnal intentions, seeking great things for ourselves and our posterity, *the Lord will surely break out in wrath against us,*

*and be revenged of such a people, and make us know the price of the
breach of such a covenant* . . .

And to shut this discourse with the exhortation of Moses,
that faithful servant of the Lord, in his last farewell to Israel,
Deuteronomy 30, "Beloved, there is now set before us life and
death, good and evil," in that *we are commanded this day to love
the Lord our God, and to love one another,* to walk in his ways and
to keep his Commandments and his ordinance and his laws, and
the articles of our Covenant with Him, that we may live and be
multiplied, and that the Lord our God may bless us in the land
whither we go to possess it. *But if our hearts shall turn away, so that
we will not obey, but shall be seduced, and worship other gods, our
pleasure and profits, and serve them; it is propounded unto us this day,
we shall surely perish out of the good land whither we passed over this
vast sea to possess it.* Therefore, let us choose life, that we and our
seed may live, by obeying His voice and cleaving to Him, for He
is our life and our prosperity.[3]

When the Unanimous Declaration of the Thirteen United States of
America was presented to the Continental Congress on July 4, 1776, it
included this affirmation (emphasis added): "We hold these truths to be
self-evident, that all men are created equal, that they are *endowed, by their
Creator*, with certain unalienable rights, that among them are life, liberty,
and the pursuit of happiness. . . . We, therefore, the Representatives
of the United States of America assembled, appealing to the Supreme
Judge of the world for the rectitude of our intentions do. . . . And for the
support of this declaration *with a firm reliance on the protection of Divine
Providence*, we mutually pledge to each other our lives, our fortunes, and
our sacred honour."[4]

On April 30, 1789, when George Washington took his oath of office as
first president of the United States, he concluded his address with these words
(again, emphasis added): "Having thus imparted to you my sentiments as they
have been awakened by the occasion which brings us together, I shall take
my present leave; but not without resorting once more to the benign *Parent
of the Human Race* in humble supplication that, since He *has been pleased
to favor the American* people with opportunities for deliberating in perfect

tranquility, and dispositions for deciding with unparalleled unanimity on a form of government for the security of their union and the advancement of their happiness, so *His divine blessing* may be equally conspicuous in the enlarged views, the temperate consultations, and the wise measures *on which the success of Government must depend*."[5]

We are most familiar with the First Amendment (of twenty-seven) to the US Constitution, which reads, "Congress shall make no law respecting an establishment of religion, or prohibiting the free exercise thereof; or abridging the freedom of speech, or of the press; or the right of the people peaceably to assemble, and to petition the Government for redress of grievances."

There are many other markers of the original intent of (most of) the founding luminaries of America—"one nation under God" in the Pledge of Allegiance; "In God we Trust" on our instruments of currency; the Gettysburg Address of Abraham Lincoln who said, "That this nation, under God, shall have a new birth of freedom . . .". And there are many other examples.

All patriotic citizens must actively reject subversive, slanted initiatives and philosophies which tear down America! The present-day American Marxists want you to believe an entirely inverted history based on perpetual oppressor-victim struggle.

We now consider, rather candidly, the mountain of trouble, corruption and complicity with evil that much of our federal government and many of those embedded in this leviathan are involved with today. The extensiveness of the deep state's role, coming to light in greater measure in America today, is truly sobering!

Government Tyranny

There are many erudite authors and thought leaders who write and speak on the government's departure from our founding principles, and the collusion which exists between government, business, and media. We can plainly see now the censorship and controlled messaging from leftist corporate media giants and tech oligarchs. The government has infiltrated, influences, and in some instances actually controls segments of traditional media and social media platforms. Victor Davis Hanson, Mark Levin, Robert Woodson, and Carol Swain are some of the voices of truth who provide clarity in the howling wind tunnel of state-influenced and disseminated "information." They use their platforms to appropriately and repeatedly tell Americans to wake up and get involved.

Below, I have listed a few points of concern, each of which reflect the tentacles of various branches or departments of the US government which are slowly squeezing and canceling our God-given freedoms as enshrined in our Constitution.

- Open borders with millions of immigrants entering without restraint or procedure
- A flawed, corruptible and voter ID-less voting system for elections
- The demeaning, defunding, and therefore defanging of law enforcement officers
- Dark money funding corrupt judges, AGs, DAs, and other so called justice officials
- The imposition of a globalist agenda to the detriment of national sovereignty
- Climate change fanaticism and the death of energy independence
- The hate-America drumbeat, which says *every* BIPOC is a victim of systemic racism
- The myth that white supremacy is the greatest threat to America
- Government-initiated propaganda, censorship, and subversion
- The radical trans agenda—where did all the women's rights voices go?
- The COVID years, fear-mongering, masking, and mandated vaccines
- An *undeniable* two-tiered system of justice, looking more like one tier, for one side
- The destructive DEI cultural metastasis
- The unconstitutional weaponization of the government against parents, conservatives, Christians, and everyday working Americans
- Crushing national debt and intentionally foolish monetary policy
- The enticement to remain a dependent recipient of the welfare state
- Term-limitless, self-serving, bureaucrats-for-life
- Turning the US military into a social experiment rather than a fighting defense force

What follows are selected quotes or events—most in America, a few in Canada—which give form, shape, and context to the destructive pattern of the increasing tyranny just identified:

- The Committee on the Judiciary is conducting oversight of how and what the extent of the executive branch has coerced and colluded with companies and other intermediaries to censor speech. Of particular interest is the Center for Countering Digital Hate—CCDH has admitted to directly engaging with the executive branch and big tech about content moderation.[6]

- During the COVID-19 crisis, the nationwide quarantine, and the protests and subsequent rioting over the death of George Floyd, we witnessed the ideal incubator of socialist ideas that in calmer times would have little resonance. Petty county officials, mayors, and governors used the quarantines to enforce often incoherent social-distancing and other edicts, which seemed designed as much to emphasize their authority as to ameliorate the effects of the corona virus.[7]

- In a December 30, 2021 letter, a January 6 political prisoner Jeremy Brown asks, "Are you ready to light brushfires of Liberty in the souls of men? Then don't do nothing. I am a 20-year retired US Army Special Forces Combat Veteran. On January 5th and 6th, 2021 I was in our nation's capital as part of an all-volunteer protective detail tasked with providing security for organizers and speakers at a legally permitted political rally. On September 30, 2021 I was arrested at home in Tampa, Florida by approximately 30 to 40 heavily armed Federal Agents and local law enforcement. They came in full force to serve a misdemeanor arrest warrant for being in an 'unauthorized area.'" These were no ordinary agents. They were agents working as part of the FBI's Joint Terrorism Task Force (JTTF). According to Brown, the same JTTF agents who arrested him on Sept 30, 2021 had tried to recruit him as a confidential informant (CI) on December 9, 2020. Their "pitch," he said, was intended to gauge his "willingness to infiltrate law-abiding citizen groups that had no criminal history and certainly were not designated terrorist groups."[8]

- On October 8, 2020, one month before the 2020 general election, Muskegon Michigan City Clerk Ann Meisch noticed a black female, whose name was later redacted from the police report, dropping off between 8,000–10,000 completed voter registration applications at the city clerk's office. Clerk Meisch immediately noticed that the stacks of registrations included the same handwriting, nonexistent addresses, and incorrect phone numbers. The Muskegon Police Department was contacted and an investigative task force was formed. During their investigation, the state police discovered the woman worked for GBI Strategies with temporary offices in numerous Michigan locations. They identified Gary Bell as the head of the organization. When the police inspected the Muskegon GBI Strategies office they found semiautomatic guns, silencers/suppressors, burner phones, a bag of prepaid cash cards, and incomplete registrations in an office space that was styled as an eyeglass store that had gone defunct. There were never any arrests! Michigan State Senator Ruth Johnson, who is herself a former secretary of state, said, "My estimate is over 800,000 ballot applications were sent to non-qualified voters in Michigan.[9]

- Multiple FBI offices targeted American Catholics. New evidence suggests that the FBI's attempts to spy on American Catholics were more pervasive than originally stated and that the agency's director may have lied under oath. According to a letter from Rep. Jim Jordan (R-OH) and Rep. Mike Johnson (R-LA) to FBI director Christopher Wray, documents that the federal law enforcement agency provided to legislators show that an FBI memo detailing plans to spy on "radical traditionalist Catholics" did not originate solely with the Richmond field office, as Wray insisted under oath. Instead, multiple field offices were reportedly involved—namely, offices in Portland and Los Angeles.[10]

- Dr. Jordan Peterson (Edmonton, Alberta, Canada) is a Mensa IQ author, clinical psychologist, marriage health and restoration expert, foster parent, and truth-teller. He was slapped with an Ontario Superior Court of Justice ruling that the College of Psychologists of Ontario could mandate Peterson to go through a so-called "specified continuing education or remedial program." Some of Peterson's supposed offenses, according to the College of Psychologists, included retweeting Conservative Party leader Pierre Poilievre's criticism of

Canadian Prime Minister Justin Trudeau criticizing a former senior Trudeau aide, and expressing opposition to the idea of the Ottawa police taking custody of the children of Trucker Convoy protesters. Peterson said, "I'm going to do everything I can to make all of this as public as I possibly can. I want to make this 100% transparent, and let the public decide for themselves who exactly is acting, let's say, in an unprofessional capacity."[11]

- The Canadian government's persecution of Christian pastors for expressing views not in line with socialist ideology has become very onerous. Pastor Artur Pawlowski from Calgary, Alberta represents just one of hundreds who have suffered for their faith in Jesus Christ and direct expressions of biblical truth. Pawlowski, a Polish immigrant in 1995, founded Street Church Ministries which had its religious charitable status revoked. He now faces incarceration for any number of matters angering the Trudeau government.

- What does the US Government, in tandem with one or more of our seventeen intelligence agencies, still have to hide about the 9-11 hijackers and the role of Saudi Arabia? Of the nineteen Al Qaeda terrorists who hijacked four US commercial airliners, fifteen were Saudi citizens. Gold Star families, first responder families, every resident of the five boroughs of New York City, and Americans at large see a pattern of obfuscation and something sinister!

LCpl Jared M. Schmitz

- On August 29, 2023, "Gold Star Dad" Mark Schmitz of Wentzville, Missouri gave a riveting testimony to the House Foreign Affairs Committee (not broadcast by any leftist media outlets), His twenty-year-old son Jared was one of thirteen American service personnel needlessly killed by a suicide bomber at the Abbey Gate entrance to the Kabul Airport during the chaotic handling of the US withdrawal. Forty-seven additional U.S. personnel were injured and, tragically, 170 Afghan children and adults were also killed. This was a completely avoidable tragedy because the Biden/Harris administration ignored the near-unanimous advice of the military and intelligence recommendations in favor of the armchair quarterbacks in the State Department; also, one of our military snipers had the bomber in his sights and was denied permission to terminate him! All actionable digital information was withheld—video footage from land-based cameras and drones, even the SIM cards from all service personnel were removed before leaving. It is nothing short of stunning how complicit and reprehensible our government acted in this matter.

- Do both or either of our major political parties operate with full transparency and fairness? They do not. Democrat Bernie Sanders was maneuvered out of the 2020 presidential race for the predetermined candidate, Hillary Clinton. Democrat Robert F. Kennedy wasn't even allowed to enter the 2024 race as a Democrat. Republican Larry Elder and other 2024 Republican presidential candidates didn't make the debate stage. I believe the biblical term "brood of vipers" is quite applicable to those who control the levers of political power.

- *Every American should expect and demand election integrity.* I distinctly recall Democrats raising issues related to election integrity—Al Gore (2000), John Kerry (2004), and Hillary Clinton (2016). They did so with the full support of the corporate media. But when Republicans raised the same type of concerns in 2020 the media excoriated them as election deniers, insurrectionists, deplorables, and people clinging to their guns and religion. M*any* groups are now focused on leveling the playing field.

- One of the most evil and despicable realities of our present open border situation, where millions have crossed the border or been flown in without restraint, is the trafficking of children, women and some men in the commercial sex trade—as well as the forced labor industry. This includes outright sale of babies and young children. This has resulted also in organized criminal gang activity from the Tren de Aragua of Venezuela and Mara Salvatrucha (MS 13) from El Salvador. 2024 is replete with cases of the rape and murder of American girls and young women by such people.

Is anyone surprised, after considering these specific examples of government malfeasance and in some cases tyranny, *why* we are in the condition we are in?

Military Depletion and Degradation

As any herpetologist (and well-trained outdoorsman) knows, you must cut off the head of the snake to end its purpose and direction. One translation: who we choose to lead us defines the journey. John Maxwell said, "A leader is one who knows the way, goes the way, and shows the way."[12] There is no coincidence that the senior military leaders in every branch of service, selected by both the Obama/Biden and Biden/Harris administrations, comport with the leftist, Marxist policies of the present era. Many of our senior military leaders are woke and weak. Contributing factors to or indicators of our depleted condition of military readiness include:

- The deleterious effect of our pull out from Afghanistan—billions of dollars of military armaments and equipment now in the hands of global terrorists
- The removal of patriotic career officers for spurious reasons
- The decimation of morale
- Recruitment well below basic maintenance levels
- Forcing service personnel to leave the military if they refused the unnecessary vaccine mandate, some losing their pension just prior to retirement
- The promulgation of gender transition surgeries at taxpayer expense
- Putting arbitrary quotas on the racial percentage of particular specialties—for example, the limitation to 46% of Air Force pilots who can be white

- The mission creep of our armed forces from defending America to becoming a forced social engineering experiment
- Critical Race Theory books as mandatory reading
- Indoctrinating recruits with pronoun videos
- DEI hiring quotas at the Department of Defense
- Military funded travel for service personnel abortions
- Subsidizing family friendly drag shows and travel to pride events; pride night on deployed ships at sea
- 2024 DoD Budget includes funds to "root out extremist activity"[13]

These are three examples of the leadership problems noted:

1. Complaints by veteran soldiers about younger generations who lack discipline and traditional values are as old as war itself. Grizzled veterans in the Greek phalanx, Roman legions, and Napolean's elite corps all believed that the failings of the young would be the ruin of their armies. This is not the chief worry of grizzled American veterans today. The largest threat they see by far to our current military is the weakening of its fabric by radical progressive, i.e., woke policies being imposed not by a rising generation of slackers but by the very leaders charged with ensuring their readiness.

   Wokeness in the military is being imposed by elected and appointed leaders in the White House, Congress, and the Pentagon who have apparently have little understanding of the purpose, character, traditions, and requirements of the institution they are trying to change. Actually, I believe they have understanding—they're complying with a political agenda!

   Woke ideology undermines military readiness in various ways. It undermines cohesiveness by emphasizing differences based on race, ethnicity and sex. It undermines leadership authority by introducing questions about whether promotion is based on merit or quota requirements. It leads to military personnel serving in specialties and areas for which they are not qualified or ready. And it takes time and resources away from training activities and weapons development that contribute to readiness.

   Wokeness in the military also affects relations between the military and society at large. It acts as a disincentive for many young Americans in terms of enlistment. And it undermines wholehearted support for the military by a significant portion of the American public, at a time when it is needed most.[14]

2. Keep an eye on the policies of the current chairman of the Joint Chiefs of Staff, Air Force General Charles Q. Brown, aka Charlie Brown, a Biden/Harris appointee. I've heard him called "Al Sharpton in uniform." According to the Heritage Foundation's latest, highly regarded *Index of U.S. Military Strength*, the Air Force is assessed to have gone from "marginal" in 2021, General Brown's first year as chief of staff, to "weak" in his second and "very weak" in 2023. By design, the Marxists' damage is extensive:

   - Pitting races against one another, destroying unit cohesion
   - Diverting training focus and resources away from war-fighting
   - Eroding safety and willingness to serve of females "uncomfortable" with bunking and showering with intact males
   - Politicizing the military
   - Degrading readiness and deterrence[15]

3. The Biden/Harris administration is fighting back against a new provision in the annual defense spending bill that would require military promotions to be based solely on merit rather than considering race or gender. Rep. Chip Roy (R-TX) supported the move to strip DEI provisions from military promotions, adding, "What we're trying to do is move to a colorblind, race-neutral worldview, where we're focused on, you know, blowing things up and killing people, not on social engineering wrapped in a uniform. Wokeness is a cancer that will destroy our military from the inside out if we don't stop it."[16]

It is a critical time in our nation, and people of faith, family, and patriotism need to realize that we are in *existential danger*. Unless "we the people" wake up to what is happening, set aside any fear or hesitation to get involved, *and get involved* at every level of society—in very short order it will be too late to do so. One serious exercise of reflection we each must engage in early on is *to consider what people, from which institutions or infrastructures, promulgate much of this evil.* With this element of understanding, we will have a clearer path to develop a strategy for victory.

The Democrat Party

Thankfully, I discovered early that it is rather foolish to vote for an individual on the basis of likeability, personality, or his/her communication style. It is also unwise to fall into a lemming-like pattern and just keep voting for the same party. In truth, I dislike both majority U.S. political parties *almost* equally. But I also believe that it is a total abdication of our precious gift of freedom not to vote for anyone. Therefore, informed, faith-centered citizens must understand the spiritual dynamics embedded in virtually all temporal institutions, because Satan has been subverting this domain intently. The church, government, corporations, associations—each have been infiltrated.

I have a nostalgic sense of the valor of the "greatest generation" and their sacrifice in World War II (before I was born). Franklin D. Roosevelt's prayer on D-Day, June 6, 1944, brings images of a country united behind a Democratic president who had a grasp on the undeniable blessings and protection of Almighty God on our destiny—victory. Here are excerpts.

> In this poignant hour, I ask you to join me in prayer. Almighty God: our sons, pride of our Nation, this day we have set upon a mighty endeavor, a struggle to preserve our Republic, our religion, and our civilization, and to set free a suffering humanity. Lead them straight and true; give strength to their arms, stoutness to their hearts, steadfastness in their faith. They will need Thy blessings . . . some will never return. Embrace these, Father, and receive them, Thy heroic servants, into Thy Kingdom .. . . With Thy blessing we shall prevail over the unholy forces of our enemy. . . . Thy will be done, Almighty God. Amen.[17]

Can you imagine any Democrat president in the last forty-two years (i.e., since the Carter era) publicly proclaiming this prayer or anything close to it? Not a chance!

And how many of us can remember the inspiring oratory, encouragement to conquer the future, and affirmation of the American people often spoken by John F. Kennedy?

- If not us, who? If not now, when?
- Ask not what your country can do for you, but what you can do for your country.
- Every accomplishment starts with the decision to try.
- As we express our gratitude, we must never forget that the highest form of appreciation is not to utter words, but to live by them
- The ignorance of one voter in democracy impairs the security of all.[18]

Of course, all presidents have speechwriters. But JFK "had it" and motivated a nation. His life, cut short, was a national tragedy. However, *the most important point of this section is that those who control the levers of power in today's Democrat Party do NOT represent the historic platforms or values of the Democrat Party.*

Since the days of Roosevelt, Truman, Kennedy, Johnson, and Carter, *and* including the legitimate, heterodox policies of 2024 formerly Democrat presidential candidate Robert F. Kennedy Jr., one can understand how Democrats have maintained their appeal. Post-Carter Democrats are a different story. Again, this consistent appeal to about half of the US voting population would not be possible without the unequivocal influence of the majority corporate-owned media.

It is time for historic Democratic voters, who pull the lever out of habit, to take a hard, serious look at the platforms they espouse and how it aligns with or betrays their faith, values and commitment to maintain a stable civil society. There is clear evidence that the Democrat Party has been taken over by Marxist, extremist radicals! The Democrats are now the party of the elite. There is an awakening taking place which emphasizes:

1. The overwhelming need to put God first in all decisions, especially in voting, and
2. The increasing exposure of longstanding corruption which must have greater bearing on who we vote for

An interesting shift is underway in the historic voting base for the two major parties. Republicans are now strongly supported by the working-class including Union members (not the bosses), with increasing transitions of people from historically consistent Democratic voters - Latin, African, and Asian Americans as well as Jewish voters. Regarding the latter, more than 40% of donations received by the Democratic National Committee has been from liberal Jewish voters. With the stunning (but not surprising) strength of anti-Semitism in large sectors of the Democratic base, this financial support is beginning to move out of the DNC as well as the so-called "elite" universities.

These are the direct links to the issues as articulated in the official party platforms of the Democrats and Republicans:

> https://democrats.org/where-we-stand/party-platform/
> https://gop.com/about-our-party/

It is vital that we clearly understand and research the position of the Democrat Socialists of America (https://dsausa.org). They have overtaken the high ground in the deliberative affairs of the Democrat Party. *Democrats have moved so far to the left that one could make the claim that they are the greatest threat to democracy!*

Please, also take the time to review the "45 Communist Goals from 58 Years Ago" (https://www.ethanallen.org/45_communist_goals_from_58_years_ago). Here are just five:

1. Capture one or both political parties in the United States
2. Get control of the schools and teachers associations
3. Infiltrate the press
4. Discredit the American Constitution by calling it inadequate and old-fashioned
5. Infiltrate and gain control of big business and unions

Finally, here are selected positions from the twenty-two-page downloadable DSA political platform. After you read these excerpts, then you decide who is in control of the Democrat Party!

- The Democratic Socialists of America are fighting to win a world organized and governed by and for the vast majority, the working class. We are socialist because we share a vision of a humane social order based on popular control of resources and production, economic planning, equitable distribution, feminism, racial equality, and non-oppressive relationships.
- A democratic socialist society must end the economic subjugation of women in the workplace, violence, and harassment affecting

women and nonbinary people, and the entire system of unpaid, gendered work.

- The fight for *socialism* is the fight for true democracy. *Our demands*:
  - A new political order through a second Constitutional convention
  - Abolish the filibuster
  - Supreme Court term limits and additional seats to break the counter-majoritarian conservative majority
  - DC statehood
  - Passage of HR 1, the For the People Act, providing for nationwide online election day and automatic voter registration, providing for nationwide early voting
  - Defund the police by rejecting *any* expansion to police budgets or scope of enforcement while cutting budgets annually *toward zero*
  - Free *all* people from involuntary confinement
  - Demilitarize the police and end colonial policing of our cities and neighborhoods
  - Disarm law enforcement officers, including the police *and* private security
  - We fight to abolish white supremacy and racial oppression.
  - Whiteness is a modern sociological construction, and its development and integration into the racial ideology of the United States is linked to the development of capitalism in the original European colonies.
  - We fight for policies such as reparations for black and indigenous communities; in the long-term, for the abolition of police and prisons.
  - End environmental racism
  - A four-day, thirty-two-hour work week
  - We fight for the abolition of capitalism and the creation of a democratically run economy that provides for people's needs.
  - Social ownership and democratic control of utilities and key industries
  - Create a unified democratic and public banking system that will socialize the fuel of the capitalist system; finance

- o DSA is a socialist feminist organization. We organize people of all genders to fight against systems of oppression and exploitation by including *patriarchy, capitalism* and *white supremacy.*
- o Free abortion on demand
- o End anti-queer violence
- o Guarantee queer-friendly and gender affirming healthcare
- o Grant all privileges afforded to married couples to all consenting partnerships
- o Decarbonize the economy within a decade
- o Democratize control over major energy systems and resources
- o Transform the rules of the capitalist global economy, through both domestic policy and multilateral cooperation toward decarbonization, the dismantling of neocolonialism, realization of global climate justice as a global Green New Deal
- o DSA operates in the heart of a global capitalist empire (for) solidarity with *comrades* around the globe.
- o Stop using economic and financial sanctions to punish other countries, such as Cuba, Venezuela, and Iran.
- o Close all US foreign military bases
- o Protect the right to asylum and safe entry; abolish ICE [19]

One final thought - Concern for our borders is not racist. The creation of sanctuary cities for migrants who did not cross legally or have necessary documentation is for what purpose? Creating new congressional districts with newly minted voters, of course! The United Nations suggests that *replacement migration* "is a solution to declining and aging populations." Is that the motivation for allowing millions coming across our borders? I don't think so. This is much too large and important a topic to just give cursory attention, but we must.

All people of faith, who trust in our sovereign God and love their country, *must pray as never before!*

Pray for . . .

- that Holy Spirit will awaken the hearts, minds, and spirit of all people who will, to see with new eyes the evil all around us and then declare God's victory and His will be done.
- that Holy Spirit will lead as many as He has ordained to offer a heart of repentance so that America and all nations that turn to God will live in peace until the end of this age.
- discernment, protection, provision and encouragement for all of God's people in these times of peril.

CHAPTER 9

Mountain of Trouble—Business

THE INFILTRATION OF evil in one of the biggest mountains of trouble is *the domain of money*. Of course, business is only one means of generating money. This represents a global spiritual battle ground against all of humanity. The spiritual forces of wickedness, the spirit of mammon, reigns and operates significantly in this sector of our human existence. "For the love of money is a root of all kinds of evil. Some people, eager for money, have wandered from the faith and pierced themselves with many griefs" (1 Tim. 6:10).

We will first focus on U.S. public corporations including massive institutions that manage assets utilizing *some* of the publicly available wealth data. When you multiply the reach and influence of these controllers and repositories of money *and* include global wealth, you can understand the necessity of engaging kingdom principles *and* principals to operate redemptively.

Most of us do not fully realize the intrusive and interconnected effect major corporations and fund managers have on "we the people". These institutions do not work in a vacuum. They most assuredly partner with other power structures, especially governments, media, and big tech. With spiritual discernment one begins to understand the pool of piranhas that must be overcome *in the spiritual realm—*in the domain of money.

This chapter will also include commentary on three subsets of importance:

- Intersectionality / DEI
- Global warming / climate change
- COVID-19 / "Big Pharma"

Consider this:

- When you begin to understand the enormous wealth that exists in our U.S. context and globally, it is easy to understand how greed and corruption, both subtle and overt, is endemic.
- The religion of climate change ("climate justice" and other monikers) is a central tool in the planning of future societal control, especially in regard to finances.
- COVID-19, the first of additional contemporary pandemics to come, will also be used as a means for centralized control and the imposition of the state over the God-ordained freedoms of the individual.

Let's begin with some quantifiable information. There are many attractive charts and graphs which could be included, but since we are not trying to recreate Forbes, Fortune, Bloomberg or Barron's we will just use these much simplified "Top 10" and "Top 5" measures. Of course, all data is time sensitive and represents one point in a continuum of variables that fluctuates constantly. These snapshots just paint a picture.

The 10 Largest US Companies by Market Capitalization[1]

1. Apple (AAPL) .... $2.711 trillion
2. Microsoft (MSFT) .... $2.455 trillion
3. Alphabet (GOOG)... $1.757 trillion
4. Amazon (AMZN).. $1.326 trillion
5. Nvidia (NVDA) .... $804.24 billion
6. Meta Platforms (META) .... $739.32 billion
7. Berkshire Hathaway (BRK-B) .... $688.29 billion
8. Tesla (TSLA) .... $562.39 billion
9. Eli Lilly (LLY).. $488.02 billion
10. Visa (V).. $486.31 billion

Note: Six out of 10 are highly influential Big Tech oligarchies.

The 10 Largest US Hedge Funds[2]

1. Bridgewater Associates .... $124.317 trillion
2. Renaissance Technologies .... $106.027 trillion
3. AQR Capital Management.................................... $ 94.524 trillion
4. Two Sigma .... $ 67.471 trillion
5. Millenium Management....................................... $ 57.670 trillion
6. Citadel .... $ 51.574 trillion
7. Tiger Global Management .... $ 51.000 trillion
8. D. E. Shaw .... $ 45.773 trillion
9. Coatue Management.. $ 42.339 trillion
10. Davidson Kempner... $ 40.800 trillion

Note: Nine out of 10 are in NY or CT (the one in Miami was founded by a "snowbird")

The 10 Largest US Asset Managers[3]

1. Blackrock .... $9.425 trillion
2. Vanguard.. $7.250 trillion
3. Fidelity Management & Research .... $3.880 trillion
4. The Capital Group Companies .... $2.300 trillion
5. Pacific Investments Management....................... $1.740 trillion
6. Invesco... $1.483 trillion
7. Wellington Management .... $1.400 trillion
8. Franklin Resources .... $1.388 trillion
9. T. Rowe Price Group .... $1.350 trillion
10. Blackstone Group .... $881 billion

Note: ESG, Net Zero, cashless digital monetary systems are coming

The 5 Largest Mutual Funds[4]

1. Vanguard Total Stock Market Index Fund Admiral Shares (VTSAX) .... $1.3 trillion
2. Vanguard 500 Index Fund Admiral Shares (VFIAX)........... $808.8 billion

3. Vanguard Total International Stock Index Admiral Shares (VTIAX)......
$385.5 billion
4. Fidelity 500 Index Fund (FXAIX)...$380.7 billion
5. Vanguard Total Bond Market Index Fund Admiral Shares (VBTLX) .....
$305.1 billion

Note: It is vital to understand *where* these funds are invested!

The 5 Largest US Retirement Funds[5]

1. Federal Retirement Thrift...$774.2 billion
2. California Public Employees ....$496.8 billion
3. California State Teachers...$313.9 billion
4. New York State Common ....$267.8 billion
5. New York City Retirement ....$266.7 billion

Note the political orientation of these two "blue" states and, the federal "deep state."

Most people are unaware that three mega-asset management groups— Black Rock, Vanguard, and State Street—own 88% of the Standard and Poor's 500. *Another sobering projection is that by 2030, 60% of single-family homes will be owned by corporations who pay cash.*

With so much accumulated, centralized wealth, what does your natural mind, but especially your spiritual discernment, tell you? *Yes*, this is a mega-battleground between good and evil.

> The spirit of mammon attaches itself to money, and this spirit has one, overarching goal: to get us to trust it more than God. Mammon constantly suggests to us that maybe God's promises in this area aren't true, and it tells us it can do things for us that God can't. Jesus had plenty to say on the subject and, during His ministry, He warned against being enslaved to it. "No one can serve two masters; for either he will hate the one and love the other, or he will stand by and be devoted to the one and despise and be against the other. You cannot serve God and mammon (deceitful riches, money, possessions, or whatever is trusted in)" (Matthew 6:24, AMPC).

There's nothing wrong with having money, as long as money doesn't have us. We can't trust it, because it can let us down. Loving it more than anything else is a sign that we've developed a wrong relationship with it. The rich young ruler with whom Jesus had a conversation was ruled by mammon; this spirit is still prevalent today.

Stockpiling wealth and valuing it above everything else is a mistake due to spiritual short-sightedness. "Then he said to them, Watch out! Be on your guard against all kinds of greed; life does not consist in an abundance of possessions" (Luke 12:15). Money is fickle, and putting our full trust in it sets us up for disappointment. Greed can cause us to abandon common sense and do foolish things.

We can take authority over the destructive spirit of mammon when we're aware of its presence and how it operates. Mammon is insidious; it uses deception to make us think we need money more than God. We only hurt ourselves when we desperately cling to it. God is well aware that we need money, and He won't let us down in this area. "But seek first his kingdom and his righteousness, and all these things shall be added unto you" (Matthew 6:33).[6]

Intersectionality/DEI

Business and government, in coordination with media and technology companies represent a formidable cabal of trouble—and intense opposition to kingdom principles.

One of the tools employed in this spiritual battle comes under the banner of ESG, which stands for Environmental Social Governance. It is a classification system now used by many of America's biggest corporations and global ones as well. It has become a political tool to promulgate a radical agenda. An ESG "score" is applied on a graded scale, which rewards or penalizes a company based on an agenda contrived and controlled by . . . *well, that is the million-dollar question.*

ESG was developed by the United Nations Environmental Programme Initiative. Please refer to the Freshfields Report of October 2005, created by team leader Paul Clements-Hunt. "It was subsequently 'concertized' into sustainable finance and responsible investment in the ECOSOC Chamber at UNHQ. . . . A recent Deloitte's Insights study showed that ESG now account for 25% of total market assets. . . . Many forecasters believe this momentum will continue in the coming years with a 50% market share an achievable goal."[7] Clearly, this mutated well beyond the UN.

So, what exactly is dangerous about ESG? To start with, "ESG rules are requiring companies to appoint board members based on race and sex and requiring greenhouse gas emissions to be reported. Other ESG rules require:

- Cancel culture for "wrong thinking"
- Racial quotas in the workplace
- Corporate donations for abortion
- Pushing the trans issue onto children
- Critical Race Theory
- Corporate welfare
- Anti-oil, "green new deal" mandates"[8]

A rather recently exiled member of the "green community," Elon Musk, called ESG "the devil" and "a scam" perpetrated by "phony social justice warriors." One month after he angered the left by his acquisition of Twitter (now X), he was removed from the S&P 500 sustainability index, receiving only 37 out of a maximum 100 points, versus the 84 score by cigarette giant Philip Morris International with 8 million deaths annually from smoking (author's comment - not all PMI-related, of course). Musk's firing of his LGBTQ+ president was a factor, as was insufficient embracing of diversity, equity, and inclusion.[9]

One poignant example of this nonsense is the change in selecting fully trained air traffic controllers. The FAA is being sued (April 2024) for selecting candidates based on race instead of aptitude test results. A class action law suit led by Adam Laxalt, former Nevada attorney general, represents one thousand qualified air traffic controller applicants who completed the two-hundred-hour training program with high AT-SAT test scores required. Candidates selected in their place were high school graduates who were first given a "biographical test" *as a pre-screener to determine who were selected* to take the subsequent qualifying requirements.

But there is "a quiet revolution against woke," as described in The Epoch Times dated June 21–27, 2023:

> Consumer boycotts against 'woke' corporations such as Target and Anheuser-Busch (Disney, Oreo cookies owned by Mendelez Int'l and many others) are the key to reversing race, gender, and environmental activism in corporate America. . . . That's because companies ditching companies that are pushing left-wing policies have given conservative groups the traction they need to fight them legally. . . . ESG, which started as just guidelines, has now turned into heavy-handed mandates on controversial "social justice" ideologies . . . Shareholder lawsuits could be the key to stopping ESG—and prolonged consumer boycotts are making it possible by inflicting huge losses on woke companies. . . . The boycotts hit the companies' market capitalization. . . . Woke business practices aren't going away without a fight, according to Will Hild, executive director of Consumer's Research, a nonprofit protection group. Consumer's Research started a public information campaign on BlackRock and recently created a "woke alert" for consumers. Consumers and citizens to have the power—they just have to stand up and use it, Hild said.[10]

Let us not forget the landmark 9–0 Supreme Court decision (*Muldrow v. City of St. Louis*) definitively reinforcing support for Title VII of the Civil Rights Act, which forbids "race, color, religion, sex or national origin" discrimination with respect to employment "compensation, terms, conditions or privileges."

It is no surprise that 970 U.S. corporations moved their headquarters to Ireland—reflecting issues of taxation, overregulation, and DEI (among other factors).

Global Warming / Climate Change

What is the *simplified*, core message of the disparate, passionate proponents of this field of endeavor. The "whole system" reduction of greenhouse gases (GHG) is necessary to achieve the macro-goal of saving the planet from self-destruction. The foundational document which explains this in a more erudite way comes from the International Resource Panel of the UNEP (United Nations Environmental Programme, www.unep.org/resourcepanel). It is well worth reading this informative treatise entitled "10 Key Messages on Climate Change." In fact, there are reams, volumes, libraries, entire ocean tankers (not carrying petroleum, of course) filled with more information than you will ever need.

From this document, let me cherry-pick a few phrases from their list of ten:

- Mitigate GHG emissions *urgently* (#1)
- *Decouple* economic growth from environmental degradation (#2)
- Achieve the two-degree Celsius *target* (#3)
- A more sustainable *food* system (#6)
- Large-scale deployment of *low-carbon* technologies (#7)
- Rethinking of *societal values* (#10)

Lots of truly well-meaning people are members of this community. Unfortunately, lots of wack-a-doodles reside here also. Scripture *does* affirm our responsibility and necessity for the care of Creation—but where do these two belief systems, aka religions, parallel, and where do they vector in magnitude and direction?

In response, there are a few more references related to these climate disciples:

- "[US] Treasury Department Releases Principles for Net-Zero Financing and Investment: Principles Focus on Scope #3 *Financed and Facilitated Greenhouse Gas Emissions*. Although the release states that use of these principles is 'wholly voluntary' and that these principles 'do not impose legal requirements on any activities or institutions.' [They] *should consider . . .* to begin the benchmarking of existing practices against the 'emerging best practices' identified by the Treasury."[11]
- California is always out in front (of the leftist steam roller)—yes? This message from the California Public Utilities Commission was delivered to my mailbox, entitled, "What Are the California Climate Credits?":

"Your utility bill will [now] include a credit . . . paid as a flat rate twice a year. . . . The credit is your share of the payments from the State's program."[12] In the blink of an eye this credit will be assessed against some new conservation benchmark requirements and will morph into a tax or a penalty of some type!

Greta Thunberg

- Swedish teen sensation—no, not one of the 1970s pop music idols from ABBA— Greta Thunberg, climate activist extraordinaire: "Greta Thunberg, who has been propped up by global elites and central planners since she was a child, is finally admitting her activism isn't about saving the environment. Instead, it's about tearing down capitalism and implementing communism, government-controlled systems around the world. She now admits it's to overthrow 'the whole capitalist system,' which she says is responsible for 'imperialism, oppression, genocide and . . . racist oppressive extractionism.'"[13]
- It has been an emerging light in a dark tunnel to learn of the grass roots civil disobedience of farmers in Europe, protesting the net-zero, high-yield agricultural demands of their governments. Meat eating is being transformed into an inadvisable practice. Informative resources can be found at https://climatedepot.com.

- According to emissions analytics, "pollution from tire wear now 1,850 times worse than exhaust emissions. Electric cars actually emit more particulate pollution, because today most vehicle-related particulate matter comes from tire wire"[14] Heavy double battery electric cars are heavier than most gas-powered vehicles.

Question: What do pizza ovens, flatulating cows, light bulbs, eating crickets, gas stoves, electric vehicles, and China building one hundred new coal plants to manufacture all of the batteries and solar panels that the green economy wannabes will need - have in common? You got it: climate alarmism. *The cult of climate hysteria is a false narrative built on deceptive models promoting fear and ultimately preparing the world for additional societal controls.* Let's ease into this alternative reality:

> It is estimated that by 2030 150 million electric cars will be on the road and the demand for EV batteries will soar. The high-capacity lithium-ion batteries that are used in electric cars . . . are made using carbon or graphite, a metal oxide and lithium salt, combined with electrolytes. The key elements inside . . . are the anode, cathode, separator, electrolyte and lithium ions. The battery cells in EVs contain roughly 17 pounds of lithium carbonate, 77 pounds of nickel, 44 pounds of manganese, and 30 pounds of cobalt. . . . Nearly 500,000 gallons of water are used to extract one ton of lithium.[15]

> An EV battery's weight is determined by its size and energy capacity. A Tesla Model S has a roughly 544 kg (1,200 pound) battery and contains about 62.6 kg (138 pounds) of lithium. A Tesla Model Y has a 771 kg (1,700 pound) battery and contains a similar amount of lithium; but both batteries also require graphite, cobalt, manganese, aluminum and nickel.[16]

Holy hamlet, Batman, how many young child laborers in the Congo does it take to extract all of these minerals, sell them to the Chinese, and ship them back as a finished product to the good ol' US of A at inflated prices?

Now let's move from the sublime to the really ridiculous:

I recently bought a new SUV Toyota FJ Cruiser. According to the www.carbonfootprint.com calculator, my FJ Cruiser will produce about 3.25 tons of CO2 over a year of driving my average of 6,000 miles. If I had purchased a Toyota Prius, I would produce 1.17 tons over the same year, a savings a just over 2 tons of CO2.

That sounds like a big reduction in CO_2 emissions, but how does it compare to some other choices that we might make? A round-trip flight from LAX to JFK produces 2.41 tons of CO_2 per passenger when the effects of water vapor are taken into account. Thus, a single airline flight obliterates the benefits of driving a hybrid for a year. Another choice that has a big environmental impact is eating meat. According to the Nature Conservancy's calculator, eliminating meat from one's diet reduces one's yearly carbon footprint by 3.2 tons; again, more effective than buying a hybrid.

The choice that has the largest environmental impact by far is having children. According to a study published last year, the lifetime carbon footprint of an American child is estimated to be more than 9,000 tons of CO_2. Thus, the environmental impact of having just one child in the United States is equivalent to 1,450 people each driving a Cadillac Escalade 10,000 miles over one year. Another way to look at it is that the yearly CO_2 savings due to all of the hybrid vehicles sold in the US . . . [290,272 according to www.HybridCars.com] is enough to offset the lifetime carbon impact of about 64 American children.[17]

No one disagrees that the earth's climate is changing, and that the past few centuries human pollution has made things worse. Thousands of climate scientists refer to the powerful effects of the natural cycles of the sun and the changes which occur in the earth's magnetic field. The climate has always changed, before God breathed life into humankind, and it continues to change. The earth *is* a giant greenhouse. The more carbon dioxide molecules that come off of the earth, the more they are trapped in the protective layer of oxygen, nitrogen, and yes, carbon dioxide. Climate scientists use long, thin ice-core samples from Antarctic glaciers to measure past levels of carbon dioxide. These drillings confirm *the earth's level of CO_2 has gone up and down in regular cycles for thousands of years.* These teaser headlines reference further investigation:

1. "World Climate Declaration: There Is No Climate Emergency"[18]

    Primary messages: 1) Natural as well as anthropogenic factors cause warming; 2) warming is far slower than predicted; 3) climate policy relies on inadequate models; 4) CO_2 is plant food, the basis of all life on Earth; 5) global warming has not increased natural disasters; 6) climate policy must respect scientific and economic realities.

2. "Over 1,600 Scientists Sign 'No Climate Emergency' Declaration"[19]

    Primary messages: 1) A total of 1,609 scientists and professionals from around the world have signed the declaration, including 321 from the United States; 2) the earth's climate has varied as long as it has existed; 3) it is no surprise that we are now experiencing a period of warming; 4) warming is happening considerably slower than projected; 5) climate models have many shortcomings and are not remotely plausible.

3. "Meteorologists, Scientists Explain Why There Is 'No Climate Emergency'"[20]

    Primary messages: 1) The group is an independent "climate watchdog" founded in 2019 by emeritus professor of geophysics Guus Merkhout and Marcel Crok, a scientist journalist; the organization's objective is to generate knowledge by objectively looking at the facts and engaging in scientific research; 2) the declaration signatories include Nobel laureates, theoretical physicists, meteorologists, professors, and environmental scientists worldwide; 3) "I [Haym Benaroya, Rutgers Univ.] signed the declaration because I believe the climate is no longer studied scientifically. Rather, it has become an item of faith"; 4) the earth has warmed about 2 degrees F since the end of the Little Ice Age around 1850, but hardly constitutes an emergency—or even a crisis—since the planet has been warmer yet over the last few millennia; 5) "'The climate emergency is fiction,' he [Benaroya] said unequivocally."

4. "Two Princeton, MIT Scientists Say EPA Climate Regulations Based on a Hoax"[21]

   Primary messages: 1) Physicist and meteorologist testify that the climate agenda is "disastrous" for America; 2) "Climate is a self-regulating process, more clouds form when temperatures rise. Atmospheric carbon dioxide is increasing [but] the gas's effect on global warming is swamped by the natural cloud cycle"; 3) there is this huge fraction of the population that has been brainwashed into thinking this is an existential threat to the planet; 4) Richard Lindzen, who holds the most distinguished chair in meteorology, was pushed out of academia once he began to question the climate narrative; funding and publication became almost impossible; 5) the initial predictions of climate disasters had New York flooded by now, no ice left at the North Pole, England like Siberia. Nothing they predicted actually came true. You have to do something to keep the money coming in, so they changed "global warming" to "climate change."

5. *Global Warming: The Great Deception*, by Guy K. Mitchell. Jr.

   Primary messages: 1) The triumph of dollars and politics over science and why you should care; 2) a definitive work on the subject of anthropogenic (man-made) global warming; 3) there has been no significant warming of the world's oceans, atmosphere, or land mass since accurate satellite measurements were initiated in 1979; 4) the average temperature of the earth is an abstraction; it is a figment of imagination of climate scientists; 5) Why do the UN and certain politicians in the US and Western Europe continue to promote the fraudulent global warming hypothesis? It is all about the money—money for research and *to affect socio-economic change.*

6. *Red Hot Lies: How Global Warming Alarmists* Use *Threats, Fraud, and Deception to Keep You Misinformed*, by Christopher C. Horner

   Primary messages: 1) Liars: Al Gore, the United Nations, *The New York Times*; 2) the global warming lobby—relentless in its push for bigger government, more spending, and more regulation—will use any means necessary to scare you out of your wits, as well as your tax dollars and your liberties, with threats of rising oceans, deadly droughts, and unspeakable future consequences; 3) the next time somebody in the media denies that there is media bias, ask how they explain the fact that there are at least a hundred stories about the shrinking ice cap for every one about the expanding Antarctic ice cap, which has now grown to record size; 4) America's National Academies of Science, the UK's Royal Society, and the acronym jumble of United Nations agencies have increasingly abandoned traditional roles as science advisers in favor or actively lobbying for the quantitative models and scenario extrapolations to be public policy planning tools; 5) we can thank the French for many things: great whiners like John Kerry, and of course their former president Jacques Chirac outing the Kyoto Protocol with praise of it as *"the first component of an authentic global governance."*

7. "Globalists Are Engineering a Financial Shock, and Here's the Proof"[22]

Primary message: Globalists are now using the climate change issue as a trojan horse for their plans to increase control over international finance and monetary authority. They are even suggesting that the threat of climate change be used as a springboard for giving global banks even more power to control the distribution of wealth and pull down the existing system so it can be replaced with something else. It goes something like this:

- The purpose of the global financial system is to redistribute wealth
- One aspect of every crisis is financial loss (direct and indirect)
- Central banks, can address financial loss, usually through money-printing so central banks use crisis response as an excuse to engage in monetary inflation
- Which makes crisis victims more dependent on centralized government giving central banks a compelling argument to increase their own power

As we know all too well, in the absence of a media-friendly crisis, globalists are perfectly happy to invent one. I believe there is no man-made climate crisis, no "anthropogenic global warming."

We can only fit one more area of bamboozlement into this chapter. But since the Chinese Wuhan virus created by gain of function research funded by Anthony Fauci killed 1,136,920 Americans, and 6,974,473 globally as reported by the World Health Organization (as of June 2, 2023), it seems important to include here.

COVID-19 / "Big Pharma"

China is a vast country with many decent, hardworking people. *It is the Chinese Communist Party which controls China to which any aspersions in this section are ascribed.*

The Chinese directly head four of the fifteen principal agencies in the UN and have deputies present in nine of the fifteen. They are a charter member and permanent member of the Security Council. There is reason to believe (with no footnote attached to this comment) that the Chinese have undue influence over the World Health Organization. Some critical voices have suggested something a bit more sinister: "the WHO is bought and paid for."

We have already documented the close collaboration of the mega corporations and investment titans. The US government had just as big a role in the economic outcomes of its policies, as it did control of both the messaging and personal liberties of its citizens. *Major issues were manipulated by these four power structures* (don't forget media), including:

1. the origin of COVID
2. the efficacy, or lack thereof, of vaccines, masks, and policies related to their use
3. the realized benefits derived from centralized control and emergency powers
4. the many punitive measures of those in power, which created a template for future planning for the next pandemic, already in place!

We will address #1 and #2 here and deal with #3 and #4 in Chapter 12.

RFK Jr. has paid a stiff price for going against the established narrative. He pushed back on the direct collusion between government and business, with a sycophant corporate media hammering anyone who raised legitimate scientific issues of concern. His banishment from running as a legitimate Democrat alternative to J. R. Biden, and now Kamala Harris, was punctuated at a news conference with a gaggle of grinning Kennedys betraying their own kin and endorsing Joe! Here we include a few minutes from the transcript of RFK's excellent speech:

> Then I realized, Okay, these guys either don't know what they're doing or they're lying about it deliberately. Then I realized these agencies were captured on steroids. The FDA gets 50% of its budget from the pharmaceutical companies. CDC is a 12-billion-dollar budget and 5 billion of that, goes to buying vaccines from these companies. So, if you work at the CDC you do not get promotions by finding problems with vaccines. You get promoted by increasing uptake. Then NIH is just an incubator, so it develops vaccines, hands them over to the industry, who hands it over to universities, which then gets money from the NIH (200-300 million) for phase one and phase two trials. Then *if* successful, which they always make successful, they turn them over to the pharma companies to complete phase three; oh, and they all divide up the royalty and control the patent rights. Then Tony Fauci walks it through the regulatory process at MTA and CDC where he's picked the members of the panels who are all taking money from him. Their job is to rubber stamp this. Then any inquiries into this closed system or objections are fed into the media echo chambers as vaccine disinformation![23]

"I represent science"

The Origin of COVID

Rand Paul, in late October 2023, published his book *Deception: The Great COVID Cover-Up*. He was the senator most focused and an appropriately virulent critic of Anthony Fauci, MD, recently "retired" director of the National Institute of Allergy and Infectious Diseases, and highest paid employee of the US government. Fauci's denial of engaging in (*funding and authorizing*) COVID gain-of-function research in the Wuhan Institute of Virology, if adjudicated in a court of law and convicted, *might* include any number of felonies. On August 8, 2023, Dr. Paul officially referred Fauci to US Attorney Mathew Graves for criminal investigation after repeatedly lying to Congress about his role in funding dangerous gain-of-function research in Wuhan pursuant to 18 USC § 1001. And in May 2024 ex-NIAID senior scientific adviser Dr. David Morens, who served under Fauci from 1998 to 2022, was outed by his own communications confirming that he violated federal recording keeping laws by deleting emails before a FOIA (Freedom of Information Act) request was submitted *and* urged many associates in the national health sphere associated with Fauci to use their personal emails. So what were they hiding? *The truth will come out sometime.*

I recommend you do a DuckDuckGo search (Google may block it) to locate the transcript of a speech given by Epoch Times senior editor Jan Jekielek on May 19, 2023, at a University of Chicago symposium titled, "Academia's COVID Failures." There is much to ponder here, both for a reflective "looking back" but more importantly for the *inevitable* next pandemic scare with even more onerous societal controls.

Multiple "committees" (Senate, Congressional, UN) have either determined that the origins were of natural zoonotic means (animal-related, crossing over to infect humans) or that the origins were sufficiently indeterminate—perpetuating the obfuscation. What is blatantly obvious is that China did not cooperate one iota with allowing investigation or producing specimens, data, or "patient #1" information to any authorities—which in the main was whitewashed by the WHO.

Robert F. Kennedy Jr. wrote one of the best books on this topic. The title alone paints a very encompassing picture of the collusion which contributed to this global travesty, and equally importantly, events leading up to it: *The Real Anthony Fauci: Bill Gates, Big Pharma, and the Global War on Democracy and Public Health.* A few chapter titles will illustrate: "Pharma Profits over Public Health" (Chapter 2); "White Mischief: Dr. Fauci's African Atrocities" (Chapter 8); "Hyping Phony Epidemics: 'Crying Wolf'" (Chapter 11). I recommend you read this treatise, because you will likely never trust those in authority again, unless the Almighty grants a spiritual cleansing of repentance in our nation.

Kennedy said, "I wrote this book to help Americans—and citizens across the globe—understand the historical underpinnings of the bewildering cataclysm that began in 2020. In that single *annus horribilis* liberal democracy effectively collapse worldwide. The very governmental health regulators, social media eminences, and media companies that idealistic populations relied upon as champions of freedom, health, democracy, civil rights and evidence-based public policy seemed to collectively pivot in lockstep assault against free speech and personal freedoms."[24] And he poignantly referenced those who paid a price for speaking out: "I dedicate this book to that battle-hardened cadre of heroic scientists and physicians who have risked their careers, their livelihoods, and their reputations to champion evidence-based science and ethical medicine."[25]

The Efficacy of "PPE" Products and Policies

The messenger Ribonucleic Acid (mRNA) vaccines for COVID were, as we all recall, produced in an accelerated manner, without the normative time for clinical trials and evidence-based documentation. The fear factor in the general population was at DEFCON 1! So as our complicit health authorities (CDC, NIH, etc.) rolled out mandates never before seen, and the public talking heads assured us of the journey ahead, the general population kicked into lemming-like obedience. Unfortunately, nearly every recommended PPE (personal protective product) had marginal value; some were detrimental.

And the policies were just as horrific. We have yet to fully document the long-term damage for these vaccines affecting some pregnant and lactating women (yes: women, not birthing people), and causing myocarditis and pericarditis in some healthy young men. The value of preventative or non-vaccine-based therapeutics such as hydroxychloroquine were ridiculed. Mandated masks did not have the composition to prevent penetration of the virus. And masking children as young as two years old was ridiculous. The social and psychological damage of totalitarian lockdowns, loss of employment for not complying with vaccines mandates, military personnel given dishonorable discharges, emergency powers granting legislators over-the-top authority to close churches, arrest people on the beach, destroy the reputation and livelihood of any dissenting professional voice . . . it was all so Orwellian. And make note that China is now fighting IP (intellectual property) protections in the WTO (World Trade Organization) on behalf of "developing nations." This would give them access to further dominate the global pharmaceutical market. Much more could be said—we must end and will do so with three prayer requests.

Suffice it to say here Black Rock and Vanguard were the top two investors in the massive production of Pfizer and Johnson & Johnson COVID *mandated* vaccines, and #2 and #3 top investors in Moderna vaccines. These same two players were the top investors in Gilead's Remdesivir as well.

More investigations now, over time, reveal new information on a range of politically motivated pharmacological decisions.

> Former officials in the U.S. Department of Health and Human Services and the Food and Drug Administration condemned what they described as the FDA's duplicity in allowing off-label use of so-called puberty blockers while loudly condemning the use of far safer drugs to treat COVID-19. In (a) Jan 25, 2022 email, Shannon Sullivan, clinical team leader at FDA's Division of General Endocrinology, noted that the agency's Division of Metabolism and Endocrinology Products performed a "safety review of the GnRH agonists class in pediatric patients in 2016/2017." (GnRH stands for "Gonadatropin-releasing hormone." GnRH agonists prevent the natural release of testosterone and estrogen that initiate puberty.) "We found no effect on bone", she noted. "We did find increased risk of depression and suicidality, as well as increased seizure risk." David Gortler, a Yale University-trained pharmacologist who previously was a senior advisor to the FDA commissioner on policy and drug safety, raised the alarm about GnRH agonists for minors. "The FDA relied heavily on the reporting system's data to declare that

hydroxychloroquine was unsafe after finding only a few hundred reports of adverse events, but the agency dismisses 70,000 adverse reports for GnRH agonists."[26]

As America-first run companies (or practically anyone not America-last), governing boards, CEOs and legislators become familiar with these incestuous relationships, they are making divesture decisions and pulling out of these financial behemoths. Florida, Missouri, Louisiana, and South Carolina have moved investments. States with new laws tracking these developments include Alabama, Arkansas, Florida, Idaho, Indiana, Kansas, Kentucky, Montana, New Hampshire, North Carolina, North Dakota, Texas, Utah, and West Virginia. The tide is turning. But tides ebb and flow according to atmospheric and other conditions! The *ekklesia* needs to pray for God to change the atmosphere!

Pray for . . .

- the exposure and removal of corrupt leaders, CEOs, and elected officials—that God will replace them with people of faith and integrity.
- the wealth of the wicked that has been stored up for the righteous to be identified and deployed for accelerated kingdom business.
- the Holy Spirit to place a hedge of protection around Israel and for the peace of Jerusalem, as His ordained will is brought to completion. Your kingdom come and your will be done!

CHAPTER 10
Mountain of Trouble—Media and Technology

THE ENEMY'S INFILTRATION and influence in the media is one of the most insidious and effectual tools in his arsenal. *Media* involves traditional print, digital, and broadcast delivery systems. Technology controls social media, financial, entertainment, opinion, and a multitude of other platforms in many genres. Rest assured they don't operate separately, but rather in one universe of messaging dominance! Traditional media and social media *almost always* parrot each other. And the corporate interests, the money behind most of these purveyors of synchronized "newspeak," are controlled by a small group of ideologues.

Belgian clinical psychologist Dr. Mattias Desmet began to study the disparate reactions to COVID-19 measures from both mainstream and alternative media. With a strong background in statistics, he expanded the concept of "mass formation" through his book *The Psychology of Totalitarianism*. What he surmised, then documented, is that most people accepted the "authorities" pandemic mitigation measures without question and were significantly influenced by corporate and social media which denounced those who were critical of these measures and questioned the accuracy of their counter claims, to what those authorities portrayed as "science."

> Desmet's focus on pseudo-scientific literature and "studies" was a natural outgrowth of his doctoral dissertation, which explored the increasingly sloppy, error-filled, and downright fraudulent work that has been an ongoing scandal in the scientific community
> but with very little reform or correction. The errors continue to roll on, and scientists often seem unaware of their own flawed thinking, leaving the public confused, suspicious, or blissfully

ignorant. The 2020–2022 corona crisis has been the latest in a series of similar panics followed by increasing fear driven control: terrorism, global warming, coronavirus (the reader can plug in other manias whose advocates call for more action, more security, more control); every time there is a shock wave of fear, the tool sought is tighter control—but unfortunately, coercive control increases stress and damages health, a problem largely overlooked by those calling for stricter and stricter measures.[1]

Messaging greatly influences our perception of reality and the ability to differentiate truth from what is false. That is why it is so important to understand who and what messengers (voices, influencers, media) we let into our thinking, our emotions, and our spirit. Again, we were created with three distinct elements to our "being" and all three are fertile receptors to input. My bachelor's degree (from Oral Roberts University, Tulsa, OK) was in dyadic (a fancy word for interpersonal—between persons) communication. Therefore, I have a keen interest in understanding all elements of the sender, the message, and the receiver *and*, ultimately, whether God or the enemy is the predominant influencer in what we hear from a particular media source or influencer.

The casual consumer of information—the uninformed, disengaged, and/or inadequately educated —seldom looks for alternative sources (messengers) who may give them a more well-rounded understanding of an issue. By and large, *the masses* take in a steady stream of one-sided half-truths or sufficient falsehoods to poison the true story. Remember, rodenticide bait stations for vermin only contains 1.14% arsenic. Since there are only two spiritual sources that affect *everything* in life—good or evil, light or darkness, God or the rebellion—then each piece of communication ultimately comes from persons vis-à-vis entities who serve one or the other. Thus, at this existential level, *the medium* (source, messenger) *is* (represents) *the* (truth or falsehood of the) *message*, per Canadian philosopher Marshall McLuhan. Remember also the blunt wisdom of actor and comedian Groucho Marx: "Who are you going to believe, me or your lying eyes?" Truth should be questioned in every sector of society, and media should *not* be consumed like pablum. So where do we go from here?

Consider this:

- "This is a battle for the future of civilization. If free speech is lost, even in America, tyranny is all that lies ahead."[2]
- "The crushing weight of our wayward culture is almost suffocating. America's instruments of media, Hollywood, corporate board rooms, government bureaucracies, and even the new woke military have taken a turn toward an unrecognizable America – in fact, if you do an online search of the official National Archives for copies of the Declaration of Independence and Constitution, you are met with a warning – right at the top of each document - that says 'Harmful Language Alert.' I'm not kidding."[3]
- "A study of OpenAI's ChatGPT, conducted by researchers at the University of East Anglia in the UK, shows that the market-leading IA chatbot has clear bias towards leftist political parties. The study, published in the journal *Public Choice*, shows ChatGPT under its default settings favors Democrats in the US, the Labour Party in the UK, and President Lula da Silva of the Workers Party in Brazil."[4]

We will now consider three primary subgroups in this chapter:

- A short diagnostic on the "media" in the USA
- It's all about influence and control:
  - Intentionally selective coverage
  - Censoring, shadow-banning, dis-, mis-, and mal-information
- Artificial intelligence and transhumanism

Here we go again, huge topics with insufficient capacity to deal with any of them sufficiently. Again, my goal is to broach these issues for your further consideration, and especially to pray.

Media in the USA

When we say "the media" we are talking about a leviathan serpent, a ten-headed hydra. Actually, six heads would be more accurate: the "Big 6" companies that own *almost all* (90% by some estimates) of the disseminators of communication and entertainment are described in the following. With mergers, acquisitions, and name changes it can get confusing, but this snapshot is worth it! Combined, they control $430 billion in media revenue. (In comparison, the country of Poland's GDP is $467 billion.) The first, *added entry* here is a hybrid:

- Apple (AAPL), i.e., Tim Cook. A $2.74 trillion market cap, with the acquisition of streaming and news media to its portfolio, now fits into both the media and technology categories. *Now for the "Big 6"...*

- National Amusements / Paramount Global (PARA), i.e., Sumner Redstone. They control assets in television, film, print, video games, and internet including, but not limited to: CBS/Viacom, BET, MTV, Nick, Showtime, 24/7 Sports, Pocket Books, Simon & Schuster, Tech Republic, Game Spot.

- Disney (DIS), i.e., Bob Iger. They control assets in television, film, print, video games, theme parks, and cruise lines including, but not limited to: A&E, ABC, ESPN, History Channel, Lucas Films, Pixar, Touchstone Pictures, Marvel, Hyperion, Game Star, Lifetime, SEC Network, Military History, and that bastion of vacuous infecundity, *The View*.

- Time Warner—now WarnerMedia (WBD), i.e., Jeff Bewkes. They control assets in television, film, print, music, print, internet, and "investments," including but not limited to: CNN, Accent Health, HBO, Warner Brothers, Hulu, TNT, Time, Water Tower Music, Time Warner Cable, Bluefin, Turner Broadcasting.

- Comcast (CMCSA), i.e., Brian L. Roberts. They control assets in television and film, internet and "ventures" including but not limited to: NBC, MSNBC, DreamWorks, NHL Network, Golf Channel, Fandango, The Weather Channel, Xfinity, Vox Media, FanDuel, Peacock, NBC Universal, Telemundo.

- Sony (SONY), i.e., Kazuo Hirai. They control assets in television, film, music, internet, non-media and "investments" including but not limited to: AXN, Animax, Sony Pictures, Image Works, True Channel. Sony Music, Sony Bank, EMI, So-Net, Play Station, Mad House (animation) Screen Gems.

- News Corp (NWSA), i.e., Rupert Murdoch. They control assets in television, film, wireless and print including but not limited to: Fox News, Fox Sports, Nat Geo, National Geographic Channel, BTN,

Regency, Real Estate TV, Wireless Group, Harper Collins, Zondervan, *The Wall Street Journal, The New York Post.* [5]

We have just described the "elephants in the room." There is an entire next tier of money from individuals who *also* "have an agenda." An understandable target for conservatives is the devious George Soros (heir apparent, son Alexander, is just as insidious). The following are a few points of interest regarding this "dark money" source.

> On April 8 [2011] House Democrat Leader Nancy Pelosi headlined a Boston conference on "media reform." The 2,500-person event was sponsored by a group called Free Press, one of more than 180 different media-related organizations that receives money from liberal billionaire Goerge Soros. Pick an issue and his Open Society Foundations likely fund the liberal-position—pro-abortion, pro-illegal immigration, pro-national health care, pro-drug legalization, pro-Big Government, anti-Israel and, ultimately, anti-America. This has given Soros far more influence that even many of his harshest critics realize. He has direct ties to more than 30 mainstream news outlets—including the *New York Times, Washington Post*, the Associated Press, NPR, CNN and ABC. Each one of those companies has employees, often high-level ones, on the boards of Soros-funded media operations. [6]

More sinister than this is the recent Soros majority-ownership purchase of bankrupt radio network Audacy, the second largest in the US behind iHeart Media. He has his investment eye on other radio networks as well, which effectively could contain or outright control the reach of conservative broadcasts and programs. If there was doubt about this assertion, his team has filed a petition to the Democratic-majority FCC to fast-track the approval of this acquisition—this despite existing FCC rules limiting foreign ownership of US radio stations. And Soros' larger agenda is hiding in plain sight. "Free Press, a Soros-funded media group is actively pressuring major Big Tech platforms to ramp up their censorship efforts before the 2024 U.S. presidential election, The group issued a letter endorsed by over 200 anti-free speech groups advocating for stricter speech controls. The letter was distributed to top executives at Discord, Google, Instagram, Meta, Pinterest, Reddit, Rumble, Snap, TikTok, Twitch, YouTube and X. Notably, at least 45 of the signatories to the letter have been recipients of Soros's funding, amounting to over $80 million, Free Press (ironically named) claimed to have had a leading role in the ban on conservative social media platform Parler and in coordinating the blacklisting of former President Donald Trump on Twitter."[7] All of this should cause everyone who understands this as a spiritual battle to pause—and to pray!

Legacy media represents an almost monolithic ideological community with a giant megaphone yielding a steady stream of "information" that is usually selectively framed and often outright false. The leftist social agenda is pervasive in all Big 6 corporations and their many subsidiaries. We arbitrarily reference one corporation's "values"—Warner Media, with nearly all other companies similarly oriented:

> Creating a culture of equity, inclusion, and belonging is imperative to our company's success . . . we remove barriers to opportunity . . . and help shape the most inclusive and equitable world for all." (Two of six "initiatives" include global DEI data gathering and DEI learning. Their DEI leadership includes seven executives.) "The Warner Bros. Discovery Board provides oversight of Environmental, Social and Governance (ESG) . . . our strong focus on ESG is core to who we are."[8]

There are also nefarious ties to the US government that factor into the messaging of these media behemoths. Here are a few examples:

- Section 230 of the Communications Decency Act of 1996 and the Digital Millenium Copyright Act of 1998 provides immunity to these giant media companies by legislating that an interactive computer service can't be treated as the publisher or speaker of third-party content. It sounds good on the surface, but has been twisted into a pretzel and used as a bludgeon to allow these companies to exercise *unfettered censorship, of their own determination*. One common malpractice is via the ubiquitous "fact checkers" that claim X, Y, or Z is false when that is often not true. Censorship of objections to the handling of COVID based on purported "science" is a tangible example previously mentioned.

- Operation Mockingbird sounds like a Jennifer Lawrence movie, but it represents a more sobering reality. Wikipedia begins its article by stating it is "*the alleged CIA program to influence the press.*" Beginning in the early years of the "cold war," the United States Central Intelligence Agency recruited American journalists, working through a network of front groups (for instance, the National Student Association) to propagandize the US and global audience. Democratic Senator Frank Church chaired one of the most important investigations of the Senate Foreign Relations Committee in that era, which implicated not only the CIA but the NSA and the FBI.

- The development of technology for "defense" purposes, which later becomes commercialized, is a common trajectory in certain sectors of product development. One of the central creator/developers in this arena is DARPA, the Defense Advanced Research Projects Agency. Writers like Sharon Weinberger, author of *The Imagineers of War* and global fellow at the Woodrow Wilson International Center for Scholars, brings light to this symbiotic relationship. Whether DARPA is a national security agency that does science or a science agency that does national security is a moot point. They are conjoined twins. One could make a case that Google (Alphabet) is a DARPA creation; some have done so, though their Mountain View, CA leftist employees would highly object to this assertion.

Influence and Control—Selective Coverage

I have a longtime Christian friend who, I believe, predominantly consumes nightly information from MSNBC and CNN. In my view, few US media companies are more blatantly and consistently biased than these two among the rest of legacy media. I am certain he feels the same way about the media I allow into my conscious thinking. Is it any wonder we now, sadly, avoid discussing the substantive issues of our time? How can Americans, patriots, Christians—just decent people of whatever definition—come together to see how absolutely infiltrated by malfeasance most of the media giants are, and what questionable "information" they dispense?

Consider this train of thought: the forever loser and liar *IS the enemy of the people*. Therefore, purveyors of lies on a regular basis *are enemies of the people*. Much of the global and US-based media are purveyors of lies on a regular basis. Therefore, (fill in the blank) *is an enemy of the people!* Since the orange-haired guy said this first, it is automatically rejected. But think about this more carefully: bias, influence, and control in the media is quantifiable.

One of the pioneers who has battled media bias for years is L. Brent Bozell III. These are a few acknowledgements of his truly redemptive efforts: founder/president of the Media Research Center (with an average of more than 515 million "impressions" per week); founder of For America, an organization committed to restoring America to its founding principles; founder and first president of Parents Television Council, dedicated to restoring decency to Hollywood (yikes, is that even possible?); and a *curriculum vitae* that just goes on for pages. A must-read is "Media Bias 101: What Journalists Really Think—and What the Public Thinks about Them." There are twenty-eight "exhibits," with titles that range from "The People and the Press," "Journalists Denying Liberal Bias," "More Journalists Denying Liberal Bias," and, "Still More Journalists Denying Liberal Bias." Here are some excerpts:

- "I have worked for CNN for almost 26 years, Mutual Radio for 20 years, in the business for 57 years. I have never seen a bias on or off the air. . . . I've never seen it. . . . Fox News is a slanted network."—Larry King (*Honestly, I can hardly stop laughing as I type this!*)
- "We've never had an ideology. An ideology is a single thought across all programs."—MSNBC president Phil Griffin (*Oh, of course, that was before Rashida Jones took over—not!*)
- "I can see how the intensity of coverage on certain issues may, to some people, seem to reflect a liberal point of view. But I actually don't think it does."—*New York Times* executive editor Jill Abramson (*Ditto previous comment, now that Joseph Kahn is Executive Editor - not.*)[9]

Doesn't my selective choice of these three examples of claims that "bias denial"—as well as my italicized commentary—itself represent bias? It most certainly does. And that is my point. Truth, without bias, only comes from the Creator of heaven and earth. *No one* has the same batting average, the same capacity to *absolutely* discern what is misinformation or outright lies. But that same Creator has given *all* of us minds capable of inquiry, hearts sensitive to intangibles, and a spiritual core that, if we follow it, will lead us closer to the truth than the megaphones of corporate greed which daily fill our receptors with nonsense!

Has the media covered these following topics, people or events with truth and parity?

- *Bidenomics*. Is this "build back better"? Dollar Tree closing 1,000 stores. Macy's closing 150 stores. The Gap closing 350 stores. Regal Cinemas closing 429 locations. Walgreens closing 900 stores. Foot Locker closing 400 stores. Burger King closing 400 sites. Kroger closing 413 stores.[10] Joe has said multiple times that inflation was 9% when he became president, when in fact it was 1.4%."lies, damned lies, and statistics" (Benjamin Desraeli).

- *Obama*. Highly beloved *and* highly reviled. As a confirmation of his "beloved" status, watch, listen to, or read every organ of the legacy media. To them he is the silver-tongued mamba, wise and measured. For examples of his "reviled" status, refer to Appendix 1, an opinion piece by Victor Davis Hanson. Too controversial? Not to those who believe it to be true. What follows are a few events that have occurred in the life of this forty-fourth president of the United States:

  1. His central role in Iran's renewed funding and ability to engage in its current jihadist global chaos, mostly hidden from media coverage.
  2. What was his involvement in the circumstances related to the death of his personal chef, Tafari Campbell?
  3. His twice-intimate encounter with Larry Sinclair and the tawdry allegations of homosexuality and drug use broadcast in his interview with Tucker Carlson.
  4. Circumstances related to the death of Doug Young, ex-choir director for Jeremiah Wright's Trinity United Christian Church.

- US intelligence agencies are banning "hurtful" terms, including "Islamic extremists," "radical Islamists," "Salafi jihadist," "jihadist," and "Sunni/Shia extremism."[11] And why is this?

- Why has no one located and reported on the Supreme Court leak in advance of their 2022 decision on *Dobbs v. Jackon Women's Health Organization*? Does this not seem highly suspicious?
- Why did the White House Secret Service have no information on the discovery of cocaine in the West Wing? No fingerprints, no DNA? This branch of civil service is usually highly professional. The markings of a cover-up?
- Why has no information been released on the relationship between Paul Pelosi and his "hammer attacker" on October 28, 2022? No curious media chasing this down?
- Why has the US government not released information on the credible, significant number of UFO sightings, now called UAP (Unidentified Aerial Phenomena)?
- Why wasn't the Nashville shooter's "manifesto" released to the public after a reasonable amount of time following the close of the investigation?
- What was the US chain of command and where are communications related to the Chinese spy balloon that was characterized by the media as *not* a spy balloon, after it was allowed to traverse the entire land mass of the United States?
- Why was the "undocumented new arrival" (not)—in truth, the senseless murderer of Laken Riley initially released with no charges or incarceration? *Are you kidding me?*
- Why are all the violent "summer of love" rioters free, and peaceful pray-ers outside abortion clinics in jail?
- Why are Trump's *actual* Charlottesville comments regularly obfuscated with false narratives bouncing around the echo chambers of *all* the mainstream media?

I respectfully submit to you that selective coverage in the media is a standard practice, not an exception. There is a significant percentage of the American electorate that believe the majority of corporate media serve as the propaganda arm of the Democrat Party, providing cover by ignoring critical information and following herd-mentality coverage when disseminating *intentionally* coordinated messages that are indisputable truth to some, and outrageous lies to others. You get to choose.

One last point. One methodology used in the effort to influence the masses, employed by the media, is called DARVO. This refers to a reaction that perpetrators of wrongdoing may display in response to being held accountable for their behavior. DARVO stands for "Deny, Attack, and Reverse Victim and Offender."[12] This seems, to me, blatantly evident in our 2024 context. Who is really a threat to democracy? Who really should face charges for wrongdoing? Who will make America the best it can be? Who should go to jail for their behavior? I have an opinion! My opinion makes no difference to anyone except me. But why I bring up this media practice of influence and control is because it is effective. Again, if all you are taking in is the likes of corporate media conglomerates you have no real understanding of what is actually happening.

Influence and Control—Censoring, Shadow-Banning, Etc.

Do you remember that childhood rhyme, "Sticks and stones may break my bones but words will never hurt me"? It was a well-intentioned tool for parents to try to minimize some hurtful story or incident that their young son or daughter expressed after coming home from school or playing with friends. This may have offered a momentary salve for a slight or insult, but did not bring a solution to bullying or abuse.

This reflects a deeper truth found in Scripture (Prov. 18:21a): "Death and life are in the power of the tongue" (KJV); "The tongue has the power of life and death" (NIV). The words that *come into us* as well as the words that *come out of us* are powerful indeed. Cursing or blessing. Declarations of faith versus expressions of doubt, fear, or anxiety. All these are a direct result of our words—because words are expressions of the heart.

In the previous subsection on the "selective coverage" media engages in, we read bullet points with issues that were clearly crafted for the purpose of influencing and controlling our awareness or response. This section addresses intentional, purposeful influence and control. It is no accident that "the father of lies" has so effectively taken over the commanding heights of the media and technology.

This is the essential difference between censoring and shadow-banning. To censor means to *overtly* suppress or prohibit (fill in the blank); whereas to shadow, ghost, or stealth-ban something is to apply influence and control surreptitiously. It is important to understand, however, that they have the same goal *and* the same effect.

Alternative media is now reporting much more extensively on the "censorship-industrial complex." It's about time! With a slim Republican majority in the House of Representatives, there is more "discovery" being pushed out into the public domain. One case in point is a report from the Select Subcommittee on the Weaponization of the Federal Government titled, "The Weaponization of 'Disinformation' Pseudo-Experts and Bureaucrats: How the Federal Government Partnered with Universities to Censor Americans' Free Speech." In short, the Department of Homeland Security (DHS), Cybersecurity and Infrastructure Security Agency (CISA), and the Global Engagement Center (GEC) within the State Department coordinated with Stanford University and other entities to create the Election Integrity Partnership (EIP) to censor Americans speech in the lead-up to the 2020 election, in hopes of bypassing both the First Amendment and public scrutiny.[13] Basically how this operated was EIP "stakeholders," including the federal government, would submit "misinformation" reports, the EIP would "analyze" the reports across different platforms, and then submit their recommendations to Big Tech on how to censor. This is a can of worms that requires a whole lot more fishing!

There is unequivocal evidence that our intelligence agencies work intimately with the legacy media to shape public perception and opinion. This is true in America, of course, but their tentacles include global populations to also shape their perception/opinion in the interests of . . . well, that is another million-dollar question!

There are also new "hate speech" laws which threaten freedom of expression across the western democracies. "One of the first things you learn—or should learn—in Civics 101 is that there is no freedom at all without freedom of expression. Free speech is the essential freedom from which our other rights flow. It's a right that we have taken for granted in the West."[14] Of course, these new laws rest on, depend on, chilling redefinitions of what "hate" speech consists of. In many cases Scripture is the *direct source* from which this alleged hate speech is derived! The Justin Trudeau government in Canada is implementing draconian new laws in this sector. In the UK a post on X that "transwomen are men" can facilitate police coming to your door. Scotland is set to become one of the most censored countries among western democracies with the passing of the Hate Crime and Public Order Act. And let's not forget our own US Department of Homeland Security creation of the "Disinformation Governance Board." This movement reaches, of course, into all the global one-world-order crowd. One example: Melissa Fleming heads the United Nations Department of Global Communications. Do your own online research of what these fine folks are up to!

Under the guise of 'improving digital safety' a major global control mechanism over free speech was launched in Cannes, France in November, 2019. GARM, the Global Alliance for Responsible Media was formed by the World Federation of Advertisers as a 'flagship project of the World Economic Forum', now with over 60 of the industry's heavy weights. Their Global Media Sustainability Framework outlines collaboration to control advertising dollars through the lens of monitoring "hate speech" and "harmful content", but, by whose definition? There are, of course, other goals which should be reviewed on multiple websites.[15]

Accelerating rapidly (from this writing in September 2024) is this global jihad against free speech. Elon Musk's X has been banned by a corrupt government and Supreme Federal Court in Brazil; more countries will follow. Telegram CEO Pavel Durov was arrested and thrown in jail on a refueling stop in France for specious reasons. Rumble is no longer available in Brazil, France, Russia and China. Truth Social will follow a similar trajectory. Like Islamic jihad, media jihad must be confronted – with prayer (and likely a few other exercises of a free people)!

Allow me to identify "three big fish" in this theater of the absurd—the coordinated control of the masses—that is you and I and what we are *not* told! This includes dis-, mis-, and mal-information. These reflect a cauldron of complexity and, as yet, undisclosed depths of collusion and corruption that will eventually be revealed—Lord willing!

- Election integrity
- Anthony Fauci
- Christian nationalism

The year 2016 was a gut punch for the Democrats. There was no way in hell-o they would allow that MAGA Nazi insurrectionist to return to the

White House in 2020. And by golly, they succeeded. I refer you to a critical Tucker Carlson interview with Mike Benz @MikeBenzCyber on February 16, 2024 titled, "Everything You Need to Know about the Government's Mass Censorship Campaign." America will not survive without election integrity. There has always been cheating—from the beginning of time. But we have now entered the Twilight Zone and something needs to be done quickly, before it is too late.

Regarding Dr. Fauci, inquiring minds should look more closely at the presentations of Senator Rand Paul; the Fox News reporting of Jesse Waters on Fauci's connections with the CIA; or the testimony of a CIA whistleblower who alleges they paid the COVID discovery team to alter the Wuhan lab findings.[16] Then look at the transcript of the testimony of Lara Logan at Senator Ron Johnson's roundtable discussion on the topic "Federal Health Agencies and the COVID Cartel"; or two other blockbuster Tucker Carlson interviews with Bret Weinstein, on January 5 and 15, 2024.

A well-known tactic of a Las Vegas magician is to have you look away from what she/he is doing with their other hand. A standard practice in warfare is to create a disruptive diversion in a direction opposite the intended action. Media mouthpieces proclaim regularly that white supremacy and Christian nationalism, and therefore, white Christian nationalism, is the greatest danger facing America today. *It is not!* This is a sleight-of-hand trick of the magician trying to get us to look elsewhere. Almost any rational person could make a list of many things—in graduated scales of urgency— that could be included on a list of what is most dangerous to America. When terrorist attacks begin in the homeland, and they will eventually, it won't be from the media-reviled MAGA crowd. It will be perpetrated by any number of nefarious characters, single adult military-aged males, among the millions that came across our border to collect their free stuff!

There are lots of small fish too, besides these three "Bigs":

- Israel didn't bomb the hospital in Gaza; it was an errant Hamas rocket.
- Kirk Cameron was denied the opportunity to read about faith and family in public libraries, while drag shows and pornographic books are allowed.
- Catherine Herridge, current CBS (former Fox) employee, was terminated by parent company Paramount Global and had her

computer and materials confiscated after her reporting on the FBI's investigation of Chinese scientist Yangping Chen. *Why?*

- NPR suspended veteran senior business editor Uri Berliner, after he wrote a critical essay detailing how NPR succumbs to liberal groupthink.
- More inquiries must be made into financial platforms like PayPal, Venmo, and others, which cancel accounts and freeze assets of conservative individuals and organizations regularly.
- Check out this X Post from October 29, 2023: "Media Blackout: 10 Stories They Chose Not to Tell You."
- Here is a twisting tale of intrigue: US Secretary of State Antony Blinken is the stepson of attorney Samuel Pisar, who is the lawyer and confidant of Robert Maxwell, who is the father of Ghislaine Maxwell, who was the accomplice of Jeffrey Epstein. *Say what?*

This author is only a watchman on the wall, not an adjudicator or judge. Thus, I am sharing what I am watching. *Time will tell what time will tell.*

Artificial Intelligence and Transhumanism

The rise of artificial intelligence (AI) is transforming industries and society at an unprecedented pace. From self-driving cars and intelligent virtual assistants to sophisticated medical technologies and advanced manufacturing systems, AI is increasingly being used to automate and improve a wide range of functions and processes. As AI continues to advance, it is raising important questions about its potential impact on the workforce, privacy, and the very nature of intelligence itself.

Americans need news grounded in a biblical worldview. Help shine the light of truth by partnering with . . .[17]

Both of these quotes were *not* written by a human being, but rather entirely by ChatGPT from OpenAI. So, to begin, what is one indicator of this technology? The first and most obvious is that what has been "put in" determines what will "come out." The orientation and intention of the programmer affects the message. Here is one example: "Now Google's 'absurdly woke' Gemini AI refuses to condemn pedophilia as wrong—after being blasted over 'diverse' but historically inaccurate images [both the Nazi and Viking were black] . . . fresh controversy for its response on pedophilia, suggesting individuals cannot control their attractions. The bot termed pedophilia as 'minor-attracted person status' and emphasized the importance of distinguishing attractions from actions."[18]

Obviously, the prevailing issue is not a specific topic that AI will exposit, but the range of predisposition that one will receive in response to one's inquiry. Other AI indicators involve ethical considerations, how it will affect employment and human interaction, the fear factor of it "taking over," privacy issues, and much more.

> The big technical question is how soon and how thoroughly AI engineers can address the current Achilles' heel of deep-learning—what might be called generalized hard-reasoning, things like deductive logic. Will quick tweaks to existing neural-net algorithms be sufficient, or will it require a fundamentally different approach. . . . Data used to train generative AI models comes not only from textual sources such as Wikipedia and Reddit, but also from videos on YouTube, songs on Spotify, and other audio and visual information. With the new generation of multi-modal large language models (LLMs) powering these applications, you can use text inputs to generate not only images and text but also audio and video. [19]

Transhumanism is *much* too complex an issue to do anything except offer a cursory summary and encourage your further research and reading. There is much good that AI will achieve. There is also, admittedly, a dark side of what artificial intelligence can become. And since we have documented that Satan, the enemy of God in all things, infiltrates every human endeavor and institution, we must mention it. The simplest definition of transhumanism is, "the belief or theory that the human race can evolve beyond its current physical and mental limitations, especially by means of science and technology."[20] That sounds fairly benign, but look further.

I encourage your reading of the 482-page treatise on this subject titled *Dark Aeon: Transhumanism and the War Against Humanity* by Joe Allen. Before you even get to the introduction, his endorsers paint ominous images: the planned post-human future; a clear and present danger to every man, woman, and child on earth; what every human must do today to save our freedom . . . indeed, to save our humanity; it posits that life will be made better by an embrace of the destruction of humanity as we know it; transhumanism is Satanism with a brain chip. Now that we have your attention, I will simply identify the titles of four chapters: "Into the Electric Antfarm," "Cultural Eugenics and Digital Darwinism," "Countdown to Gigadeath," and "My 55-Point Plan to Stay Human." This is not a read for the faint of heart, or the easily distracted.

> "Know in order to believe," wrote Saint Augustine, "believe in order to know." Philosophy can play with divine symbols—the intellect can categorize and analyze them—but it cannot reason out their deepest secrets. Science cannot prove or disprove sacred symbols as hypotheses. Technology cannot improve upon them. The infernal can only ape their outward expressions. The sacred demands our faith. Our faith demands a degree of submission. True understanding means abandoning logic as the sole path to ultimate reality. Only the heart can grasp that truth. This is my anchor in a world of illusions, approximate truths, and theological sophistry. [21]

We conclude with an important connection again to our Creator in this, and all matter(s):

> Our worry is not where machines become self-sustaining and can think for themselves. Our caution should be a familiar one—that we're not putting our hope in the created. The created will fail us. It's only a matter of time. Contingencies are infinite, and even the most intelligent AI is still *artificially intelligent*. Hope in the *imago hominis* (image of man) is just as perilous as hope in humanity itself. Isaiah warned those who put too much stock in the created, "When you cry out, let your collection of idols deliver you! The wind will carry them all off, a breath will take them away" (Isaiah 57:13, KJNV). We who were created in the *imago Dei* (image of God) need only look to him for deliverance. And his enduring Word provides us with an intelligence that creates out of nothing,

needs no programming, and can lead us through any contingency. He isn't the droid we're looking for but His is the intelligence we need. "For who has understood the mind of the Lord so as to instruct Him? But we have the mind of Christ" (1 Corinthians 2:16 ESV).[22]

OK, so we've quoted one book and a few sources that casts aspersions on artificial intelligence. What other sources of information can we consult? I commend to you Bride Ministries International (https://bridemovement. com), focused on strategic equipping, powerful teaching, and cutting-edge revelation. One of their cutting-edge resources is a listing of "evil AI sites," which can be found on their website.

The media and technology world requires us to tread carefully, listen with supernatural discernment, and pray with targeted intercession! May God give us grace to do so.

Pray for . . .

- the exposure of all lies, corruption, and nefarious activities in every medium of communication.
- the rise of and protection of platforms within the greater sphere of the media that will offer as much truth as possible in the corrupted world in which we live.
- the Holy Spirit to grant supernatural discernment in all communication that we receive from all people and platforms, and that we test the spirits to see that they are of God.

CHAPTER 11
Mountain of Trouble—Arts and Entertainment

THE PHYSICAL LOCATION we know as Hollywood represents an enormously powerful center of cultural influence around the world. But influence of what kind? In the spiritual realm, Hollywood is a domain where supernatural beings of wickedness and deception have long-held authority and jurisdiction.

Much of what goes on in Hollywood is well hidden . . . to most. For the spiritually discerning, we understand that gatekeepers and nefarious influencers pull the strings and control money, opportunity, and access to the upper echelons of stardom. But there is a severe price to pay for participating in their deviant control. We will develop a clearer picture of who these hidden maestros are in this world of so-called entertainment. But first, two personal stories that my spiritual brother and friend George Bell lived through and survived, by the grace of God. He was in the belly of the beast for a time, but it did not consume him.

Consider this:

- The big Hollywood studios prescreen their films and TV shows for GLAAD's (Gay and Lesbian Alliance Against Defamation) Board of Censors, who determine whether or not the product is "acceptable" based on how much LGBTQ content the studios are squeezing into their product.[1]
- Would you believe me if I said that a mother watched videos of her daughter having sex with her boyfriend and picked which one her daughter looked best in to sell? Because that is exactly what happened: Kris Jenner watched and hand-picked which sex tape her daughter

Kim Kardashian would release. It is not an exaggeration to say that Hollywood is satanic.[2]

- Olivia Rodrigo (21 years old), a former star actress on Disney Channel, is promoting abortion access on her "GUTS" concert tour and working with local pro-abortion groups to distribute free Plan B abortion pills and publish phone numbers where girls can get an abortion. The average age of her concertgoers is fifteen years old.[3]

Now my friend George shares two eye-witness, personal experiences.

True Story #1

I came from a family of musically inclined siblings, and my mother was a phenomenal classical vocalist and pianist. As a young kid I aspired to become a musician, and couldn't get the thought of those parade drummers out of my head. Each year I would go to the annual Christmas parade to see the flair of the marching bands. From that time on, I participated in school talent shows, and at the age of 13 I recorded an album with "The Blues Man," Curtis Griffin.

The opportunity to record as a drummer at a young age was gratifying and stoked my ambition to become a studio and recording musician. After playing drums with local bands from elementary through high school, opportunities on a grander scale began to manifest. In 1974 I joined a funk-pop-rock band, Friends and Family, who had international connections to a Los Angeles–based club and promoter, Mavericks Flats. After our long days and hours of rehearsing we were finally on the road. Friends and Family embarked on an international tour; our first performance was scheduled for a nightclub named Zapatas in Regina, Saskatchewan, Canada. We were booked for one month. It was great; Canada in the winter, the brisk air and snow of our new surroundings was a change from the mild winter days of Southern California. Three of the guys I traveled with all attended California State University Northridge. We were known as the party band on campus. Whenever there was an occasion for students to gather, our Righteous Right-On Band was there to perform. In addition, we often gigged on the weekends in various venues around Los Angeles and the San Fernando Valley.

Being in Canada away from family and friends was quite an experience, unlike the short junkets of local and regional performances in northern and southern California. Of course, we also had to do the tourist routine. Meeting new people, site seeing, exploring new vistas, and the slight cultural differences between the US and Canada was enjoyable. I began to relax and settle into this new milieu.

We performed for three weeks and were close to wrapping up our performances at Zapatas, when the owner of the club invited our band to a performance featuring the ten-time Grammy-nominated, and winner of three Grammys, Blood, Sweat, & Tears. Wow, one of my favorite bands (besides Chicago). All of us were excited to go to the concert and have Halloween night off to hang out with B, S, & T. The concert was classic vocalist David Clayton-Thomas, that awesome melodic horn section, and an in-the-pocket rhythm section. The audience was alive with the sounds of the '70s emanating throughout the arena, and people were really enjoying the event.

As the concert ended, and we were preparing to return to our hotel, the owner of the nightclub invited us to his home for an after-party. Well yeah, of course we went. After arriving, we all gathered and introduced ourselves; there were conversations, and there were people sitting around the indoor pool laughing, having a great time. So, a band buddy and I went out to the pool and sat down talking and enjoying the superstar life. Suddenly a gun shot rang out from across the pool in a room with a glass window, and we saw a female fall to the floor. Those who were outside of the bedroom became frantic, wondering what was happening. My band buddies began to run away from where the shot came from, going out the back door. When I opened the back door, there was a man dressed in black coming through the back door. It struck me as odd that he had on a collar like a minister, but the collar was black not white. He entered the room where the woman had been shot, and others went into the room.

We were in shock, wondering what to do because we didn't know where we were. There were no cell phones to call 911 in 1974. We had no idea how to get back to the hotel. In addition, the leader of our band was in the room where the woman was shot, with Blood, Sweat, & Tears, the nightclub owner, and other partiers. My band buddies and I were frozen, just standing in the kitchen away from the commotion in the bedroom. We knew something very bad was going on in the bedroom, but had no choice except waited for this horrific situation to end so we could leave. Eventually, people began to exit the bedroom, hurriedly leaving the house. Among them was the B, S, & T band with others including our lead vocalist. All of them had blank expressions on their faces. My three close friends looked at each other in disbelief at what had transpired in just a few hours. When we returned to our hotel, we finally admitted what we had witnessed: a human sacrifice on Halloween night in 1974! We kept silent about that horror-filled night, but now and then when get together we ask the question. *Did it really happen?* The answer is always *yes!*

Interestingly, a couple of years later 1 made a visit to my dentist, and while waiting for my turn, 1 picked up a magazine with an article about the many witch covens along the California coast. It pin-pointed areas along the coast with a second part in the article disclosing various rituals conducted by witches and satanist. Then, there it was, a paragraph describing the "ritual of Blood, Sweat, & Tears." For decades I've tried to warn family, friends, church members, and students that Halloween is not just an evening when children go out saying "Trick or Treat," to receive candy and apples. It is, in fact, a counterfeit high-holy time for the occult to perform sinister rituals, using human sacrifices to conjure demonic powers to advance their corrupt ideations, recruiting, and to further establish themselves as an enemy of Almighty God.

True Story #2

Many people don't believe the Illuminati exists. Well, here's my story, as a young musician starting out performing in the entertainment industry. 1 did what most up-and-coming musicians did, performing locally in Los Angeles and Hollywood nightclubs and other venues. 1 was exposed at a very early age to bands like War, because one of my fellow band members was the brother-in-law of Howard Scott, vocalist and guitarist who lived in Compton, California where 1 grew up. Members from War would visit our "WWIII" band rehearsals. 1 impressed them with my drumming skills, and was invited to audition for a United Artists band called Uncle Tom. My overly protective parents wouldn't let me record or go on the road with them because 1 was only sixteen years old and in high school. This is where I began to see how the Hollywood "machine" worked, and I was impressed.

Through pursuing my performance and studio musician career I was referred to many other headliners by word of mouth or the Musicians Union Local 47 in Los Angeles. My reputation as a drummer began to circulate among musicians, bands, and around the circuit. I recorded the drum track for a demo that I never knew would eventually become a number-one hit "Get Away" by Earth, Wind, and Fire. I thought I had arrived, working and hanging out with many famous entertainers, the likes of Motown writer Willie Hutch, Smokey Robinson, Brenda Holloway, Mary Wells, Ike Turner, Billy Preston, Chaka Khan, Brothers Johnson, Eddie Harris, Lena Horne, James Ingram, Carl Carlton, Leon Haywood, and many more.

While on tour with Motown artist Willie Hutch I was introduced to the darker side of the music industry. Willie decided not to pay us our weekly salary while on tour. Two of us protested the nonpayment and reported it to the Musicians Union Local 47. It took quite some time for the union to arbitrate on our behalf with the Motown lawyers. Finally, the union reported the good news that we were awarded the unpaid wages we had been deprived of months earlier. Being naïve about how the stars and record companies operated, I found out the hard way that we were "blackballed" by Motown, preventing us from being hired by major recording studios and entertainers. It was a few years before I was able to get a gig with another topflight artist. Willie and Motown wanted us to submit to their control. But the acclaim of Hollywood meant nothing to me over my personal character.

One day, because of my working and playing with many famous entertainers, out of the clear blue I received a phone call from an agent named Mr. Pride. I didn't know him, but did detect an effeminate tone in his voice. I wondered who he was, who referred me to him, and who he represented. Mr. Pride invited me to meet with him to discuss offering me an opportunity to work as a drummer for his entertainment agency. I met with Mr. Pride a couple of days after our phone conversation in Beverly Hills at his penthouse on the Sunset Strip. I arrived at Mr. Pride's place and he invited me in, but noticed that I had brought a friend with me. I never go anywhere alone, when I'm suspicious of a person's intentions. We sat down and exchanged pleasantries, Mr. Pride offered drinks and marijuana, and we began to discuss the purpose for my invitation.

Mr. Pride stated that he represented many known artists and bands, and owned many businesses. He also stated that his reason for inviting me was to offer the opportunity for me to join one of his bands. He never mentioned the names of his artists, but it was obvious he had clout in the entertainment industry. Mr. Pride stipulated that if I signed the contract I would never have to drive again because he owned limousines. He offered for me to move into the penthouse, and I would be "compensated very well." The contract would be for seven years, and then he added, "But you will have to do whatever I tell you to do." That statement *screamed* control. It was to be a binding contract, liked the one I walked away from with Motown. That ended my interest, but for someone else would have been a great opportunity. I was still vexed, but heard a voice in my subconscious say, "For what shall it profit a man, if he shall gain the whole world, and lose his own soul?" I knew I had met with pure evil that day, a Hollywood music industry gatekeeper who was recruiting young professionals, of which I would've become a slave to the industry elite with a contract enforced by the Illuminati. I knew many others who compromised themselves for fame, and had become totally controlled. They became different people, dazed and confused, controlled by the illusion of power, prestige, and wealth.

Not long after the meeting with Mr. Pride a miraculous occurrence happened. I was performing on stage with songwriter and entertainer Leon Haywood at the Cow Palace in Oakland, California when I had an epiphany, a vision of sorts. It was as if the Lord pulled back a curtain, and I could see how I was contributing to the kingdom of darkness. As we performed Leon's number-one hit "*I want'a do something freaky to you,*" the audience was going wild, climaxing into a public display of licentiousness and debauchery. That night I came under such conviction of the Holy Spirit and vexed by whom I had become. How had I been living my life?

Shortly after that tour I dedicated my life to Jesus Christ. Strangely, the telephone stopped ringing for a year after that tour, and musicians depend on the phone to ring. The Lord removed me from my past by separating me from the entertainment industry for a time. It was a season when my gracious Father began to restore me spiritually, by reconnecting me to my family and a local church family. After a year the phone rang, but it was a phone call from a gospel artist, Sandra Crouch, who needed a drummer. As result I joined Sandra and her brother Andre Crouch, performing in concerts. Because of this new beginning I was again picking up momentum, playing with contemporary gospel artists Jon Gipson, Vernessa Mitchel, Nicholas, and others. A new vista presented itself. But this time I was no longer living by my own conceit. God Almighty then called me to ministry as a youth pastor, then an associate pastor, and now a pastor and servant of the Most High. My life is brighter than ever before due to the glory of God.

> But you are a chosen people, a royal priesthood, a holy nation, God's special possession, that you may declare the praises of him who called you out of darkness into his wonderful light. (1 Peter 2:9).

♪ ♪ ♪ ♪ ♪

There are many things in life obscured from plain sight by the great deceiver. Human trafficking, the injustices perpetrated on widows and orphans, the endemic corruption in government—these are more recognizable. But there are numerous secret societies and nefarious associations who are dedicated to Satan. For those without Holy Spirit discernment, this assertion is thought to be an unfounded conspiracy theory—or just nonsense. *It is not.* These groups entice initiates or members with initially appealing messages and purposes. But in the higher echelons of their power structures, they cross the line into the dark side. Scottish Rite Freemasons is one such entity. By the time you are a thirty-third-degree Mason you have sold your soul. Hidden in plain sight are many examples of symbols, slogans, and hidden agendas and is worth your consideration. With intentional focus you *can* confirm the signs and evident evil of people who have sold their soul. This includes triangular hand symbols, triple 6s, the all-seeing eye of Providence, pentagrams, and more. We could not possibly cover adequately these many groups, so I will focus on the one that has most effectively infiltrated the arts and entertainment world.

The Illuminati

It amazes me how thoroughly the enemy has deceived a majority of people to *only* believe in what they can see, hear, feel, taste, or touch. In earlier chapters we referenced how "the Enlightenment" has diminished our illumination to the truth, thinking that logic and human reasoning are the arbiters of what is real. Actually, the spiritual realm is very much real with two forces active, *at all times*, in everything on earth—good and evil. One demands bondage, the other offers freedom. It is our choice.

Since arts and entertainment has such penetrating societal influence and global appeal, especially on the young, it is no wonder that Satan has allocated significant divisions of his demonic realm to pull people away from God and into darkness. George's two stories are eyewitness accounts. Let us look now more deeply into this *entity*—the Illuminati—which collectively, purposefully, and actively promotes the person and work of Satan while unequivocally, but secretively, opposes all things of God. We're highlighting their command of the entertainment world, but they also most certainly retain of seats of power in politics, banking, specific industries, and the "news."

Illuminati symbol

Two books, both written by Mark Dice, are worth your consideration on this topic: *The Illuminati in Hollywood: Celebrities, Conspiracies, and Secret Societies in Pop Culture and the Entertainment Industry* and *Illuminati in the Music Industry*. Some of the chapters in his book include topics such as the Gay Mafia, sex magic deviants, the CIA in Hollywood, and spirituality of the stars. These are a few summary bullet points providing insights into this world:

- Famous stars and rappers from Jay-Z and Rick Ross to Rihanna and Christina Aguilera are believed by many to be part of the Illuminati. Satanic symbols in their music videos and clothes go unnoticed by those not "in the know." (This list is nearly endless, but also includes Beyoncé, Lindsay Lohan, Lebron James, Michael Jackson, Kanye West, et al.)
- Why did an aspiring rapper in Virginia shoot his friend as an "Illuminati sacrifice," hoping it would help him become rich and famous?
- How and why did the founder of BET (Black Entertainment Television) become the first African American billionaire?
- Les Claypool, singer of Primus, wrote a song about the Bohemian Grove. Do an internet search to see what they are up to!
- Why is rap and hip-hop filled with Illuminati puppets and wannabes more than any other genres of music, and direct demonic symbolism and words of death and mayhem?

The fact that some people don't believe this group, with such wide-reaching tentacles, even exists is testament to the effectiveness of the liar and deceiver at its center. But people involved with the Illuminati eventually share their regrets in public, when it is too late. A Facebook post about Lady Gaga corroborates in text what other genres like her Ellen DeGeneres appearance and various YouTube videos communicate clearly:

> "I truly regret selling my soul to the Illuminati Secret Organization." Recently, Lady Gaga spoke openly about her relationship with the Illuminati occult organization. It seems she regretted the adherence to this evil organization. Lady Gaga believes that the chronic illness she is suffering is actually physical confrontation of the evil forces that have begun to take control of her body.

The artist entered the dark forces of the Illuminati when she was young. It is important to note that before this pact, she was an unknown performer at small events. She sold her soul for fame and money. After having made that pact with the Illuminati, Lady Gaga was left possessed by an evil entity that she later attempted to have removed through exorcism, but the Catholic priest who did the ritual failed lamentably. It all started when, after a small concert she met a man behind the stage. He stood supported by a wall, smoking a cigarette. Then the mysterious man said, "I think you've got what it takes. Do you want it?" And when Lady Gaga asked what he was saying, he said, "Everything! Success, Fame, Money, and Power. Do you want them all?" She said she accepted his offer without thinking and donated her soul to the Illuminati. Shortly after this pact, Lady Gaga became an international star.[4]

"What good is it for someone to gain the whole world, yet forfeit their soul? (Mark 8:36); "For what does it profit a person to gain the whole world, and forfeit his soul" (NASB)?

Let's back up a step and identify the origin, blood lines, and other details of this evil association. The Illuminati was founded in Bavaria in 1776—again, during the "enlightenment" era. How (not) coincidental that a counterfeit force of destruction was birthed at the same time that our new covenant nation, America, was being born. Only five men were part of this launch. It grew to some unspecified number, then "disbanded" (or so we were told) ten years later. The Illuminati then went underground, and thus the rise of suspicion that they did not exist. A recent Reddit post said, "Stop worrying about something that will never affect you"; another source stated, "There's no real proof of a modern-day Illuminati." That is exactly what the enemy wants us to believe.

Available on the web is the master outline of the carefully researched work of Fritz Simmons called *The Bloodlines of Illuminati*. It is notable that the full online document is 298 pages (the book is 623 pages) and includes many detailed notes and even some of the donations these families made to particular institutions. "Follow the money!" You could spend hours clicking on the many subsets, all fascinating and interconnected, each shedding light on what is hidden. If we could see all that God sees, I am convinced we would sit in stunned silence! I have, actually.

What follows is the full list of the thirteen primary Illuminati family names, plus four related families for a total of seventeen. But in the interest of chapter space, I only notate one arbitrarily selected subtopic link and one statement in the larger family summary from seven families. If you do your own research, you will find the other family histories and connections to the occult to be very interesting indeed. Note the Krupp bloodline (World Bank), the Disney bloodline (amazingly evil), and of course, the Rockefellers and Rothschilds.

As you read, I trust you will understand that the Illuminati most certainly exists *and thrives* today. If you have remaining doubt, you will find even more information on these platforms: CIA, Amazon, Wikipedia, YouTube, and Google, to name a few. Lots of information for something that doesn't exist!

- The Astor Bloodline—FDR and Lady Astor
  "The process of 400 years looks like this. Various Satanic families moved into Southwest Germany in the late Medieval period. Witchcraft associated with Diana was practiced. The Astor family provides leadership in the covens in the Heidelberg area."

- The Bundy Bloodline—Ted Bundy, Charles Manson, Jack the Ripper
  "It is not publicly known why serial killer Ted Bundy killed so many innocent victims. He told his girlfriend Elizabeth Kendall that 'the force' caused him to kill. 'The force' is the very term that high level Satanists use to describe the power they believe in." And to desensitize us, isn't this a known term in all the Star Wars movies?

- The Collins Bloodline—J. Edgar Hoover, Joan Collins, Michael Collins (Apollo 11), Oliver Cromwell
  "The following is a description of a highly secret high level Satanic meeting held twice yearly, via an ex-insider who is now a Christian. The Collins family has been kept out of the limelight because they have more occult power than the Rothschilds or the Rockefellers. The Grande Mother on the throne was a Collins, all decked out with a great deal of jewelry. Two boys were taken to be her sons one of whom (Tom) was later gunned down by the Illuminati. A great discussion was had about what has happened in the last six months to bring in Satan's One-World government."

- The Dupont Bloodline—a dynasty of satanic royalty
"After immigrating from France they settled in Delaware USA, many of whom become governor and were high-ranking Freemasons. They established the Order of the Garter a secret committee of 300 within the Order of St John of Jerusalem. They were diabolical men. Lord Palmerton is an example from history who was totally corrupt, pretended to be a Christian, and practiced Satanism."

- The Freeman Bloodline—ties to other important families
"The late Grand Master of the Prieure de Sion (Priory of Zion) was Gaylord Freeman (among many Jews in the Illuminati). The book *Holy Blood, Holy Grail* provided historical proof that this organization existed since the time of the early Crusades (1099 A.D.) This blood line included the Medicis, also tied to the Black Nobility committed to Hermetic Magic a type of black magic that originated with the ancient Egyptians and is portrayed in the Egyptian Book of the Dead. . . . A descendant of Joseph Smith, Jr. who was a Satanic ritual abuse victim, has quietly told certain people that her family is indeed a Satanic bloodline."

- The Kennedy Bloodline—Marilyn Monroe, Jane Mansfield, Jackie Kennedy
"The question always arises, how are the Kennedys related to the elite of the Illuminati and the New World Order? How is this Kennedy related to this other Kennedy [and their Scottish aristocratic European roots]? If John F. Kennedy hadn't been assassinated (which is another rabbit hole of intrigue) and so much about his life examined and written about, a window allowing us to see the Kennedy Illuminati family may have never opened. JFK had three long-term girlfriends (besides his wife Jackie)—Marilyn Monroe (a Jewish girl working in striptease), and actresses Jane Mansfield and Zsa Zsa Gabor. All three were also the girlfriends of Anton LaVey, founder of the Church of Satan, whose occult grandmother was from Transylvania. Jane was a high priestess of the Church of Satan and Marilyn was a participant in LaVey's satanic rituals."

- The Li Bloodline—understanding the Chinese —triad leaders and rituals "In recent history three Lis stand out as giants: billionaire and former *de facto* ruler of Hong Kong, Li Ka-shing; former ruler of the People's Republic of China, Li Peng; and, the former President of Singapore, Lee Kuan Yew. Then there are the underworld Triad leaders with 14 families ruling, many times more powerful than the Mafia with branches all over the United States. Their satanic rituals are derived from Taoism (magic), Buddhism and Confucianism. Initiation lasts about eight hours and includes ritual dance, secret handshakes and blood sacrifice. Public ceremonies include the celebration of the Goddess of Merch and the God of the Earth. They also control street gangs, youth gangs and almost all organized crime."
- The Onassis Bloodline—Aristotle, the Peron's of Argentina, Josef Mengele, Winston Churchill, etc.
- The Reynolds Bloodline—occult books and newspapers, mind control, tobacco and drugs, Nazism, etc.
- The Rockefeller Bloodline—major funding to universities, establishing anti-Christian organizations, etc.
- The Rothschild Bloodline—co-masters of the world—clerics, czars, MI5, globalism, "Five Wizards," media
- The Russell Bloodline—Jehovah's Witnesses, Mormons, Bill Clinton, Al Gore, Armand Hammer, etc.
- The Van Duyn Bloodline—Planned Parenthood, CIA, MI6, Mossad, NSA, string of "strange coincidences"
- The Merovingian Bloodline—their all-seeing-eye represents the satanic trinity: Osiris, Isis, and Horus of Egypt
- The Krupp Bloodline—Rudolf Hess, German elite occultists, World Bank, Averell Harriman, etc.
- The McDonald Bloodline—Ray Kroc bought out the hamburger chain in 1954 founded in 1937 by Richard and Maurice McDonald. Since then, the McDonald's Corp. has been rumored for years to be connected with satanism. A book titled *Satan Wants You* (p. 140) indicates that Ray Kroc tithed to the Church of Satan.

§ § § § §

- **The Disney Bloodline**—(*This one requires a quote!*) "Who was Walt Disney? He was self-satisfied, intractable, and arrogant. He could bring his artists to tears or anger in a matter of seconds. Walt grew up in an abusive home and was fascinated with the occult. He had an intuitive sense for quality cartoons that would appeal to children. In secret, Walt became a porn king. A victim remembers that he was sadistic and enjoyed snuff porn films. His interest in children was far from altruistic."[5]

So much has been hidden, but God knows all things!

Pray for . . .

- the exposure of all lies, secrets, and evil—that we would awaken and then act.
- God's mercy on America, that we turn from our ways and repent as a nation.
- all our children, for their safety and well-being, in a media infested cesspool

CHAPTER 12

A New World Order

FOR YEARS NOW there has been quite a bit of "chatter" in different sectors of society and the church about a coming "new world order," or "one-world order". Let's take a closer look with quantifiable information from different sources. I will divide this section into three parts, each with subsets of source data:

1. *Important insights*, both biblical and temporal
2. *Existential threats*, (mentioned in the Introduction)
3. Looming *changes that will chafe*!

The information which follows is not offered dogmatically. Please research further *if* you wish. Some prophetic voices have clarified that this new world order already exists, rather than something still coming in the future. God will pour out accelerated blessing and abundance on his ekklesia in this beginning of the kingdom age. The key matter for your discernment is if this is a hard-stop transition from one realm to the other *or* a both-and scenario. Either way, *sitting idlily, doing nothing is a choice, but a foolish one.*

Important Insights

If you recall my "Occam's razor" comment, understanding that there are two realms, and *in all matters, there are only two options*—good and evil. Every person has been corrupted, "For all have sinned and fall short of the glory of God" (Rom. 3:23). Therefore, *every* human institution has been corrupted by the enemy, to a greater or lesser degree, because "fallen" people operate them.

Biblical—Positive

Archbishop Carlo Maria Viganò was the papal nuncio to the United States who rose to "fame" in 2018 when he published a lengthy letter accusing Pope Francis of covering up reports of the sexual abuse of minors in America ("allegedly" also occurring worldwide). On December 18, 2021, in the throes of COVID restrictions, he sent a letter (#185) to the American people. It was quite lengthy; these are excerpts:

Dear American People, Dear Friends,

For over two years now, a global coup has been carried out all over the world, planned for some time by an elite group of conspirators enslaved to the interests of international high finance. . . . Today more and more people are opening their eyes and beginning to understand that the emergency pandemic and the "ecological emergency" (i.e., climate agenda) are part of a criminal plan hatched by the World Economic Forum, the UN, the WHO, and a galaxy of organizations and foundations that are ideologically characterized as anti-human and—this needs to be said clearly—anti-Christian. . . . Political and religious leaders, representatives of the people, scientists, doctors, journalists and those who work in the media have literally betrayed their people, their laws, their Constitutions, and the most basic ethical principles. . . . The answer is now clear: throughout the world, in the name of a perverted concept of freedom, we have progressively erased God from society and laws. We have denied that there is an eternal and transcendent principle, valid for all men of all times, to which the law of States must conform. We have replaced this absolute principle with the arbitrariness of individuals, with the principle that everyone is his own legislator. . . . Christianity is the strongest defense against injustice, the strongest garrison against the oppression of the powerful over the weak, the violent over the peaceful, and the wicked over the good, because Christian morality makes each of us accountable to God and our neighbor for our actions, both as citizens and as rulers. The Son of God became Incarnate in time and in history in order to heal an ancient wound, and to restore by Grace the order broken by disobedience. . . . The infernal challenge of the Enemy is repeated over the centuries unchanged, but it is doomed to inexorable failure. . . . For it is absolutely impossible to hope for the end of this global tyranny if we continue to remove from the Kingdom of Christ the nations that belong to Him and must belong to Him. . . . My appeal for an Anti-Globalist Alliance—which I renew today— aims precisely to constitute a movement of moral and spiritual rebirth which will inspire the civil, social and political action of those who do not want to be enslaved as slaves to the New World Order. . . . May God bless you, and may God bless the United States of America. [1]

Biblical—Negative

My brother in Christ, George Bell, has done *extensive* research on the corruption within the Catholic church. These are excerpts from his work:

- The "beasts" spoken of throughout Scripture (which makes the average layman's eyes roll) refer to nations, earthly kingdom governments, and authorities
  - Lion with eagle's wings—Babylon (Dan. 7:4)
  - Bear—Persia (Dan. 7:5)
  - Leopard—Greece (Dan. 7:6)
  - Beast with ten horns—Rome, followed soon by a kingdom of a reestablished Rome (Dan. 7:7, 7:23; Rev. 13:1)
- The Vatican is a sovereign government unto itself, has insinuated itself into the (organization) of the New World Order, and plans to divide the world into ten regions with the Pope as the supreme leader.
- Two American presidents were killed *with intention*—Lincoln and Kennedy, both by people with ties to the Jesuit Order of the Catholic church; and Kennedy, as well, by people with ties to the CIA.
  - Charles Chiniquy, a close friend of Lincoln and "disillusioned" Catholic priest who became a Presbyterian minister, confirmed that there was an irrefutable connection—as John Wilkes Booth

was the leader of eight others in this plot who were coached by the Jesuits.

o Kennedy, an independent thinker, wanted to deescalate the Vietnam War, dismantle the Federal Reserve, and dismantle or at least reduce the reach of the CIA. (Witnesses claim that CIA agents E. Howard Hunt and Frank Sturgis were photographed near the scene in Dallas; as well as Eugene Hale Brading, an associate of Mafioso James "The Weasel" Frattiano.)

- The founders of the CIA are the Sovereign Military Order of Malta, also known as the Sovereign Military Order of St. John of Jerusalem, a "closed" fraternity of the Roman Catholic Church. The founding fathers of the CIA, William "Wild Bill" Donovan and Allen Dulles, were Knights of Malta.

- This is a portion of the Jesuit Oath: "I do further promise and declare that I will, when opportunity presents, make and wage relentless war, secretly and openly, against all heretics, Protestants and Masons (scapegoats), as I am directed to do, to extirpate them from the face of the whole earth; and that I will spare neither age, sex nor condition, and that will hang, burn, waste, boil, flay, strangle, and bury alive these infamous heretics; rip up the stomachs and wombs of their women, and crush their infants' heads against the walls in order to annihilate their execrable race." [2]

Temporal—Positive

What is the Great Reset and why should we care? Why is the Swiss-based World Economic Forum (WEF) advocating a complete "re-imagining" of the Western world's social, economic, and moral structures? Whether Western democracies will succumb to the paternalistic totalitarianism of the oligarchical Resetters remains to be seen. With the death of God—or of a god—Nietzsche sought liberation from the jiu-jitsu of Jesus: that weakness was strength; that victimhood was noble; that renunciation—of love, sex, power, ambition—was the highest form of attainment. [3]

When great is applied to a proposed transnational comprehensive revolution, we should also equate it with near religious zealotry. "The Great Reset," after all, in all its green and "woke" glory, with all of its credentialed and "expert" devotees, is still a faith-based rather than scientific effort. Its spiritual predecessor was perhaps the eighteenth-century "Great Awakening" of Protestant evangelicalism that swept the eastern seaboard of colonial America in reaction to the secularism of the Enlightenment. But this time around the frenzy is fueled more by agnostics who worship secular progressive totems such as Al Gore or Greta Thunberg.[4]

Temporal—Negative

Many institutes have debunked what they consider the false allegations of a pending new or one-world order.

> The "New World Order" conspiracy theory is an example of how misinformation forms and is disseminated amidst homogenous online political subcultures. At one time, the term was used to refer to a cabal of international organizations (the Trilateral Commission, the Council on Foreign Relations and the United Nations, amongst others), and worldwide elites conspiring to subvert sovereignty and liberties of free nations. Today adherents of the conspiracy describe the "New World Order" as an organization for back-door "totalitarian" policies.[5]

Existential Threats

This author's assertion, again, is that there are three external existential threats converging on us simultaneously:

1. Radical jihadist Islam who demand fealty to their *god* or be killed
2. Globalist secular humanism whose goal is to delude and replace *God* in all things
3. *God-less* Chinese communist hegemony with a 100-year plan to subvert then subjugate

I have already addressed global Islamic jihad in Chapter 5 and documented their sinister intentions. Therefore, let us move on to the two remaining threats.

Globalist Secular Humanism

First, we are referring to people worldwide. Their orientation is not determined by nationality, citizenship, or ethnicity, but rather by what abides in their "heart." And who determines this? It is only God who knows each person's heart and what dwells there: "man looks at the outward appearance, but the LORD looks at the heart" (1 Sam. 16:7, NKJV). *Second*, the word "secular" customarily describes a person who is nonreligious, or worldly rather than spiritual. In truth, contemporary secular humanists are just as religious; they "worship" and have faith in their belief system. The word "worship" comes from the Old English word *weorþsciepe*, which means "to give worth to." *Third*, secular humanists ascribe worth to what they believe. Much of what they believe has been documented in this book. In Chapter 7 I identified a humanist as someone who "regards the universe as self-existing and not created." Within this "man-centered" foolish universe we will now look at the WEF, WHO, and the newest "axis of evil."

World Economic Forum

Klaus Schwab

Klaus Schwab is the founder and executive chairman of the World Economic Forum, holding two earned and seventeen honorary doctorates. His book *COVID-19: The Great Reset*, is coauthored with Thierry Malleret, who has a PhD in economics. He is the founder of the Global Risk Network within the WEF. Note these two additional anecdotal items, one past, one future. Klaus' father was a munitions manufacturer for the Nazis. Also, he is rumored to be stepping down from a formal leadership role of the WEF, but his wife Hilde and son Olivier will certainly keep this movement headed toward its primary objective. One only needs to look at his book's contents to better understand the orientation of this globalist. Here are four: the fate of the US dollar; contact tracing, contact tracking, and surveillance; stakeholder capitalism and ESG; and redefining our humanness and moral choices.

These excerpts from his book further describe the WEF's "theo-political" orientation:

- "The coronavirus pandemic has no parallel in modern history. . . . It is our defining moment—we will be dealing with its fallout for years, and many things *will* change forever." (p. 11)
- "For decades, the US has enjoyed the 'exorbitant privilege' of retaining the global currency reserve, a status that has long been 'a perk of imperial might and economic elixir.'" (p. 72)
- "One of the great lessons of the past five centuries in Europe and America is this: acute crisis contributes to boosting the power of the state." (p. 89)
- "Progress is indeed possible in those global areas that have traditionally benefitted from international cooperation, like environmental agreements, public health and tax havens. This will only come about through improved global governance—the most 'natural' and effective mitigating factor against protectionist tendencies." (p. 113)
- "The corporate move will be towards greater surveillance; for better or for worse, companies will be watching and sometimes recording what their workforce does. The trend could take many different forms, from measuring body temperatures with thermal cameras to monitoring via an app how employees comply with social distancing." (p. 165)[6]

And just in case you aren't yet fully convinced what direction WEF is headed, here are two more signposts:

- "What great progress has been made since President Xi Jinping addressed the Annual Meeting of the World Economic Forum earlier. President Xi highlighted the importance of increased global cooperation as the only way to create a peaceful, prosperous and sustainable future. This One Belt One Road Initiative fully embodies this concept, and serves as a shining model for regional collaboration, development and growth."[7]
- WEF Corporate Governance Circular: *Davos Manifesto 2020: The Universal Purpose of a Company in the Fourth Industrial Revolution.* The content addresses why we need the 'Davos Manifesto' for a better kind of capitalism.[8]

Now let's also look at some people who have not drunk the Kool-Aid.

Klaus Schwab looks into the camera. He is dressed sharply in a dark suit, crisp white shirt and blue tie; he is bald and speaks with a thick German accent. The WEF is to demonstrate entrepreneurship in the global public interest while upholding the highest standards of governance. Schwab has been, since 1971, the advocate of what he terms "stakeholder capitalism." This philosophy of corporate governance is entirely at odds with the dominant corporate model of shareholder capitalism. The notion, coined by Milton Friedman, stood in direct opposition to what he termed "the social responsibilities of business." To his credit, Schwab isn't hiding the ball. The "Great Reset" of capitalism, practically, means dispensing with metrics of global progress like Gross Domestic Product (GDP), but rather what matters most: climate action, sustainability, inclusivity, global cooperation, health and well-being.[9]

Globalists, who are obsessed with societal control, decided to take advantage of the pandemic in order to increase authoritarian power. It is no secret that the WEF is focused on accelerating the implementation of central planning for the entire global population. Drastic changes to the world order like the Great

Reset do not happen spontaneously; rather, they are designed by global policy makers, including influential billionaires, politicians, celebrities, biased academics, wealthy philanthropists, and the bureaucrats of international organizations and institutions. These types of people support social engineering because it will enable them to acquire control over the world's wealth and natural resources, and strengthen their ability to shape society as they sit fit. Some of the more ridiculous controls proposed by the WEF include limiting the washing of jeans to no more than once a month, and pajamas once a week. The WEF also advocates for transforming the entire food system encouraging people to consume insects or "cultured meat" referring to meat produced by cultivating animal cells in a controlled lab environment. They want to design a societal order where sympathy and mutual assistance will be rendered obsolete and where every citizen of the world, is equally powerless, poor, and isolated so that people will be unable to oppose the organized strength of global governance and become dependent on governments and their allies for survival.[10]

Javier Milei, the president of Argentina, made a historic speech at the 54th WEF Economic Forum on January 17, 2024. Here is an excerpt:

Today I am here to tell you that the West is in danger; it is in danger because those who are supposed to defend the values of the West find themselves co-opted by a vision of the world that, inexorably, leads to socialism, and consequently poverty. Thanks to free enterprise capitalism, today, the world is at its best. There has never been, in all of human history, a time of greater prosperity than the one we live in today. The world today is freer, richer, more peaceful, and more prosperous than at any other time in our history. Now, if free enterprise capitalism and economic freedom have been extraordinary tools to end poverty in the world; and we are today at the best moment in history of humanity, why do I then say that the West is in danger? Because it must never be forgotten that socialism is always and everywhere an impoverishing phenomenon that has failed in all the countries it was tried. It was an economic failure. It was a social failure. It was a cultural failure. And it also murdered more than 100 million human beings.[11]

From the commentary titled, "The 7 Most Outrageous Moments of the World Economic Forum 2024":

1. *A pagan ritual*—WEF concluded its forum on "Climate and Nature" by inviting a shaman to carry out a pagan ritual for the healing of the planet.

2. *A digital ID to track your whole life*—Queen Máxima of the Netherlands (whose grandfather Prince Bernhard of Lippe-Biesterfeld was cofounder of the Bilderberg Group in 1954). She urged governments to adopt a "ubiquitous" ID card that is "digital" and "biometric." Such an ID not only provides surveillance over the financial industry; it's also good for school enrollment, and to see who actually got a vaccination, as well as facilitating the redistribution of wealth to see that welfare recipients and other *favored classes* get their subsidies from the government.

3. *A global tax*—Amnesty International secretary general Agnès Callamard said that governments should enact "not just [a] carbon tax; let's tax the corporate interests." The Biden administration took the first steps toward such a tax in 2021 when it supported a "global minimum tax"—a 15% tax, which would allow foreign nations to tax US-based corporations.

4. *Efforts to force social media companies to yield to government censorship*— WEF's panel on "Protecting Democracy against Bots and Plots" complained that social media titans faced "scrutiny" and sought ways to "force" companies to comply with free-speech restrictions. CEO of the Google-aligned Center for Democracy and Technology, Alexandra Reeve Givens, admonished that social media platforms are "still keeping up the good work." Editor-in-chief of *Foreign Policy* magazine Ravi Agrawal asked, "Is there a way to force them?"

5. *Reining in Donald Trump, and US sovereignty*—A persistent discomfort pulsed through the 2024 World Economic Forum: the possibility that Donald Trump will defeat Joe Biden (now Kamala Harris) this November. "How are we assessing the election risk? There is a risk the

wrong man will get elected," declared Bloomberg's Haslinda Amin. Alex Soros claimed that America had an unwritten system of checks and balances until "one man, Donald Trump, literally came in and just took that all away."

6. *The WHO, lockdowns, and pushing the green agenda to preserve "health"*—World Health Organization Secretary-general Dr. Tedros Ghebreyesus refused to answer Canadian journalist Andrew Lawton's question about whether he would reject lockdowns as a public health measure for future pandemics. Climate change will also be weaponized as "health crisis," said John Kerry's daughter Vanessa Kerry, who is cofounder and CEO of Seed Global Health. "The climate crisis is a health crisis, fundamentally."

7. The seventh "very bold, unusual, and startling"[12] circumstance at WEF 2024 was to see *actual pushback against these globalist automatons. Who let them in?* I previously quoted Argentine president Javier Milei. President of Hungary Katalin Novák pushed back against the WEF's advocacy for prolonging Ukraine's war with Russia: "We have to avoid a Third World War." Heritage Foundation president Kevin Roberts boldly confronted WEF attendees with a harsh reality: "You are part of the problem."[12]

World Health Organization

I earlier identified the United Nations as "that great temple of uselessness." Founded in 1948, the WHO is the directing and coordinating authority on international health within the United Nations system. "The objective of WHO is the attainment by all peoples of the highest possible level of health. Health, as defined in the WHO Constitution, is a state of complete physical, mental and social well-being and not merely the absence of disease or infirmity."[13]

Note these excerpts from the "Fourth Meeting of the Intergovernmental Negotiating Body to Draft and Negotiate a WHO Convention, Agreement or Other International Instrument of Pandemic Prevention, Preparedness and

Response" (provisional agenda item 3), February 1, 2023. And please remember who was US president in 2023!

The parties to this WHO CA+[1] . . .

> 5. Recognizing the *central role of the WHO*, as the directing and coordinating authority on international health work, in pandemic prevention, preparedness, response, and recovery of health systems, and in convening and generating scientific evidence, and, more generally, fostering multilateral cooperation *in global health governance.*

> 15. Reaffirming the importance of *diverse, gender-balanced and equitable representation* and expertise in pandemic prevention, preparedness, response and health system recovery, decision-making, as well as in the design and implementation of activities.

> 26. Reaffirming the importance of *a One Health approach* and the need for synergies between multisectoral and cross-sectoral collaboration at national, regional and international levels to safeguard human health, detect and prevent health threats at the animal and human interface, in particular zoonotic spill-over and mutations, and to sustainably balance and optimize the health of people, animals and ecosystems.

> 34. Reiterating the determination to achieve *health equity* through resolute action on *social, environmental, cultural, political and economic determinants of health* . . .

> 46. *Recalling resolution* WHA61.21 (2008) on the global strategy and plan of action on public health, *innovation and intellectual property* . . .

Article 4

> 3. *Sovereignty*—States have, in accordance with the Charter of the United Nations and the principles of international law, the sovereign right to determine and manage their approach to public health . . . *provided that activities within their jurisdiction or control*

do not cause damage to their peoples and other countries. Sovereignty also covers the rights of States over their biological resources.

11. Gender equality—. . . will be guided by and benefit from the goal *of equal participation and leadership of men and women in decision making* . . . using a country-driven, *gender responsive/ transformative*, participatory and fully transparent approach.

15. Universal health coverage—The WHO CA+[1] will be guided by the aim of achieving universal health coverage . . .[14]

What does all this formal gobbledygook mean? The globalist organizations are preparing for globalist control. It is that simple.

I commend Michele Bachmann, former congressional representative from Minnesota, for being at the forefront of many raising alarm bells about the danger of the United States subordinating our sovereignty to this leviathan global entity during her interview on the World Prayer Network, on the weekly "Well Versed" multi-platform broadcast hosted by Dr. Jim Garlow and Rosemary Schindler-Garlow. This show is an excellent source of information from a biblical perspective for many of the temporal challenges in our world today.

A sobering, yet very realistic prognostication, has been made by the former Director of the Centers for Disease Control, Dr. Robert Redfield. He is a leading virologist who warns Americans to prepare for the next pandemic, which he believes will be more catastrophic than COVID-19. "Redfield predicted the next pandemic will be the bird flu, also known as H5N1. Its mortality rate is significantly higher than COVID: 52% of the 888 infected patients with H5N1 have died since 2003. COVID's mortality was about 0.6%. Bird flu's mortality is going to be north of 5%, 10%, 15%, 20%. It's going to be catastrophic."[15]

So, what do you think? Is all of this one-world, Great Reset stuff nonsense?

The "Axis of Evil"

Our final focus on existential threats is China, as previously identified, but here we are using the title "Axis of Evil" because there is important connectivity between hostile state actors that must be identified. George W. Bush first used this term in his 2002 State of the Union Address. In that period, North Korea, Iran, and Iraq held this moniker. I would suggest, based on the theme of this book, that *everything* that is not with God or moving toward God is part of an axis (alliance) with those who are against God. In the present context, this assuredly includes China and Russia as the primary actors, with a satellite of other nations including Iran who serve as proxies.

China and Russia

For my predominantly Christian reading audience, here are two interesting indicators.

Ralph preaching in China

- Over the past four decades, Christianity has grown faster in China than anywhere else in the world. Daryl Ireland, a Boston University School of Theology research assistant professor of mission, estimates that during this time the Christian community there has grown from 1 million to 100 million.[16]
- Demographers have projected that the Chinese population will peak in 2030 at 1.4 billion. By then, Protestant Christians likely will constitute 16 percent of the Chinese population based on the lower rate of 7% annual growth. *Wow, that's a quarter-billion Christ-followers*! If we add Catholics into the equation, it would take fewer years for China to become the largest Christian nation on earth.[17]

This is not random information. How many "real" Christians will there be in America by 2030?

What follows is a summarized description of the mischief the Chinese Communist Party is currently up to, and will be up to. Whatever transpires in the political and economic life of America or China, God's *ekklesia* will survive and be with Him in eternity. "But our citizenship is in heaven" (Phil. 3:20a). God sees things through the lens of eternity, and his purposes are always sovereign. We must not categorize "the Chinese" as the enemy. Lots of them are our sisters and brothers! But the Chinese Communist Party *is* a godless instrument of the enemy during this time in history. Therefore, we must be vigilant in the "affairs of men." Our leaders must govern and do business in the interests of America, to protect the freedoms which God bestowed upon us.

BRICS and Other Money Matters

In June 2024 Russian Foreign Minister Sergey Lavrov announced that the BRICS nations (Brazil, Russia, India, China and South Africa) are moving closer to launching a new reserve currency, what we can consider "the anti-dollar." Russian President Vladimir Putin especially wants to get revenge on America and dethrone the dollar, to challenge the U.S. dollar's dominance. The dollar could meet its end as the global currency as early as the next BRICS summit, which is happening in Kazan, Russia, October 22–24, 2024.[18]

BRICS heads of state

More than forty countries, including Iran, Saudi Arabia, United Arab Emirates, Turkey, Argentina, Algeria, Bolivia, Indonesia, Egypt, Ethiopia, Cuba, Democratic Republic of Congo, Comoros, Gabon, and Kazakhstan have expressed interest in joining BRICS. This is only the beginning.

Chinese and Russian central banks are discussing the use of national payment systems, which will use and promote their respective currencies. Russian banks may issue cards with China, while Visa and Mastercard cut links. The use of the Mir and China UnionPay will undergird this new arrangement. Also, the Bank of Russia, led by First Deputy Governor Olga Skorobogatova, is collaborating with the UAE regulators to establish a cutting-edge system for fast payments. The digital ruble is expected to enhance transaction efficiency, fostering financial inclusivity and exemplifying a proactive approach to the future of finance. Also, Russia's SWIFT alternative is expanding quickly.[19]

By 2050, China's economy will be much larger than America's. China will be the most economically dominant nation. China will be able to shape the world in its image. What will that world look like. This question, of course, is unanswerable. Yet one thing is certain: if China's government retains its current priorities, continues its same strategies, and clings to the values it has held dear since Mao Zedong's rise to power, a world shaped in China's image will be very different from the world we know today.[20]

Many of our navel-gazing, self-enriching politicians and globalist business titans look blithely past the signs all around us, or don't look at all. These are a few of the warning signs from China's intentional actions:

- Foreign purchase of American farmland and acreage with water rights
- Fentanyl and other drugs pouring across our borders, which could kill every American, many times over
- Rampant intellectual property theft, for decades
- The microchip center of the universe, Taiwan, soon to be subjugated
- The Fauci/Wuhan virus wiping out 1.1 million American lives—or likely less than that, since dual-diagnosed patients "always" died of a COVID diagnosis so health facilities could secure more federal dollars
- Spy balloons, Chinese nationals gate-crashing military instillations, thousands of cartel-guided military-aged men coming across our borders, spies in virtually every sector
- Building a military base in Cuba at El Salao, outside Santiago de Cuba.
- Below-the-radar Chinese "police" units in NYC and six other U.S. cities keeping tabs and putting the muscle on Chinese dissidents, otherwise known as free-thinking people
- TikTok, facial recognition technology, satellite surveillance, and scores more "spooky stuff"
- Controlling much of our American supply chains for essential medicines, rare earth, minerals, raw materials, ammunition, military equipment, industrial parts and components . . . and much more
- Seeding significant amounts of money in our universities and public school system, often through the proliferation of five-hundred-plus Confucious Institutes in the US

- As part of a push to "Sinicize" religion, the Chinese Communist Party has embarked on a ten-year project to rewrite the Bible and other religious texts. In the Gospel of John, Jesus famously confronts the accusers of a woman caught in adultery, a beautiful story of forgiveness and mercy—unless you're a CCP official. Then it's a story of a dissident challenging the authority of the state. The rewritten Gospel of John excerpt ends not with mercy, but with Jesus himself stoning the adulterous woman to death. The CCP also wants the authority to select the next Dalai Lama, a sacred tradition in Tibetan Buddhism. [21]

Facts and statistics don't communicate as well as matters of the heart. I will end this section with *a true story*. Most people in our Western countries have heard stories in the media about the Beijing government's brutal abuse, conscripted labor, and genocide of the Uyghurs in Xinjiang Province in far western China. The largest population live in its capital Urumqi. This ethnically Turkic and predominantly Sunni Muslim people have lived with horrific persecution. A forty-five-page single-spaced report by the United Nations *suggests* "Crimes against Humanity." You may agree after reading this quote:

> Believed to be the only Christian family to escape to the U.S. intact, the Turdakun family have waited for years for this moment—an end to a nightmare so many Uyghurs and ethnic minorities are still living. Like so many others, their story began at home with a knock on the door. For weeks, the Chinese authorities would call their house or come by to threaten him. After a month of this nightly trauma, they finally took Ovalbek into custody, sending him to a camp where he would spend the next 10 months suffering. "Everything was painful," he remembered. Each morning, he and his 23 cellmates would wake up in a tiny, crowded, windowless room with harsh lights that never went off. Guards would order them to sing communist songs to get their breakfast. Talking to other prisoners was forbidden. If anyone was caught whispering, the entire cell was punished. The worst part were the injections—a toxic mix that left him with fevers and searing pain in his ears, hands, and feet. Other times, the shots would make him sick with diarrhea and vomiting, unable to walk, as an eerie yellow substance leaked from his ears (likely his own spinal fluid, experts

say now). The level of torture and abuses against Mr. Turdakun for being a Kyrgyz Christian in China's concentration camps is beyond imagination.[22]

Iran (Persia)

Biblical Perspective: The demonic realm has had dominion over the lands of the Persian empire for millennia. They have been a sword in the side of the Israeli people and nation throughout history. Why? Because their father of lies is behind every means possible to thwart God's purposes. The people of Israel are God's chosen people. The Persians will lose and Satan will lose. "Though we are slaves, our God has not deserted us in our bondage. He has shown us kindness in the sight of the kings of Persia: He has granted us new life to rebuild the house of our God and repair its ruins, and he has given us a wall of protection in Judah and Jerusalem" (Ezra 9:9, NIV84).

Political Perspective:

- "Tehran will continue to develop 'peaceful' nuclear capacities. We seek peaceful use of nuclear energy."—Iran's Supreme Leader Ayatollah Ali Khamenei
- "Today, the grounds for the annihilation and collapse of the Zionist regime are [present] more than ever. . . . Hezbollah has 100,000 missiles that are ready to hit Israel to liberate the occupied Palestinian territories."—Hossein Salami, Commander-in-Chief Islamic Revolutionary Guard Corps. But, oh, my, have circumstances changed in late September/early October 2024!
- And this from my friend and Christian brother, David Weston:

   Let's begin by asking, what does Iran want? Iran has positioned itself to become the next oligarch state in the Middle East. It has been using influence and lust for power over its Sunni neighbors for almost four decades. Its attainment of a nuclear weapon is paramount to the achievement of its goals. . . . It feels like this generation of diplomats is playing the "delay game." They just do not want war to break out during their watch. So, they believe that these measures contained within the JCPOA (Joint Comprehensive Plan of Action) will hopefully slow the Iranian's nuclear weapons program down. . . . Let there be no confusion. Iran is playing a dangerous game. "Do and Deny" is central to its strategy. It is the same strategy that Russian President Putin is employing, as well as Syrian President Bashir al-Assad, China's Xi Jinping, Turkish Prime Minister Recep Tayyip Erdoğan, Belarus President Aleksandr Lukashenko, North Korea President Kim Jong-un, and Afghanistan President Mullah Baradar. . . . Ask yourself what lies are you prepared to believe. One of the things that many pundits are counting on is that you will not have time to put the necessary work into gaining the truth.[23]

Changes That Will Chafe

Here I will simply list topics for which I have additional research in my files but insufficient space to describe them with sufficiency: neurotechnology microchip devices, subdermal microchip implants, frequency weapons, synthetic biology, quantum phones and computers, numerous blockchain and digital currencies, World Bank and World Food Program involvement in acute food shortages and famine, the proliferation of "The 15-Minute City," restrictive housing choices, and many dark-money individuals and secret organizations that are today, and will be in the years ahead, investing trillions to intentionally guide these next years ahead.

So, dear reader, is the "chatter" of a coming "new world order," "one-world order," or "great reset" all nonsense, a conspiracy theory? That is for you to decide. Hopefully you will receive the affirmation proclaimed in the Indiana Jones movie, The Last Crusade – "You chose wisely".

A few very important points to conclude . . .

We have part of the world trying to destroy Israel (Islamic radicals). We have part of the world trying to destroy the United States (Chinese communists and allies). And we have a cabal of financial elites and humanists—some known, many others hidden—*planning now* to create (actually accelerate what already exists) a global order that which will restrict, control, and dominate the majority world completely. There is freedom in Christ for his body!

God's kingdom warriors, the anointed leaders He will raise up in this season, *will create redemptive alternatives* in many of these areas of human endeavor where nefarious actors are scheming. Prophetic intercessors, please pray with accelerated intensity to bring down strongholds of darkness. *What will happen in the days ahead, again, are both-and, not either-or*: God's abundance and grace toward His people, and increasing bondage and fear for those who do not know Him.

EMBRACING FREEDOM—
Spiritually and Financially

CHAPTER 13
Kingdom Alliances

WITH YOUR UNDERSTANDING, I need to explain a journey before I describe the destination . . .

For decades now I have worked and traveled in about one hundred countries, serving, supporting, and sometimes rescuing precious, vulnerable children whom the Lord loves with all his being—children who are victims of war, abuse, trafficking, famine, poverty, neglect and ignorance. All children, born and preborn, are precious gifts from our Creator. After finishing my bachelor's and master's degrees I set out for what I thought would be a career in business. But in my early twenties God had another plan—which makes perfect sense now. It is out of the crucibles of our own life that the Almighty shapes a spiritual weapon against the demonic rulers and powers of this world. We become His lightsabers against their evil and for their destruction.

In fact, I also was an at-risk child, adopted at age five, those first formative years a blur of complexity. I never met my birth father. Then, as a newly married man, my firstborn daughter (on my birthday) started to show signs of a serious medical problem. Her eventual diagnosis revealed a degenerative neurological condition. By the time she died at age ten she suffered from severe, twisting scoliosis, had to eat through a gastrostomy tube, and went blind and deaf. A YouTube post of the longer story is at http://youtu.be/H2_FxW7bLjw.

Without understanding this fully in the midst of these trials, I came to realize that the challenges in my own life prepared me directly, generating the passion and commitment to pursue the path God had ordained for me. My guess is you also have discovered this truth in your own way.

Life is an interesting journey. We experience joy and pain, success and failure. We have both times of wonder and wandering. God brings us through it all, if we seek Him and trust completely in His Sovereignty and then . . . we become one of His wounded healers.

Over time it was clear that my heavenly Father had given me unusual access to places of bondage and need, especially with the people who dwelled there. My service took me to intense environments like Yemen, Somalia, Iraq, Tibet, Mongolia, North Korea, Bosnia, Ukraine, Russia, Cuba, Haiti, Nicaragua and dozens more. Without conscious intent, I embraced what became one of my life principles: *anonymity is a gift to be retained as long as possible.* A high-profile social media presence is anathema to me. As they say, the higher your head is out of the foxhole, the easier target you become. In tandem with this, I understood that my innumerable contacts developed over time were also facilitated by God because I was imbued with gifting as a connector, conduit, and catalyst. Caution and confidentiality are important to and for many of the people I have met, many in hostile environments. This brief history is part of the potter's furnace, His ceramic kiln that shaped me.

Fast-forward to 2019. I began to fast *and* pray more intensely, asking God to make clear what His plan was for the remaining years of my earthly sojourn. I deeply desire, and fully believe, that He will fulfill in me the purpose for which I was created. The Father's response, to my prayers, came to me in the form of a dream, a vision and prophetic confirmation.

First, the Dream . . .

Unlike some people, I don't often recall my dreams, and God is not usually present in them. This one was intense and vivid. I had a sense of His presence. Whether it was an assigned angel or otherwise, I was not certain. He handed me a torchlight—blazingly bright, not a standard flashlight. A door opened and I was directed out into the dark. Hearing nothing audible, somehow, I knew what I was supposed to do. Carefully and intentionally, I continued to walk over an expansive and diverse terrain, coming upon deep pits of various sizes in the barren ground. It was dark everywhere—only blacks and greys, no color. When I directed the bright light downward, there were groups of people, adults and children, silent lips moving, begging me with their eyes to help them. The pits were too deep for them to naturally remove themselves. I was not capable of helping them all myself, but I indicated through pantomime that I would return. I assured them, without speaking, that I understood and that they could count on me to bring resources.

For some period of time, I walked slowly in all directions, discovering many other pits. The condition of all the people in them was haggard and desperate. I sensed each was hampered by different types of bondage, some deeply and inextricably. This dream felt like a 1920s silent film. Suddenly I was in another place, standing up in a search boat in the icy Atlantic. My torch light again shone into the darkness. I was in the one lifeboat that returned to look for survivors of the Titanic. Most were frozen stiff, their fate sealed. But I knew, still in silence, that it was my urgent task to find the few who remained alive, who could be saved. I woke up in a sweat and prayed.

What does one do with such a dream? I asked God for discernment. It would be great if I could tell you clarity occurred in the next moments, but it came months later. While I did fast *once,* for forty days (liquids only) as a part of a larger intercessors' initiative, my long-sought-after discernment for this dream followed a one-week fast. It occurred in one of my quiet places to commune with God—the tranquil Santa Rosa Plateau Ecological Reserve in southwest Riverside County, California, just a few miles from San Diego County.

This is my discernment from the dream:

- I have been granted unique physical access to and spiritual under-standing of expansive evil which places multitudes in various forms of bondage throughout the world, especially children.

- The Holy Spirit has confirmed that I am to shine a light on, become a clarion for, and contribute to a global strategy for the acquisition and deployment of resources for these people in need.

- This is a huge, enormous assignment. God is in charge. I am preparing for it, pray for a fresh impartation of the Holy Spirit for power and boldness, and await His further specific guidance, including the "team" I will sojourn with.

Next, the Vision . . .

People who understand visions and open visions are able to follow this. My guess is that other readers will think I have lost my mind. That's fine, because my mind, heart, will, body, soul, and spirit belong to Jesus—so *if* it is lost, it is lost in Him and I am in good hands! While still physically looking at a beautiful landscape, simultaneously my mind, with spiritual eyes, were focused on a global "movement." It was not a singular event, rather the unfolding of many events over a period of time—for a "season." The following includes excerpts from a document I later constructed called "Kingdom Alliances: A Global Movement in Service to the King."

> Whomever the Holy Spirit has already called, *and* soon will be calling, to participate in this global vision, will discern that we are in the early stages of a divinely initiated "coming together" for a specific kingdom purpose which was ordained before the foundation of the world.

> We are at war, and it is a spiritual one. God's end times army, His *ekklesia,* has now been enjoined in battle coordination with the angelic hosts of heaven against *the enemy* and his minions. In so doing, we must proceed with a conquest mentality, in full exercise of the authority given to us.

> A victorious army requires ample, accessible, properly deployed resources. These have been stored up in abundance around the globe, i.e., in many countries and regions, for such a time as this. He is giving supernatural revelation to those called to this task on where to access and how best to utilize this outpouring of resources.

> The purpose of this movement is to *aggregate* and *accelerate* the *acquisition and provision* of these resources which includes: 1) human capital (Holy-Spirit–called and overflowing people); 2) *intellectual capital* (inspired human wisdom and prophetic words of knowledge and revelation); and 3) *financial capital* (cash, goods-in-kind, services, bartered value, etc.)

> Satan very clearly has accelerated evil throughout the world in the commanding heights of every institution and community. Kingdom alliances will *aggregate* types (domains) of ministry, yielding much larger interdependent plans so that the *accelerated*

release of those resources (in size/amount and frequency) will have maximum impact.

The strategic leaders for this movement are now being revealed. The magnitude of funding anticipated, globally, will become *trillions not billions*. This movement is well outside of any purely human enterprise. Whatever takes place from here is now God's plan, and only He will accomplish it!

This is my discernment from the vision:

- It is necessary that I transition from an undercover operative (so to speak, not literally) and become a member of a "tribe"—one accountable, interdependent "center of influence."

- My journey of discovery, incremental portions of revelation, and the related strategies God has shown me need to be linked to a larger body of gifted, called-out ones.

- *The critical element* of this vision, again, are the two words *aggregate* and *accelerate*. Until now we think and act on projects or initiatives. We raise funds for organizations or campaigns. Our vision is too small. God is going to rain down enormous wealth.

Affirmed Prophetically . . .

This prophetic declaration was made on December 13, 2022, by Rick Taylor, Wesley and Stacey Campbell:

We have this sense of destiny in the leading on Ralph and the calling that you put within him through wealth creation, wealth transfer and wealth provision You are named by heaven, you are called to be a plumbline for the greatest wealth transfer that the world has ever seen, which I am going to show you supernaturally.

The favor of the Lord is all over you. Divine connections are coming to you. The presence of the Lord surrounds you. Where doors are locked the angel of the Lord will open it for you.

With profound clarity this brought into focus the multiple elements of what the Lord has shown me in part, and in increments, over these last five years. In total, more than a dozen other prophetic individuals have contributed to what amounts to ten, single-spaced typed pages. I don't feel this book is the right platform to list all of these, but let me add just two additional—given directly to me from the Lord:

> "My Son, I love you. I know your heart and it pleases me. For I have a large assignment for you. It will only be accomplished by my Spirit through you. I see your life from my eternal perspective and I will take whatever time is necessary to grow your character to match my assignment for you."

> "I will bring to pass what I have promised you and what I have put on your heart to pray for every day. You desire to be used mightily against my enemy, and so you shall be."

This is my discernment from these prophecies (the larger portion of which are not included here):

- It is nothing short of amazing to discover how many in the *ekklesia* He is infilling with these same types of proclamations and affirmations! Now . . . how shall we link?
- This vision for Kingdom alliances needs to be specifically and intensely bathed in intercessory prayer by as many formal networks of intercessors as feel led to do so.
- There are "councils" of apostles, prophets, and leaders in various domains. *Soon*, there needs to be first one council then more, for this marketplace juggernaut.

I am incredulous that God would assign this to me, "Called to be a plumbline for the greatest transfer of wealth the world has ever seen." I chose a path of service, and lived on a single nonprofit paycheck my entire life. Very few would want to exchange their net worth with mine. I grew up in a 640-square-foot, one-bedroom house, where my parents slept on a foldout couch in the "living room" and gave me the bedroom. (A more complete description is found in my third published book, *My Mother, Your Mama: Stories of Caring for Aging Parents.*) Lastly, I don't live in a social stratum where I have personal relationships, *as a peer*, with lots of uber-wealthy people. Someone once called me a "marketplace apostle." I don't think so. People with that moniker, whom I have seen highlighted or speak at various Christian conferences, are all wealthy; one was called a missionary millionaire – which I believe is quite valid. It's just not me.

Despite this . . . Holy Spirit, I yield to you—and wait upon your guidance and timing!

What Is the "Movement" of Kingdom Alliances?

Succinctly stated, these are *redemptive communities* **or** *centers of influence* **or** *apostolic hubs* birthed out of and continuously supported by intensive intercessory prayer. They are directed by the Holy Spirit to penetrate, then tear down, a particular "stronghold" of the enemy. These teams will covenant together to assemble a strike force to raise a specific level of resources for this purpose.

These are additional elements:

1. *Aggregate and accelerate* the wise deployment of resources (human, intellectual, and financial) required for His end-times *ekklesia*, army, to penetrate strongholds of the enemy. Ask bigger and believe bigger. With Holy Spirit discernment, operationalize your vision both with a larger horizon and international partnerships. Then take your projected resource need, multiply it in faith believing for ten times or one hundred times and cover it in prayer.

2. *Centers of influence,* birthed from covering intercessory prayer, will identify a Holy Spirit–assembled group of people who come together to infiltrate a specific enemy stronghold. This will be geographically *or* functionally based. This "epi-center of prayer" will prophetically affirm the formation of the initial nucleus of a new "cell" or center of influence composed of key change agents and stakeholders. These will be composed of a minimum of twelve people or twelve times X, depending on the breadth of the vision. This prayerfully, operationally, and financially committed group will agree upon goals and outcomes, including a funding level. A "superfund" (with a chosen moniker; for example, the Caleb Fund) will steward the ingress, egress, and reporting

on all resources deployed.

3. *Covenantal commitments* to God and each other are essential. Each center of influence will create a self-determined covenant, agreed upon by all "members" which may include such matters as: 1) how stakeholders join or leave the group, 2) an abiding commitment to do everything in love, 3) clear conflict resolution guidelines, 4) an authority structure for the group, 5) how decisions are made, 6) reporting and transparency, etc.

4. The stewardship of *kingdom wealth* to be distributed will come from: 1) new, supernaturally inspired wealth creation, 2) inter-generational wealth transfer and, 3) what God has promised to remove from those who have labored against His will and purpose: "a sinner's wealth is stored up for the righteous" (Prov. 13:22). Each covenant community—a *de facto* center of influence—will create, populate, and carefully steward a superfund for high impact, which must have a formal relationship with a reputable fiduciary to steward, disburse, and report on all activities.

5. *Networks* of these units, as they multiply regionally and globally, will covenant together for particularly large-scale initiatives which, over time, will form "kingdom alliances" in this unique time in salvation history. A vision-casting map of what "can be" is shown in the following.

What Is Different about This Model?

Haven't people prayed, responded to the Holy Spirit, and engaged in channeling resources for specific ministry purposes before? Yes, of course. Scripture itself tells us, "What has been will be again, what has been done will be done again; there is nothing new under the sun" (Eccl. 1:9) However, this is a specially appointed *kairos* time in salvation history. God is calling us to believe for more, *much* more—and "to come up higher," as many of our prophetic voices have enjoined. We are in the midst of an emerging global movement, thus this "vision board" world map with future locations is an expression of faith.

A Vision for Future Kingdom Alliances
Centers of Influence

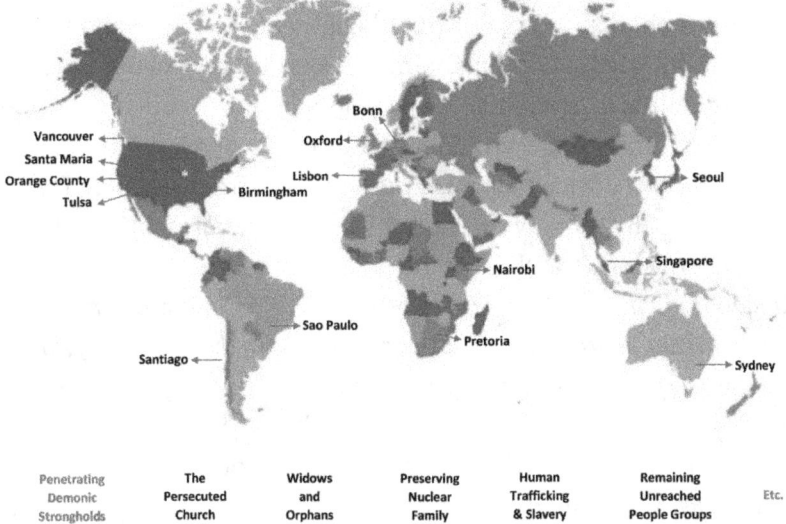

| Penetrating Demonic Strongholds | The Persecuted Church | Widows and Orphans | Preserving Nuclear Family | Human Trafficking & Slavery | Remaining Unreached People Groups | Etc. |

What follows is not an exhaustive list but an important one, helping clarify what is different. Many other scriptures could have been quoted as well.

- *Aggregate*—multiply your vision; partner with others (Eccl. 4:12)
- *Accelerate*—decree, declare, and do more; time is short (Eph. 3:20–21)
- *Penetrate strongholds*—covering with prayer continuously (Eph. 6:12)
- *Release*—the pride of ownership and control; humility is key (Prov. 11:2)
- *Covenant*—all mighty works of God are covenantal (Heb. 13:20–21)
- *Kingdom wealth*—faithfully steward Holy Spirit abundance (Luke 16:10–11)
- *Boldness*—Joining the remnant of each generation alive is an emerging, young "Joshua Generation." They will work outside of the church, be risk-takers, go where it is dark, be where the people are, will not be controlled by time or convention, are prayer warriors, are sensitive to the Holy Spirit, and have a deep compassion for the lost (Deut. 31:6).

Examples of Penetrating Strongholds

When we speak of *strongholds*, of course they are spiritual ones. The god of this age has blinded the minds of unbelievers (2 Cor. 4:4) and has in our generation, infiltrated the commanding heights of every major association of humankind: political, economic, social, and religious. Daniel 10:10–21 gives us a very descriptive understanding of the battle between the messenger angel and the (evil) Prince of Persia hindering him from reaching Daniel for twenty-one days. By the way this same evil being and his minions still retain dominion over Persia (Iran)!

Kingdom alliances, therefore, will be a replication and proliferation of this conjoining of deep, continuous intercessory prayer with the infusion of significant resources into a specific domain or type of ministry, thus bringing down a specific stronghold of the enemy.

There are many other *domains* of service beyond the seven examples that follow, as well as many *organizations* or ministries in those domains. These are intended simply as representative samples. Note: One tangible example of this "coming together" of intense prayer and a significant infusion of funding, has been the investment of the David Green family, including sons Steve, Mart, and daughter Darsee, into many initiatives related to the accelerated translation, increased distribution and promotion of the Bible, both in written and digital forms. Yes, you say, but this is a billionaire family, what can we who are of normal means and ability do? That is precisely the point! In the days ahead *God is going to do what is going to be done*! He is empowering us with His authority and revelation knowledge. And He has already pre-positioned the wealth of the nations for such a time as this! Locate the URL for each of these groups. They're amazing!

Domain	Program Type	Organization
Fulfilling the Great Commission (literally)	* Bible translation * Church planting * Evangelism	Finish the Task 2033 Lausanne Movement call2all
Defense of traditional family roles & structure	* Strengthening fathers * Empowering women * Resources for thriving	Fatherhood CoMission Nations of Women Focus on the Family

Domain	Program Type	Organization
Freedom and recovery	* Overcoming addiction * Human trafficking * Persecuted church	Lovelady Center Bride Movement Voice of the Martyrs
Apostolic movements& deploy young leaders	* Words of knowledge * Activating gift of prophecy * Supernatural manifestations	Generals International Global Awakening Iris Global
Unreached, Unengaged People Groups (UUPGs)	* Muslim world e.g. Pashtun * Hindu world e.g. Khandayat * Reaching the global deaf	Novo Reflejo "Table 71" ministries
Justice and Reconciliation	*Victim assistance * Healing and forgiveness * Policy and advocacy	Int'l Justice Mission Redeem Int'l Prison Fellowship
Penetrating the Metaverse (open and"dark")	* Social Media * Digital platforms * Virtual reality	God Tube Life Verse Cross.tv

Throughout the world there are innumerable domains, specific types of programs, ministries, and organizations that exist in service to the King and his kingdom. For example, we have not included the world of compassion ministry, which addresses endemic issues such as affordable housing, access to primary health care, clean water, disaster response, and so much more. Each one has a goal, a budget, and a finite range of resources. As envisioned, kingdom alliances will help forge aggregated, interdependent communities of service under the umbrella of intense, continuous intercessory prayer, with the acceleration of generated resources at a scale that will occur in this special time in history. Chapters 14 and 15 will expand on this overarching theme.

My Role in Kingdom Alliances

To say this five-plus-year journey of faith had its precipitous moments is an understatement. It has been a process of "progressive revelation." As someone who has always struggled with impatience, this has certainly been a 'fruit of the spirit' enhancement. In this time, I have experienced profound truths that have been shared by other persons of faith over the centuries. Among them are these:

- The level of enemy opposition is commensurate with his perception of the *danger* you pose to his earthly deception, dominion, and destruction.
- You cannot begin to embrace *true* humility, a necessary condition of the heart, without first having been refined by unexpected humiliation.
- "If at first you don't succeed, try, try, and try again." This quote from Robert the Bruce, king of Scotland in 1314, would benefit from additional language: "For the LORD your God is he who goes with you to fight for you against your enemies. To give you the victory" (Deut. 20:4).

There are some very compelling stories in my journey that accompany these truths. If we have opportunity to talk or meet in person, I will recount some of these. But to share them in writing here would require sufficient detail to reveal the individual identities or geographies of persons whom, at that time, I felt wounded or betrayed me. In fact, God used them as instruments to "take whatever time is necessary to grow your character to match my assignment for you."

Months following his counsel, I reread the wisdom shared by Sam Metcalf, founder of Novo—an excellent global ministry to support financially (https://novo.org). He solidified my understanding of where I am spiritually and emotionally now, as I write this book and await the supernatural discernment of the Lord, on how to proceed: "I've read your last book; you've had an amazing life. You do not need to subordinate yourself to someone or wait for someone else—this vision is yours to lead. With all the initiatives you have going it would be wise to set aside [and he mentions a dollar range] and remove yourself for the rest of your ministry from the distraction of earning income. Then, pray until you see who God brings to you prophetically to share in this vision and who will get behind it financially."[1]

Earlier in the chapter I shared my discernment regarding a dream and a vision from which the idea of Kingdom alliances emerged. Prophetic voices from many sectors have proclaimed this season as a time to gather the "innovators', "solutionists" and "wealth creators." It is my conviction that I am one of these. There are three specific tactical/operational elements that I will be involved in:

1. As a strategist/participant in one "council" of marketplace leaders
2. As a continuing advocate and clarion voice to promote and promulgate this movement for all other "domains" of service
3. As a dedicated member of one center of influence, *I have the burden and calling to help raise $1 billion dollars for at-risk children, of all types; and, especially to identify hidden kingdom warriors in multiple regions of the world to receive some of these resources.* This will take place under the authority of a covenant body called to attack this "stronghold" with the covering of dedicated intercessors for this purpose.

Ralph's global service to children

Who are these children at risk?

- **The Conceived**—a gestating child, alive with a spirit/soul between conception and birth
- **The Orphan**—left alone by the death or abandonment of their parent(s)
- **The Refugee (or IDPs)**—forced to flee their home and country living in dangerous circumstances; internally displaced persons are in peril in their own country
- **The Trafficked**—innocents forced into hard labor, sexual exploitation or organ harvesting
- **The Persecuted**—restricted, injured or killed by communist or Islamic jihadist Judeo-Christian-hostile authorities; radical humanists, also subtly persecute children
- **The Indoctrinated**—taught anti-God, cultural Marxist-based critical theory, gender perversion, hate America and so much more – especially in many of our public schools
- **The Enticed**—gamers, excessive internet surfers, spiritually lost in the meta verse for untold hours daily; predators traverse these digital platforms more than we realize
- **The Trapped**—those suffering from physical or emotional abuse, gang and cartel members, all types of spiritual bondage, coerced or mutated before their age of reason and maturity
- **The Resourced**—loving, economically sufficient parent(s), with a child who has a terminal illness or acute medical / psychological condition, addictions, dysphoria and other struggles
- **The Poor**—with loving parent(s) doing their best, but are underemployed or homeless, living in a car or temporary shelter, born into multigenerational poverty or unjust, oppressive societies, and many other reasons
- **The Chosen**—The children of the lineage of Abraham, David, Jesus – in Israel and throughout the diaspora; Satan is the reason for rampant antisemitism
- **The Apprentice**—*children of destiny*, in every country and territory on earth, who are eager, bright and need opportunity, education, vocational training and spiritual guidance to thrive

Allow me to share a few stories of beautiful children—one from the US and one from Iraq—to illustrate two groups who were at-risk for different reasons.

I have already reflected briefly on my firstborn daughter Bristol who died at age ten from a debilitating regressive neurological condition. It is contrary to the prevailing laws of nature that a parent should bury a young child. Actually, it is a heart-wrenching travesty. Each of us who has experienced such a thing must go on with life, and we push this pain . . . somewhere . . . into our inner consciousness or better yet, give it to the Lord and release it, as best we can.

It was during a particular period of meeting people involved in raising funds for kingdom purposes that I met Dave. His beautiful ten-year-old daughter Kelsea had passed into eternity after two brutal rounds of treatment for leukemia, including replacing—*twice*—all the blood in her cardiovascular system. I also met Rob, whose beautiful daughter Haley had committed suicide at seventeen. Who can describe, let alone understand, what debilitating pain and hopelessness each man had to deal with? Each of us was crushed by the unique crucible we had to face, *as well as* our loved ones around us. But again, we had two choices: continue to trust in God and follow Him, or allow ourselves to be dragged into a black hole of despair. Dave, Rob and Ralph, indeed, are now wounded healers!

I have mentioned the ministry of Novo in different sections of this book. It was my privilege to support them during a trip to the plains of Nineveh and its ancient capital, now modern-day Mosul, Iraq. During the ISIS reign of terror, eventually taking over the entire region, the Islamic jihadi fighters were allowed to capture women and make them their "wives," aka their conscripted consorts. One particular "source" for these women were the Yazidis. Over the course of their insurgency more than 6,400 Yazidi women were captured; another 5,000 were murdered and 2,700 remain missing. At least one thousand children were birthed during this tragedy and most are still alive today. They live with their mothers in camps operated by the UN. Various international charities are allowed to provide services for them. Fortunately, some Yazidi moms with their children, had the proper paperwork and were able to immigrate. The US state with the largest Yazidi population is Nebraska. Unfortunately, most of these women and children are still "stateless," because they retain no documentation for their legal processing.

These two photos show actual women who were enslaved and children who were born. As we interacted with them, our hearts were overwhelmed.

Yazidi women and children in Mosul (Nineveh) Iraq

One horrifying story was told of the cruelty perpetrated on one of the mothers in this photo. She, her sister, and two friends tried to escape from their "husbands" one night. They made it partway, but not far enough. Their captors roughly brought them back to their compound, tied them to chairs, and the mom with kids was made to watch as her children were killed, slowly, by poisoning.

The evil perpetrated on innocent children around the world, which I have seen first-hand - is impossible to comprehend and extremely painful to share – so much so that it overwhelms the senses. We don't have adequate chapter space to fully describe the 20,000 "Lost Boys (and girls) of (South) Sudan", most just six or seven years old who fled their communities while two million of their parents and relatives were killed by the genocidal forces the Khartoum government. They started in groups of 3-4 then collectively walked 1,000 miles for months to make it to refugee camps in Ethiopia and Kenya. Today, many ministries involved in anti-trafficking can confirm the pure evil of the estimated 500,000 children crossed by the cartels who are unaccounted for, due to the open-border polices of the Biden Administration. As you read this very page, they are being sexually exploited, and more are crossing every day. *This is why* we all must wake up and be engaged. It is why

God wants us to aggregate and accelerate our work. This is not a time for timidity or staying safe. It is a season for boldness!

Since we are at WAR against the principalities and powers of darkness, please pray that kingdom alliance leaders will be all blessed with:

Wisdom • Allies • Resources

The next two chapters will bring further detail and clarity to the role and function of Kingdom alliances, which I believe you will find interesting. We will identify some of the particulars of the greatest *transfer of wealth* in history currently underway. And we will reference one unique company and methods for *creating wealth* where commitments for realized profits are made, *in advance*, and invested in Kingdom "business." By way of clarification, this author does not separate commercial business from Kingdom "business," since God calls each one of us to a unique role within the larger whole of His will and purpose.

CHAPTER 14
Aggregate and Accelerate

ALLOW ME TO emphasize an important message from the last chapter:

> We are at war and it is a spiritual one. . . . A victorious army requires ample, accessible, properly deployed resources for such a time as this. He is giving supernatural revelation to those called to this task on where to access and how best to utilize this outpouring of resources. The purpose of this movement is to *aggregate* and *accelerate* the acquisition and provision of these resources. *Kingdom alliances* will aggregate types (domains) of ministry, yielding much larger interdependent plans so that the accelerated release of those resources, in size, amount and frequency, will have maximum impact.

It may seem unnecessary, but a simple definition of both words will enhance this faith decree and declaration.

- *Aggregate*—a whole formed by combining several elements; formed or calculated by the combination of many separate units; to collect many units into one; gathered into, or considered as a whole[1]
- *Accelerate*—increase in amount or extent; undergo a change in velocity; increasing in speed or rate of occurrence; to cause something to happen sooner or more quickly[2]

Spiritual Intelligence

We live in a time of accelerated evil, clearly evidenced all around us. We affirm that God is enjoining his end-times army, in battle formation with the hosts of heaven, to reclaim the territory the enemy has stolen. And since we have been given an "open door" into a season of abundance, the miraculous, and a billion-soul harvest—then these two words and their intrinsic meaning take on supernatural meaning and importance! In this season the Holy Spirit is intending for us to labor together: "to collect many units into one" and "to cause something to happen sooner and more quickly." I believe part of "that something" describing my "assignment" for these latter days. I am certain many of you also have an important assignment!

Does this word which follows resonate with you? It did for me.

> Since 2020, there has been a recession constantly trying to make the church back pedal on faith amidst so much shaking. It [has been] the season where finances have felt tighter because the enemy is anticipating great wealth transfer and he dreads [this] coming to the church. That's why financial systems have been shaken, [costs and] interest rates have skyrocketed, and people have gone into survival mode. Yes, the enemy has tried to bring back a poverty mindset upon the body of Christ and a hope-deferred spirit to cause us to feel deeply let down by God and doubt His promises. It has felt like a deep cloud of discouragement and soul-sickness has hit many because the enemy has been delaying these plans for so long now. *This is all changing.* We are coming into a time where the Lord is repaying that which the locust ate in your life. We're entering into a time again when the Lord is restoring the joy of sowing. [And] the Lord is about to release the resources to build. He's releasing the provision to finally build [the vision] He has given [each of] us. [3]

As I listen to prophetic voices—on multiple platforms, there is amazing commonality from spiritual intel being shared. These prophetic messages address both the exposure and judgement of those opposing God as well as the blessing and provision for those trusting in God. These are a few examples:

- come up higher
- a reset of America
- returning America to its covenant roots
- flipping
- turning the tables

- boomerang
- tide is turning
- tearing apart evil schemes
- supernatural reversals
- overturning the injustice
- transformation
- awakening
- rescue operation
- "Haman reversal"
- bells of freedom
- exposure of the lying media
- all falsehoods will be shaken
- all that is hidden will be revealed
- signs, wonders, and miracles everywhere
- restitution
- recompense
- vindication

The Great Commission Fulfilled

The most important task to benefit from *aggregating* and *accelerating* is fulfilling the mandate of Jesus recorded in Matthew 28:16–20. *The Passion Translation* reflects this beautifully: "All authority of the universe has been given to me. Now wherever you go, make disciples of all nations, baptizing them in the name of the Father, the Son, and the Holy Spirit. And teach them to faithfully follow all that I have commanded you. And never forget that I am with you every day even to the completion of this age."

At the nine-day Amsterdam 2000 conference convened by Billy Graham for "preaching evangelists," attended by more than ten thousand people from *nearly* every country on earth—Graham challenged the assembly to complete what Christ had commissioned. Christians have carried this mandate since the day Jesus spoke it. Today, with *accelerating* technology and *aggregated* strategy, this is closer to fulfillment than ever before!.

In God's providence at this conference, one particular group of leaders scheduled a strategy session to focus on the specific plan and action steps needed to reach the five hundred remaining UUPGs (unengaged, unreached people groups). A majority of these two-plus-billion people live in the 10/40 Window—i.e. the land area of North Africa, the Middle East, and Asia approximately between 10 degrees north and 40 degrees north latitude. Reaching them with the gospel of Jesus Christ would hasten the day of the Lord's return (2 Peter 3:12). Attendees filled one hundred tables, with a particular group of global mission leaders at Table 71. Their focus included taking on some of the major unmet challenges— reaching the deaf (some 465 million) and developing an "orality" strategy for those who are illiterate (more than 775 million, most of whom are women). This particular leadership group continued to be referred to as "Table 71."

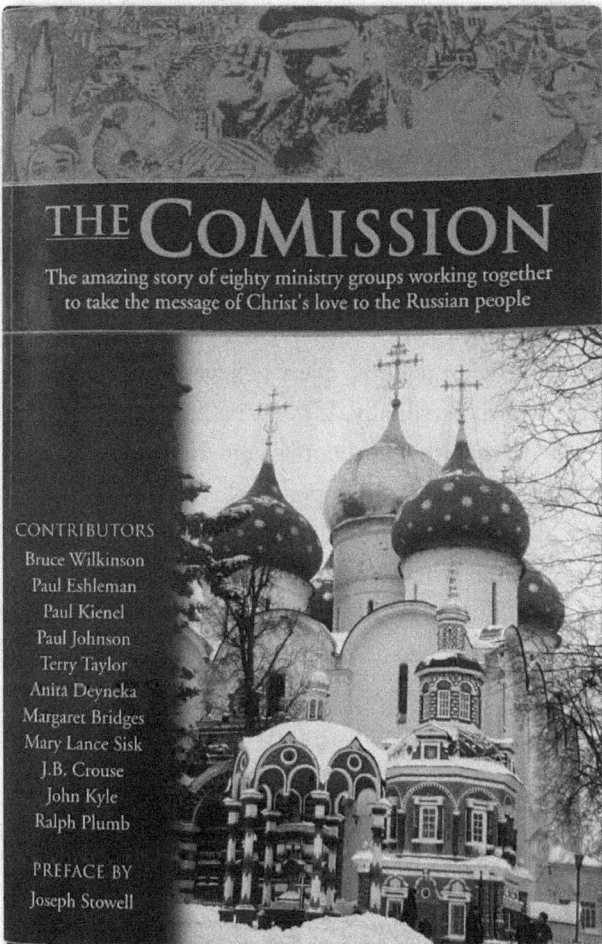

THE COMISSION

The amazing story of eighty ministry groups working together to take the message of Christ's love to the Russian people

CONTRIBUTORS
Bruce Wilkinson
Paul Eshleman
Paul Kienel
Paul Johnson
Terry Taylor
Anita Deyneka
Margaret Bridges
Mary Lance Sisk
J.B. Crouse
John Kyle
Ralph Plumb

PREFACE BY
Joseph Stowell

The leadership at Table 71 included Paul Eshelman, who directed the Jesus Film ministry under the Cru banner. I had the privilege of serving with him and ten others on the Executive Committee of the CoMission, "the amazing story of eighty ministry groups working together to take the message of Christ's love to the Russian people" after the disintegration of the USSR. In total, 42,000 Christian volunteers served on short-term teaching assignments in 142 cities in the former USSR over a five-year period.

In God's providence he brought another anointed leader to this massive global task. Rick Warren, founding pastor of Saddleback Church in Lake Forest, California, now contributes a significant portion of his time as executive director of Finishing the Task, a Christian consortium of 1,600 mission agencies, each one laser-focused on fulfilling their role in the Great Commission in our generation. In his simplistically profound way, Rick, crafted "The Three Bs" to indicate the overall global framework to achieve the Great Commission: 1) *believers* in every people group on earth, 2) a *Bible* available in every language, and 3) a *body* of believers, i.e., a church (within reasonable distance) for worship, discipleship, and fellowship:

- *Bibles:* We want every person on Earth to have access to the gospel translated into their heart language. We will also empower believers around the globe to engage with Scripture in new and expanded ways.
- *Believers:* We want to equip every believer— all 2.6 billion of them—to share their faith personally. If every believer in Jesus Christ just shared the good news with two people who had never heard it, the whole world would hear the gospel personally.
- *Bodies of Christ*: We want every existing church to sponsor and plant a daughter church where there is no church.
- And now, a fourth "B" has been added. . . . *Breakthrough Prayer:* We want to have every person on planet Earth who doesn't know Jesus yet prayed for by someone who does know Jesus. This means billions of believers will need to be praying for billions of nonbelievers.

Ralph with Rick Warren

Please review this website intermittently (https://finishingthetask.com) for updates on the fulfillment of the Great Commission! In one particular two-and-a-half-hour meeting Rick shared their strategy with key major donors we had invited. He acknowledged, as Scripture states, that no man knows the day or hour of Jesus return, only the Father. But he reminded us of the significance of the year 2033. Knowing, as we do from the historical record, that Jesus died at age 33 (AD 33) and had challenged his disciples with the words of the Great Commission just before his death, that means the year 2033 represents the two-thousandth anniversary of that mandate! Wow, a coincidence? So far, I haven't observed too many coincidences in God's original intent and grand design!

Our generation now has a strategy, and a calendar—and He has prepositioned the wealth of the nations at our disposal—soon to be transferred to His *ekklesia* for this very purpose. With the timely *aggregation* and *acceleration* of tools at our disposal, and the greatest transfer of wealth in human history—this will become a reality soon—in Jesus' name!

A final thought on fulfilling the Great Commission. I refer you to the small, but powerful booklet titled "*Word, Deed and Power: Three Dimensions of the Gospel,*" by Sam Metcalf founder of Novo. This word derives from an Old Galician-Portuguese word (Latin *novus*) meaning "to make new." Most of the Christian church understands the importance of the Word and the tangible expression of the love of Christ in deed. Yet many have lost the full meaning and application of the power of the Holy Spirit, through signs and wonders. This is one of the most significant changes, to be made "new" in this coming kingdom age. God's power, through His people, will be on full display—to His glory!

Aggregate and Accelerate in Kingdom Alliances

The COVID years of 2020–2022 were the least auspicious time to launch a new ministry initiative. We had reached out to many ministries with the inference of generating resources for them. I will avoid commenting on the specific members of the team that were part of this effort except to say that I was unequally yoked, and that sustained intercessory prayer was not in our collective DNA. Thankfully, these last two years have been a period of intense prayer, waiting on the Lord's direction and *distinctly sensing new divinely inspired intelligence*. God is good!

"We know that in all things God works for the good of those who love him, who have been called according to his purpose" (Rom. 8:28). There *were* some very important discoveries during this test launch period. I was invited multiple times to two venue sites, where mostly men, usually wealthy, gathered for a time of relaxation and comradery. Both venues were managed, at that time, by Young Life. Tudor Farms, named after hedge fund guru Paul Tudor Jones, was a 6,400-acre site on the Eastern Shore of Maryland that he sunk millions of dollars into creating a high-end hunting and fishing wonderland. Free-range Sika deer and pheasant, along with everything the Chesapeake Bay can offer, and a premier 14,000-square-foot hunting lodge were part of the attraction. After a partial day in a hunting blind (*terra firma* or in a tree) or on a deep-sea fishing boat, and following an afternoon of conversation, dinner was provided by a world-class chef. The woodsy dining facility was in the round with framed photos and mounted heads of trophies past overlooking the massive, custom-built table. But it was the conversation that ensued which was divinely ordained and most important to my growing understanding of what kingdom alliances will become.

Tudor Farms, Cambridge, Maryland

On the financial side of the upbeat talk were some stunning disclosures. One father-and-son team had liquidated their waste disposal company, with continuing mineral rights, for a low ten-figure sum. A man who owned a dozen companies had sold just one, his medical products division, for a handsome nine-figure price. And among the dozens of others, many seven and eight-figure sales or generational family wealth transfers were in process. I heard many passionate stories about their challenge with how not to ruin their children or grandchildren with this abundance.

But the most important discovery for me was on the personal side of conversation. As we went around the room, each had opportunity to share, which surfaced some poignant stories. The man to my immediate right (again, at a table in the round in which we went clockwise) spoke just before me. He struggled to keep his tears in check as he described the immense pain over his son's drug addiction and the sobering journey of emptying his accumulated wealth on multiple recovery facilities. Another powerful impression came from one particular man who responded to the open question, "Tell us something about your father." Many credited their dad with being their hero or the person who first told them about Jesus. But I watched this man across the table from me grip his water glass and say, "I am not . . . going to say *anything* . . . about that bastard!" As some of the conversation turned to philanthropy and charity, a question was asked of those nine-figure guys: "If some ministry asked you for $100 million, would you be open to giving it?" One response came after some thought, "I am always asked for help to contribute to a capital campaign, or a new program, or sponsor a golf tournament . . . $50,000 here, $100,000 there. But yes, if there was a solid plan and my life partner felt that this is what we should do . . . I believe we would." Some of these men were Christian, others were not.

A similar experience took place at an annual ski trip, with many more people, and therefore in a less intimate setting, the Crooked Creek Ranch in Winter Park, Colorado. Over time, I have now met scores of men and women of means who frequent other venues—moose hunting in the mountain West, big-game hunting in Africa, specialty islands and hideaways in the Caribbean, luxury cruises to exotic places, just to name a few.

These are a few of my important takeaways from these meaningful times of discovery:

1. There is more wealth in the world which could (and will) be available for kingdom purposes than *anyone* fully realizes. I know people like this in multiple countries! Many of them are not known or included in the major wealth-screening indicators or investment platforms which fund developers and consultants are familiar. It is hidden wealth, and it truly exists on a global scale which, in the aggregate—only God is fully aware!

2. Some individuals or couples have a clear understanding *and* plan for where their wealth will be directed, either as God leads them or by their own determination. This means that a vital need to identify and release more mega-wealth at this *kairos* time in history will require Spirit-led "discernment and engagement tools" and processes for those who need it. There are many new people who will be motivated to kingdom investment through prayerful discernment.

3. God has already entrusted, imbued, and enormously blessed specific people for such a time as this. We must come together now to create *aggregated and accelerated mega-plans* (plural) that will steward the overflowing abundance of resources this kingdom age requires. But we also must remember "the widow's mite" and "the fortune at the bottom of the pyramid." All will be part of this amazing season!

A commander does not send a squad or platoon to confront a brigade or division. And the warriors he sends must have the provision and infrastructure they need to win. In this spiritual battle in which we are engaged, we need to be wise as serpents, aggressive as eagles, and yes, innocent as doves. Our battle plans must have military precision. I am thankful for my friend, Ron Maines, a former Marine Officer and colleague of mine at World Vision. He helped me better understand the support structure and division of labor needed in a victorious fighting force. After all, I was a noncombatant Navy chaplain (1981–1989) without his level of operational knowledge. He said that today's military fighting units operate with a 10-to-1 ratio, which has increased from 3-to-1 during the Revolutionary War, as armed conflict became more complex. That is, there are ten "support" personnel for every front-line soldier: S1 (personnel), S-2 (intelligence), S-3 (operations), S-4 (supply), and so forth. "Support" does not mean "secondary." Each has an interconnected and irreplaceable role in winning! Ron went on to give tangible illustration:

> The large bases in the Vietnam War, the bases in Iraq and Afghanistan, were all small cities with all the infrastructure, transportation, and resupply lines that reached all the way back to the United States. Anything that you can list in a small city was replicated on those bases, and is needed on the more than 850 bases in 110 countries that we now have abroad. During the Vietnam War, I flew off of the helicopter carrier, LPH-11, the USS New Orleans. This was a ship that had an estimated 2,500 sailors, all in support of a battalion of 400 Marines, flown on missions in the I Corps by a squadron of 21 aircraft with 42 pilots, 80 crewman, and 130 maintenance technicians and operations support staff. All of this on a self-contained floating airport. And, this does not account for the several logistics groups providing fuel, food and ship repair in the Philippines and Japan.[4]

My friends in the Finishing the Task working groups use different language, with some variable strategies, but have a similar objective— completing the mission:

- What tools do we need to finish the task?
- What kind of people with what skills do we need?
- What resources and funding do we need?
- We need to mobilize all the allies and let them fly their own flags.

- We need a simple and clear target (objective).
- We need a time specific deadline (not just a dream).
- We need to recruit, train, and engage an ever-increasing number of participants.
- We need a Nehemiah Strategy—restructure, recommit, and redeploy during times of discouragement and slowdown.
- We must have a decentralized strategy—pushing authority and implementation to the lowest level.
- We must understand that this global task will be filled with young people, women, indigenous leaders, and "former" everything—athletes, musicians, educators. and more.
- There is untapped energy "out there." Talent that sits on the shelf rots.
- We need to focus on people in pain (which motivates them), not the cautious who don't get involved
- Remember, only one in four are open to the gospel; 75% are not. It is not our job to prepare people's hearts, it is the Holy Spirit's task.
- We *must* emphasize a sense of urgency; two people die every second. There are millions without a saving knowledge of Jesus Christ [5]

And I will add (from Tim Sheets and other prophetic voices): God's end-times army *will* include returning prodigals—a young Joshua generation who operate outside of the established church, who are unconventional, sometimes full of tattoos and metal accoutrements, not controlled by time, sensitive to the Holy Spirit, bold and direct, willing to risk, are pray-ers, have a deep compassion for the lost, and go where it is dark (where the people are trapped in those pits of bondage I saw vividly in my dream)!

It is time to aggregate and accelerate divine plans to acquire and deploy these pre-positioned kingdom mega-resources!

What follows are 12 Principles of Commitment, created for future participants in kingdom alliance centers of influence which will be birthed in the months ahead. I utilized and restructured similar principles that were effective during our Russia CoMission days:

Principle 1: Make prayer the center of everything (Eph. 1:15–18; Col .1:9).

Principle 2: Admonish repentance and a commitment to holy living in all participants (2 Cor. 7:1; 1 John 1:9).

Principle 3: Expect opposition from spiritual forces and sometime from our own networks (John 10:10; 1 Thess. 2:2).

Principle 4: Give *all* glory and credit to God for this work and the results (Ps. 96:1–9; Rev. 19:1).

Principle 5: Do the work under an inclusive banner acknowledging multiple stakeholders (Gal. 6:4; Phil. 2:1–5).

Principle 6: Professionally invest, manage and disburse funds with transparent guidelines and controlled checks and balances (Acts 6:1–6; 1 Tim 6:10).

Principle 7: Respect the unique value, gifting and calling of each stakeholder and partner in this global movement (Rom. 12:4–8; Eph. 4:11).

Principle 8: Be flexible. Leave Holy Spirit room beyond our own plans and understanding (1 Thess. 5:18; James 4:13–15).

Principle 9: Disburse funds only to vetted and trusted organizations and individual kingdom workers within understood "domains" of service (1 Cor. 7:17; Eph. 4:16).

Principle 10: Respond to open doors quickly, under the leading of the Holy Spirit (Isa. 22:22; 1 Cor. 16:9).

Principle 11: Work with visionary leaders first, then with operational leaders (Ex. 18:21; Luke 12:48).

Principle 12: Express love in tangible ways, always linking the Great Commission and the Great Commandment as Jesus modeled (1 Tim 6:18–19; 1 John 3:18).

Sheep Nations, Cities of Refuge, and Persons of Peace

It is outside of my ability to fully comprehend, with my natural mind, *how* God determines whether a person will live with Him in eternity or be removed from His presence. Two Scriptures help illuminate this for me: "You know when I sit down and when I rise; you perceive my thoughts from afar. You discern my going out and my lying down; you are familiar with all my ways. Before a word is on my tongue you, Lord, know it completely" (Ps. 139:2–4); "And he who searches our hearts knows the mind of the Spirit, because the Spirit intercedes for God's people in accordance with the will of God" (Rom. 8:27). The bottom line is: no one falls through the cracks, gets overlooked, or is stuck in the middle. Every person alive is on one of two paths, a binary choice—no exceptions. After we die, we will either be with God in eternity or we will not. Therefore, in the Father's original intent and grand design, He is the only one who knows the heart, directing His will and purpose through our free will and freedom to make decisions. Since individuals lead cities and nations, this applies collectively as well.

The term "sheep nations" can be ascribed to Matthew 25:31-33, when the Son of Man comes in his glory. With all the nations gathered before him, he will separate them as a shepherd does between sheep and goats. It is a metaphor, a parable, which refers to judgment and the destiny of each individual among those assembled.

I am not attempting to create a theological rabbit trail here. In the context of our emerging kingdom age, as we participate in and steward the greatest transfer of wealth in history through a period of restoration and repentance—there *will* be a season when embracing freedom becomes difficult as we draw closer to the emergence of the Antichrist. These points are key:

- A sheep nation is one that is influenced by the kingdom of God reigning in and through the hearts of a people within a particular geography and/or people group.
- No other kingdom will be able to rule over the members of a sheep nation, no matter how much they may try to impose their agenda.
- Dissenters who reject the new world order and the mark of the beast will find refuge in sheep nations that have risen up. They will be fortified by supernatural power from heaven to stand in the days of adversity. (I realize this statement identifies a pre/post or amillennial position.)
- Members of sheep nations will work together with the brethren in resisting the rule of the Antichrist.
- Sheep nations will receive favorable judgment after the return of Jesus.[6]

Today, a careful observer will see the movement and realignment of leaders of *nations*: the president of Iran dies in a helicopter crash; multiple conservative governments voted in during the European Union elections, joining Hungary, Poland, and Italy; election fraud in Brazil, despite months of massive protests, ushered in left-wing Worker's Party Lula da Silva; France's conservative party headed by "Marine" LePen wins round one of voting then gets sidelined by a clever maneuver by Emmanuel Macron and the leftists keep control of the people – weeks later the opening of the Olympics includes a bizarre transgender re-depiction of the Last Supper; African leaders are rejecting the woke/DEI demands of US global policy with African church leaders doing the same; Russia and China are spearheading a BRICS+ alternative to Western democracies; Saudi Arabia declines to continue using the US petrodollar. God is sovereign. Sheep nations are being formed today to prepare for the onslaught of the globalists in the near future. We who hear his voice will be guided by supernatural discernment.

Cities are also taking one of these two paths. US sanctuary cities now exist for abortion seekers, undocumented and unvetted immigrants, transgender-related surgeries—with other states banning or restricting same. Certain cities are "pink" or have legalized drugs. Others have banned pornographic books in schools, and given their law enforcement the necessary authority to maintain civil order. Some cities, with corrupt prosecutors, let the bad guys go free with no consequences. The two sides are aligning now more clearly than ever. When our world becomes ever more threatening to Christ-followers, we will also need to become aware of cities of refuge. They are an ordained part of God's plan.

As we continue to live in this dynamic season, also be alert to discover *persons of peace*:

> Missionaries and church planters talk about finding "persons of peace" in a neighborhood, city, or marketplace. Often the person of peace will have friends and relatives who are open to gospel witness and are welcoming to followers of Jesus. Finding them is but one tool of the trade that assists us in locating those in whom God may be at work in a community. Often, these people or "households of peace" are like a gateway relationship into a family, neighborhood, or community. Consider prayerfully seeking them out as you go about living more intentionally.

We can see this principle in the New Testament:
Luke 7:1-10 (The Centurion)

John 4:1–30 (The Samaritan Woman)
Acts 8:26–40 (The Ethiopian Eunuch)
Acts 10:9–11:1 (Cornelius)
Acts 16:13–15 (Lydia)
Acts 16:22–38 (The Philippian jailer) [7]

Elders at the City Gates

In the next chapter I will address the significant spiritual *mantle of destiny* that women of the kingdom have in these very poignant years ahead. God has a special assignment for you! Here, I will comment on men of the kingdom, beginning with a prophetic insight from my Christian brother Steve Magnuson of Kansas City:

> I have been thinking about the Kingdom Alliances strategy you presented. We know that God cares about people. That is undeniable. But it is also clear throughout Scripture that God cares about where people live. The strategy God gave you is really about raising up elders, men of wisdom, who will sit as part of a governmental counsel in the spirit realm and establish God's purposes on earth.
>
> I find it interesting that for decades we as a church have been emphasizing and teaching about the Proverbs 31 woman. They are very important. Have you ever noticed where the husband of a Proverbs 31 woman sits? As an elder at the city gates. God has been raising up Proverbs 31 women so that men of wisdom could arise and sit as governmental leaders at their city gates.
>
> The idea of city elders, or leaders at the gate, is a concept from the tribal communities that God is going to raise up again. Men with spiritual authority that spills over into the natural realm as they come together to transform the very cities where they live. Yes, you can't have my family or my kids. But you can't have my city either. As for me and my house, my city, we shall serve the Lord. We shall manifest the very Kingdom of God and be a refuge from the storm. [8]

As we hear the numerous clarion calls of today's spiritual elders—the apostles, prophets, evangelists—one of their consistent points of emphasis is: in this new season we must come up higher; we must *accelerate* what God has ordained for us to do. The additional element of *aggregating* is a critical piece to this puzzle. A big vision requires a comprehensive, integrated strategy and a significant infusion of resources. As I stated earlier, one element of spiritual intel that I gleaned from these men of means is that *if* there is a big vision *with* a comprehensive plan, they *would* consider a big investment of resources.

Every ministry, organization, church has needs. They have a budget and a plan. They need X dollars. But what if there was a vision and plan for 12X, or 12×12X? This, I believe, in the sector of "marketplace ministry" led by "marketplace apostles" *must* be part of our strategy moving forward. Let's use the "domain" of ministry—men and fathers.

I now refer to three (of many) ministries to men, led by strong brothers in Christ, each of whom I know well—in their own words.

Fatherhood CoMission (https://fatherhoodcomission.com)— Mitch Temple, Founder

"We are a group of ministry and business leaders working together to champion fatherhood, both inside and outside the Church, through clear, compelling evidence of God's design for dads as noble difference makers in their families and the world. We view fatherlessness as the heartbreaking cultural evil of our generation and vow to raise awareness that every child needs and deserves a loving, involved, committed, and intentional father or father figure in their lives."

Every Man Ministries (https://everymanministries.com)— Kenny Luck, Founder

"Our mission is to create a movement of God's men who are empowered to lead others on a meaningful journey into personal character and leadership, ultimately having a positive impact on generations of women, children and families. The war for spiritual freedom is the battle of battles in a man's life because evil has a stake in every man's heart. The greatest gift you can give a city, a community, women, children, employers are Spirit-empowered, emotionally grown up, and relationally committed men."

10X Better Man (https://johnnyparker.com)—Johnny Parker, Founder

"No man dreams of living an average life. Does your story reflect the life you were designed to live? The making of a 10X better man involves all of these elements: Spiritual (Mark 8:34), Physical (I Corinthians 6:18-20), Emotional (2 Timothy 1:7), Relational (Ecclesiastes 4: 9-10), Mental (Philippians 4:8), Monetary (Malachi 3:10). In my 30s I lived by the motto, 'Do as much as I can, go as fast as I can, to be as successful as I can.' Then I learned what a terrible thing it was to get what you want and still be unfulfilled."

How many hundreds of ministries are there which focus on men and fathers? Broken, addicted, or incarcerated men? Workaholic, absentee, or inadequate fathers? Likewise, God-honoring and dependable men and fathers? I believe what is needed in this season of "come up higher" is a "Table 71" group of leaders who will rally 16 or 1,600 related ministries, as there are in Finishing the Task. Then, instead of each organization raising $500K or $1M each (and protecting their own donor base), create an aggregation of like-minded men's ministries (yes, work together!) and develop an aggregated plan, with a mega-fund goal of, say, $100 or $200 million. This is a global vision for which I have yearned for many years now!

Apply this same principle with the same rationale for other ministries which focus on:

- preserving the traditional family.
- crushing the backbone of human trafficking.
- sharing the gospel with the Muslim world.
- serving widows, orphans, and at-risk children.
- etc.

I believe the intercessory bathed and birthed centers of influence, under a movement of kingdom alliances, is one component of God's intended purpose for this season!

Supernatural Networks and Affiliations

On the back of my business card is this simple statement: "I connect need with resource, utilizing the significant networks and relationships God has entrusted to me." Collectively, each of us possesses exponentially more networks and relationships. *God wants us to make bigger plans and expect bigger results, thereby providing mega-solutions for macro-problems!*

In this section I will simply list a few fiduciary entities and consultants or platforms who monitor or disburse some of this abundance, including a few thought leaders and associations in the "wealth" space. This list is arbitrarily selected, and I have intentionally not included names, contact information, or assets held, for those who manage assets. When considered strategically, they open entire vistas of new relationships.

This is just a snapshot of *one small segment* of the influencers and gate keepers in global wealth which God has stored up for the righteous for this very season. There is *so* much more available, including the restored wealth of the righteous which the wicked have stolen: "I will give you the treasures of darkness and the hoards in secret places, so that you may know that it is I, the LORD, the God of Israel, who call you by your name" (Isa. 45:3, ESV). That promise is for *us*!

- Thrivent Charitable Impact & Investing—Minneapolis, MN
- National Christian Foundation—Alpharetta, GA
- Ron Blue Trust—Alpharetta, GA
- WinShape Foundation—Rome, GA
- Unter Leham Uber Lehman Group—Stuttgart, Germany
- "Connected Strategy for Asian Wealth Management"—Wharton School, PA
- "Index of Family Offices in Asia"—Singapore
- "Europe Wealth Management Companies 2024–2029"—Hyderabad, India
- "The Africa Wealth Report 2024"—fifty-five offices worldwide (much more on the divine role of Africa in Chapter 15)
- "Giants for God"—website only
- David Green and Mary Winton Green Foundation—Northbrook, IL
- Maclellan Foundation—Chattanooga, TN
- Impact Foundation – Overland Park, KS

- Tiger 21—offices in Asia, Australia, Canada, Europe, Middle East and USA
- Pinnacle Forum—Scottsdale, AZ
- Westfall Gold Group—Chamblee, GA
- Halftime Institute—Irving, TX
- Strategic Resource Group—Irvine, CA
- Economics of Mutuality Alliance & Foundation—Oxford, UK
- Gibraltar Giving Group—Burnet, TX
- New Village Initiative—Newbury Park, CA
- The Fellowship Foundation—Arlington, VA
- Million Dollar Roundtable—Park Rudge, IL
- Giving USA—McLean, VA
- Donor Search—Marriottsville, MD
- 360 MatchPro—Atlanta, GA

To develop mega-solutions for macro-problems, it will take intentionality, prayer, and a committed tribe of people around each domain of ministry. I believe the centers of influence in a movement of kingdom alliances will become such a centrifugal force! I envision these initiatives taking shape, Lord willing, soon:

- Creating more social media platforms that circumvent current control mechanisms
- Creating alternative fund groups to offset the likes of Blackrock and Vanguard et al.
- Strategically investing in initiatives that counterbalance areas of dark money
- Intercessors praying for the titans and market apostles who will be raised up as generals
- A macro-strategy for home and charter schools; national strategy for schools of choice
- Making available "at street level" values-based strategies for buying and investing
- Many regional strategies for defeating spiritual strongholds which include a Kingdom wealth component
- and much more!

Everything of importance begins and ends with God

This is the backdrop before investigating further, in the next chapter, some examples and models for wealth creation and provision with a closer look at wealth transfer. And, these are important prayer points for those readers who will **pray.** . . .

- for those called to intercede for this kingdom alliances movement to be identified, confirmed, and interconnected with other intercessor networks.
- for supernatural wisdom and discernment for those stewarding this vision.
- that the Holy Spirit will quicken the spirit, mind, and heart of those he is calling to participate in this kingdom alliances movement.
- that the necessary human and financial resources be bestowed in overflowing abundance.
- for a divinely inspired name, plan, fiduciary agent, and partners to be revealed for the "At-risk Children" center of influence.
- that multiple centers of influence and abundant financial provision be multiplied around the world as the Holy Spirit leads and directs.

CHAPTER 15

Kingdom Wealth Creation, Transfer, and Provision

AFTER READING FOURTEEN chapters we arrive at this juncture. On the one hand, we are being warned by a significant number of leaders in economic spheres of influence. Their predictions include severe economic hardship, hyper-inflation, the collapse of the US dollar and its dominance as the world's reserve currency, the forced transition from a global cash-based financial system to a centrally controlled digital one, and more. On the other hand, there are *many* prophetic decrees and declarations about our entering into a period of abundance, the return of ill-gained resources to their rightful owners, and the greatest transfer of wealth in history. Do these seem to be contradictory elements? Is one set of predictions wrong and the other right?

In a chapter with this title, these questions must be addressed. As I stated earlier, my discernment regarding what will happen is "both-and", not "either-or". *However,* there are two dynamics to keep in mind: 1) these decidedly different set of events will affect different groups of people; and, 2) the timing of when and how these events parallel or intersect is only fully known by the Father. What we anticipate is these days ahead will be *both* a time of judgment/removal/reversal of those opposed to God, *as well as* a time of recompense and reward for those who follow Him. The ekklesia is entering a time of peace, plenty, and power that will provide stability during the increasing times of global peril. I will leave the pre-, post-, or amillennial argument out of this discourse!

Four topical subsections follow:

- A biblical framework
- A historical framework
- An economic framework

- Kingdom wealth creation, transfer, and provision

And two *very important* destinies of this era will conclude the chapter:

- The mantle of destiny *for* women
- The mantle of destiny *on* Africa

Biblical Framework

There are more than 2,300 verses in the Bible that concern money. Eleven of the thirty-nine parables that Jesus taught were about money. These are a few cursory points, on a very complex topic, that deserve more detail than we have space to provide.

> The gospel of Jesus Christ and the gospel of the Kingdom are two different things. The gospel of the Kingdom is the government of God. It is established through covenants. God established covenants throughout the Bible. The new covenant allows us to ascend to Mount Zion, God's kingdom. The resources of the Kingdom are made available to man, *right now*, to oppose the kingdom of darkness. God is interested in liberating people and nations (Isaiah 56:7). God wants his people interceding for nations. *He plans to change things.* He will give us authority over nations (Revelation 2:26). In order to liberate nations, God needs the gospel of His government demonstrated to nations. God is bringing correction. God's plan, going into these latter days, is big and magnificent. He is training us to be agents of His government. [We will be engaged and deployed in this season for much more than we yet fully understand.]

> Trade is a concept that is pre-Adamic. On the side of good, trade underlies salvation, prayer, giving and much more. Trade is a foundation of economics. It occurs acrossdimensional planes. The heart is a trading floor. Trade is an agenda to liberate nations.

> On the side of darkness, Lucifer was a trader. He was filled with violence because of the abundance of his trading. Trade has been used to enslave nations. So much of what is going wrong in

the world is a result of a broken economic system—the central
banking system, a debt-based economic system. In the Kingdom
Age trade will again become a key resource to liberate nations.[1]

These Scriptures add insight describing key principles involved in stewarding Kingdom wealth:

- When the righteous thrive, the people rejoice; when the wicked rule, the people groan (Prov. 29:2).
- The earth is the LORD's, and everything in in, the world, and all who live in it
- (Ps. 24:1).
- "The silver is mine and the gold is mine," declares the LORD Almighty (Hag. 2:8).
- The soul of a lazy man desires, and has nothing; but the soul of the diligent shall be made rich (Prov. 13:4, NKJV).
- Remember this: Whoever sows sparingly will also reap sparingly, and whoever sows generously will also reap generously (2 Cor. 9:6).
- So that when you give to the needy . . . your giving may be in secret. Then your Father who sees what is done in secret will reward you (Matt. 6:2, 4).

We need to *fully discern* the intent of the Holy Spirit in the realm of kingdom wealth. There is so much more He has yet to teach us!

Historical Framework

The Roman Empire began in 27 BC when Augustus (also known as Octavian) became the first emperor. At its peak, the Roman Empire held up to 130 million people (a significant number two-thousand-plus years ago) and covered a span of 1.5 million square miles. Rome had conquered most of the known western world. The Pax Romana allowed the empire to build fifty thousand miles of roads, aqueducts, amphitheaters, and more, some of which still exist today. Our alphabet, calendar, literature, languages, and architecture borrow much from the Romans. And some of our justice system, including the concept of "innocent until proven guilty," comes from them. Trade was a vital part of their economy. But costs kept rising; heavy taxes were levied; constant wars, hyperinflation, and an elite bureaucracy weakened the system. As long as their common monetary unit, the denarius, remained tied to the value of silver, and the aureus (used mostly by the wealthy) remained tied to the value of gold, the equilibrium of their money remained stable.

In the early years of the empire the denarius, between the size of a nickel and a dime, contained 4.5 grams of high purity silver. One denarii equaled about one day's wage for the common citizen. Then the debasement began. The denarius was first devalued with a 25% reduction in its silver content; eventually it only contained 5% silver. A smallpox plague killed 10% of their population. They were invaded by hordes of "undocumented new arrivals." Civil disorder increased. The economy shrank and splintered. Every city and every frontier under their control was breached. By 476 A.D., after just five hundred years, the Western Roman Empire ceased to exist.

I won't tax your patience by drawing direct links to the United States on each of these individual talking points. *You get it.* In 2026 America will celebrate our two-hundred-fiftieth anniversary—*or will we*, given the deleterious intentions of many of our elite university enlightened graduates, the paid agitators from multiple dark money sources, and the unknown number of hostile actors who just walked across our borders to receive their government provided goodies and ticket to anywhere. What is your guess that America will even make it to our five-hundredth birthday?

From this author's point of view, *there is no effective political or economic solution*, in and of itself, that will move America out of the same trajectory of the Roman Empire. But there is "prophetic anticipation" that we will receive the grace and mercy of our heavenly Father, as He accepts our repentance and hears our prayers of intercession. We are entering a time of transition and completion of God's created order. We must continue to focus on Him, not our circumstances.

Economic Framework

Though the percentages are changing in a positive direction, much of America is still like a family of deaf people attending a large concert. They see movement and gyrating colorful lights in a darkened arena, but cannot hear the music. For the economically and spiritually discerning, we/they have been hearing this music playing for quite some time now.

Consider the wisdom of these six persons of influence:

- I sincerely believe that banking institutions are more dangerous to our liberties than standing armies, The issuing of power should be taken from the banks, and restored to the people to whom it properly belongs—Thomas Jefferson
- History records that the money changers have used every form of abuse, intrigue, deceit, and violent means possible to maintain their control over governments by controlling money and its issuance—James Madison
- The American Revolution was a revolt against the bankers. Men called bankers we shall hate, for they enrich themselves while doing nothing—Benjamin Franklin
- Most Americans have no real understanding of the operation of the international money lenders. The accounts of the Federal Reserve system have never been audited. It operates outside the control of Congress, and manipulates the credit of the United States—Senator Barry Goldwater
- We have in this country, one of the most corrupt institutions the world has ever known. I refer to the Federal Reserve Board. This evil institution has impoverished the people of the United States and has practically bankrupted our government—Congressman Louis T. McFadden
- The government will come after corporations. They will come after individuals . . . They're going to have to raise lots of money—Warren Buffett[2]

This is not an encouraging place to start. Our baseline reality is that we now live in an intrinsically corrupted American system, tied to a globally corrupted system *and then* add the enormous number of knuckleheads who run these systems. Where do we go from here? Trust in God at all times!

Kingdom people who have been called to steward kingdom wealth in this age must understand that we are entering into a major financial crisis *soon*. Among the voices of warning is ultra-wealthy entrepreneur Bill Bonner. He cites two runaway trains that will collide, leading to the breakdown of global societies and tremendous social upheaval: 1) the obsession with ending the use of fossil fuels and taking carbon emissions to net zero; 2) the greatest hyper-inflationary period in world history. What follows is additional information to better inform us.

We have heard media outlets refer to the huge petroleum reserves in Alaska, though usually from a "green" perspective. These details provide opportunity for new kingdom (not just secular) wealth creation: Outer Continental Shelf (OCS), 26 billion barrels; National Petroleum Reserve-Alaska (NPR-A), 8.8 million barrels; Arctic National Wildlife Refuge (ANWR), 7.8 billion barrels; North Slope, 22 billion barrels and 124 trillion cubic feet of natural gas.[3]

Our Creator has blessed America from coast to coast. "Large portions of New York sit atop massive but untapped sources of natural gas. The Utica Shale . . . contains an estimated 38 trillion cubic feet of natural gas, 940 million barrels of oil and 208 million barrels of natural gas liquids."[4]

Why are those in power strangling our energy independence? The climate disciples say it is to save the planet. The globalist goal is to "deconstruct" the US and "evil" capitalism, and build a new world.

Here are three additional components to this financial crisis that spiritually discerning leaders must pray carefully about and factor into when creating new kingdom wealth strategies:

1. *Food*—Behind every revolution in world history, you'll find soaring food costs. Food scarcity and civil unrest are conjoined twins. Consider this headline: "U.N. Secretly Working with Banks to Crush American Food Industry." It follows with a longer description; this is an excerpt: "A group of 12 Republican state agricultural commissioners are now setting their sights on six big American banks over net-zero ambitions, presenting a brand-new front in the war on woke investing. . . . *Wokeness is completely obliterating our society, rotting it from the inside out.*"[5] Did you notice who is buying up so much US farmland? Bill Gates and the Chinese!

2. *Debt*—Joining our soaring food prices is soaring debt. You already know America—in fact, the world—is swimming in debt. Download this helpful App —https://usdebtclock.org, to keep track of this travesty. Many new onerous controls are coming that we *must* prepare for. Keep alert for these restrictions: more government mandates,

laws forbidding ownership of foreign currencies, restrictions on hoarding food, price controls, enormous bailouts of state pension funds, income security handouts, shortages of everything, continued excessive printing of money, and more. It's time for George Orwell's next book, *2084*.

3. *Cash*—Last but not least is the long-anticipated demise of the US dollar, and the actual disappearance of paper money other than as a keepsake in our scrapbook or time capsule. Here again, the Chinese are still on the chess board. "Talk of de-dollarization is back on the table after new data from the U.S Treasury Department revealed that China offloaded close to $50 billion in US Treasuries in the first quarter of 2024. Belgium, which is often referenced as a proxy custodian for China's debt holdings, reportedly disposed of more than $20 billion of Treasuries in the same period."[6] The cataclysmic consequences for this eventual reality are difficult for the average American citizen to absorb. *Again, we must prepare!*

    The government of the United States and many of its global allies are fighting a secret war—a war to destroy your right to own and use cash. You need to know why this battle is underway. . . . You and your family are already in this battlefield, whether you know it or not. . . . The U.S. is quickly going cashless, with consumers buying most things from automobiles to hamburgers via bank loans and credit cards. . . . When a "cashless" government turns authoritarian, it can not only monitor everything you buy, but also can ban purchases. . . . The cashless economy is racing ahead in China . . . and advanced nations around the world are rushing to do likewise. "Gold is money. Everything else is credit," said banker J. P. Morgan in 1913. Gold needs nothing else to give it value, but paper money needs backing—usually from a government that makes it "legal tender." China's cashless society will be based on financial credit combined with *political* credit. China now has a state-imposed system of "social credit" called *shehui xinyong*.[7]

The United States is well on its way to this cashless system: "Let the official records show . . . when President Biden signed a death warrant on American freedom, without the approval of Congress, the states or the

American people. . . . Executive Order 14067, Section 4 ordering *urgent development* of the digital dollar . . . the most treacherous act by a sitting President in the history of our Republic. Some call the digital dollar Biden Bucks—actually, these new electronic currencies are called CBDCs or Central Bank Digital currencies."[8]

It was necessary to describe these impending financial tsunamis to properly set the stage for God's plan and purpose for kingdom wealth creation, transfer, and provision! Like we've done with each significant topic previously surveyed in this book, I refer you to two centers of spiritual intelligence that offer invaluable insight into the realm of kingdom wealth. I will cite a few quotations from these two sources, but strongly recommend that you investigate the deeper wisdom they provide through their many materials. This is heady stuff!

I. From *Building Your Business from Heaven Down: How to Receive Heaven's Input for Your Business*, by Dr. Ron M. Horner:

Isaiah 9:6–7 sets Yahweh's divine order in place. First and the highest level of divine order of establishing is in Heaven. It rests upon His Shoulder. The second order of establishing is on earth, upon the throne of David. Whatever you do, it must first come from your heavenly scrolls of destiny and then worked out on the earth following His divine blueprints, otherwise there will be little to no favor and grace upon your efforts.[9]

While Donna, my assistant and I were exploring the Business Complex of Heaven, the question coming from the Help Desk of Heaven was, "Would you like a lesson on Heaven's commerce and trade?" "Yes," we replied, whereupon we soon found ourselves in a conference room. "We would like instruction on Heaven's commerce and trade," Donna explained. "I am not even sure what we are looking for. We are open to anything that you want to share with us; we feel we need to come further in our understanding of commerce and trade." A man walked into the room carrying what appeared to be an encyclopedia. He immediately began to teach us concerning trade, which is essentially the exchange of goods and services. "Trade from Heaven's realm is galactic. It spreads through all the universe, all timelines, and all dimensions. It is accessed by faith in Jesus Christ, the Son of God."[10]

2. *Building Kingdom Business*—Christian Duval carries something in the business realm that few people do. As a passionate entrepreneur with a full career in the business world, Christian's CV is as good as anyone's. She has qualifications in engineering from Stanford University and an MBA with distinction from Harvard. She has launched several brands including the premium beauty company Ayur Luxe. But it is Christian's kingdom understanding of business that is truly revelatory, which she teaches through Bride Ministries International, founded by her husband Daniel Duval. Christian doesn't just talk about biblical principles in business; she talks about business from the perspective of the spirit realm, and what that means for your true, God-given identity and purpose.[11]

This is one sample of a multi-structured lesson (out of six):

Lesson 1 Four Levels of Entrepreneurship
- Level 1 Entrepreneur: The Call
- Level 2 Entrepreneur: The Chosen
- Level 3 Entrepreneur: The Faithful
- Level 4 Entrepreneur: The Overcomer[12]

Kingdom Wealth Creation

As we consider the creation of new channels of Kingdom wealth it is vital to remember God has promised that *we are entering a season of the release of overwhelming abundance.* Yes, resources, but also knowledge—Holy Spirit-inspired relationships and partnerships, new ideas, patents and discoveries, redeemed people back in control of the commanding heights of the seven mountains of society, the acceleration of goodness and wholesomeness, reestablished kingdom authority, and the proliferation of the miraculous—to name a few.

For many years now, the faith community has been aware of terminology that identifies areas of specialization in economic activity. This includes people engaged in "business as mission", "redemptive entrepreneurship", "market place ministry", "social enterprise", "charitable earned-income", and one of my favorites, "business by the Book." Some thought leaders, separate this area of engagement to operate outside of what they consider "ministry".

In fact, these activities *do* represent ministry, when engaged in by members of the ekklesia. What I want to emphasize here is the vital importance of

> ➢ pre-meditation
> ➢ pre-planning, *and*
> ➢ intentional covenantal commitment.

I will provide one example of each, as described through four separate lenses: 1. Available resources, 2. Existing companies, 3. Future companies / enterprises, and 4. Redemptive entrepreneurship.

Available Resources

In terms of frequency of use, and abundance of written material BAM, business as mission, is the front runner. "BAM is inseparable from the Great Commission. It is part of God's global mission – to all nations and peoples. The BAM call is clear and remains from generation to generation. It (comes) from Christ himself. And he has promised a paraclete – a helper; the Holy Spirit will give us strength and wisdom to do BAM among all people – to the ends of the earth. Focusing on 'the ends of the earth' is not holier than working in Jerusalem, but it is certainly more complex and often more challenging. That may mean crossing national, cultural and linguistic barriers. Tough and usually never anyone's default mode. But following Jesus in the marketplace of all people is not a matter of convenience, but of choice and obedience. There is need for job creation and for multiplication of businesses all over the world, aiming at the quadruple bottom line: spiritual, economic, social and environmental transformation."[13]

One – of a myriad of resources comes via the Business as Mission Global Think Tank. The Lausanne Movement and BAM Global organized a Global Consultation on *The Role of Wealth Creation for Holistic Transformation*. This March 2017 conference attended by representatives of 20 nations took place in Chiang Mai, Thailand. Among their outputs was the "Wealth Creation Manifesto" also, now available in 20 languages. You can access many papers, videos and engaging resources through a number of websites including"

> ➢ https://bamglobal.org - "Join a global network of business people transforming people and nations for God's glory"

> ➤ https://matstunehag.com/wealth-creation - "BAM reports, wealth creation" et al

> ➤ https://www.solvingtheworldsgreatestproblems.org – "The world has problems – Entrepreneur. Investor. Christ-follower. Solving problems is what you do"

Creating wealth is God's business!

My one example in both the existing and future company categories, both fall in the energy sector. This was inadvertent, not planned.

Existing Companies

Cerilon (https://cerilon.com) has developed unique partnerships and an innovative technology to pioneer a new era of highly profitable clean energy. Cerilon is building the first US-based (North Dakota) large-scale gas-to-liquids (GTL) production facility which utilizes capture and sequestration technology. *This is a kingdom solution in the green energy space*—not a phrase one often hears in this combination!

Does this mean God cares about reduced flare gas pollutants and environmental protection? Well, of course. But, the reason why this business truly *is* an appropriate example of kingdom wealth creation is their documented commitment to make this a God-honoring enterprise vis-a-vis tangible outcomes and a detailed plan. Their company predetermined kingdom investment at the front end of their company's founding. In my occasional presentations at Christian conferences, I call this "A Covenant of Connected Investment and Intentional Return." Found in Appendix 2 is their vision for the Cerilon Kingdom Fund. Here, I identify their five "Kingdom Guiding Principles":

1. We follow a kingdom perspective and world view
2. We are guided by the Holy Spirit
3. We are part of one body of Christ, one kingdom
4. We love people to Jesus
5. We are stewards of God's resources

I would encourage every kingdom-minded follower of Yeshua who currently own one or more companies to either: 1) Review and improve your own version of a kingdom fund that you had prepared, or 2) Prayerfully develop one. I believe every economic enterprise, submitted to the authority of Jesus Christ in this season ahead *will prosper with accelerated outcomes* because this will be one of the key funding sources for accelerated kingdom activity.

Future Companies (and Enterprises)

I chose both words in the title even though these terms are often assumed to be interchangeable. In kingdom business there are important differences. A company (or corporation) has a legal status, pays taxes, hires employees, enters into contracts and other distinctives. An enterprise is essentially any business, *but* even a single person business can be an enterprise.[14] When considering "the fortune at the bottom of the pyramid", "the widow's mite", or the Scriptural dichotomy of the foolish versus the wise, the weak versus the strong, and how God is and will use these differing populations (as described in 1 Corinthians 1:27) this is an important differentiation.

The Holy Spirit, through many prophetic voices, has foretold the acceleration, the explosion of favor and creativity in this generation of kingdom wealth builders. Unlike any time in history, we will see success and abundance blossom.

Of course, there will be many new companies/enterprises launched, where more leaders/founders will include an intercessory prayer–birthed covenant—connecting the initial capital investment with an "intentional return for a specific kingdom purpose(s)". Others will not, but their product can be a resource that kingdom people can and will use for kingdom purposes.

Quantum Energy Corporation [OTC:FLCX] (https:qree.energy)

In May 2024 the executive leadership voted to change its name to Quantum Energy Corporation until then it operated as flooidCX Corp. They created a disruptive technology that could address the world's acute shortages and prohibitive costs of energy supply. Quantum manufactures a transformative photonic, magnetic propulsion, capacitor and battery energy systems for the direct generation of electrical energy produced and used by the consumer. Their "gismo" is a unique combination of photonic, magnetic and rare earth processing and manufacturing.

Why did I place this company in the "future" category. They exist. But their sustainability, funding and global market penetration is still in process and under developed. As a future thinker I can envision their sustainable energy production unit, which I called a "gismo" that approximates the size of an A/C unit in a residential home, to be able to power, say – for example – modular housing units – in remote regions of the world. To my knowledge Quantum was not founded by faith-oriented people or on kingdom principles. But this is an important qualifier - with Holy Spirit inspired knowledge and spiritual discernment, and "favor" kingdom people *will be* significant players in these years ahead, at times transforming the use products and services in service to the Lord.

Redemptive Entrepreneurship

For a short time, I was an adjunct professor (under a tenured professor) in the Marshall School of Business at the University of Southern California, teaching social enterprise to MBA students. One definition is, "Businesses with primarily social objectives whose surpluses are principally reinvested for that purpose in the business or in the community, rather than being driven by the need to maximize profit for shareholders and owners." I have written multiple papers on the topic, as well a chapter in my fifth published book (coauthored with Dr. Robert Logan, my doctoral advisor), *An Undivided Heart: Living and Loving Like Jesus*. I much prefer the term "redemptive entrepreneurship." It clearly indicates a faith orientation, since redemption means an action of saving or being saved *from something*, and in the biblical sense involves restoration and salvation. Let me illustrate.

Two excellent organizations that "do" redemptive entrepreneurship particularly well are Joy Corps (https://joycorps.org). and Praxis Labs (https://praxislabs.org). I encourage you to investigate these innovative organizations. Their framework is simple but effective:

1. Find visionary local entrepreneurs doing good work in tough places
2. Ignite an ecosystem of support, mentoring and investment around them
3. Create good work for local people in their community
4. The community thrives[15]

Since I have worked globally in the field of compassion ministry for decades, I have seen firsthand many of these "communities" which benefitted greatly from redemptive entrepreneurship. A community can be a specific geographic area. Or, a community can be, for example, a group of women freed from sexual slavery (as I saw in India) of from addiction (as I saw in Alabama). They were mentored through trauma-informed curricula and have now learned to live independently, economically and emotionally—free from bondage!

There is *huge* opportunity for commerce, trade, income generation, microloans, collectives, church-based enterprises, and redemptive entrepreneurship blessing millions of people all over the world! And this generated revenue will come from the "least of these." I commend the book *The Fortune at the Bottom of the Pyramid: Eradicating Poverty through Profits*, written by Wharton School–trained C. K. Prahalad. He reminds us that the vast majority of the world's people have both earning power *and* buying power, scaled to their environment. This is *the* biggest global market segment! God will bless and proliferate these as well as new businesses.

Kingdom Wealth Transfer

Four obvious factors in managing intergenerational wealth transfer include: 1) life expectancy, 2) family legacy, 3) charitable intent, and 4) tax implications. It is important to remember that each country and state has its own laws and regulations. Volumes of material exist on wealth management, estate planning, and every element under the banner of finance and planning. There are more than one hundred Bible verses on "wealth stored up for the righteous." God has provided sufficient wisdom and knowledge to train His *ekklesia*.

In the U.S. ten thousand "baby boomers" (born between 1946–1964) reach retirement age every day! This does not suggest that they are *all* retiring, nor that they *all* have sufficient resources to transfer in significant amounts. Yet, $84 trillion in assets is set to change hands over the next twenty years. The recipients are: primarily members of Generation X (those born between 1965–1980); millennials (1981–1996); and, Gen Z (1997–2012) expected to inherit $72 trillion of that amount, mainly from baby boomers, with the rest going to charity.[16]

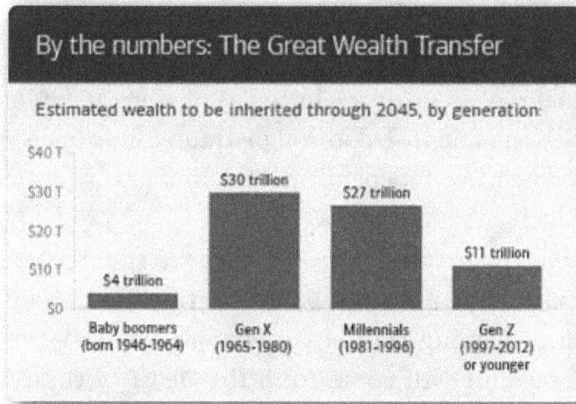

By the numbers: The Great Wealth Transfer

Estimated wealth to be inherited through 2045, by generation:

	Baby boomers (born 1946-1964)	Gen X (1965-1980)	Millennials (1981-1996)	Gen Z (1997-2012) or younger
	$4 trillion	$30 trillion	$27 trillion	$11 trillion

Now imagine the *global wealth* available for kingdom purposes! Take these U.S. numbers and multiply them a hundredfold, likely more. Many countries are noted for building wealth and wise generational transfer of wealth, including Switzerland, Germany, UK, Japan, and Singapore, among others. Also, there are many uber-wealthy people who live, and do business transnationally.

Remember again God's promise that "the wealth of the wicked is stored up for the righteous" (Prov. 13:22). There is no way we can quantify exactly how much dark money exists—although I believe, we will begin to find out! These are a few sources: money through transnational crime syndicates, money laundering, drugs, prostitution, human trafficking, counterfeit goods, arms and light weapons sales, counterfeiting, organ harvesting, crude oil theft, illegal logging, mining and fishing.[17]

Finally, there are "legitimate" or informal channels where massive amounts of funds are transferred:

1. The global Hawala Money Transfer system, which essentially is money without physical or digital movement. Hawala originated in South Asia during the eighth century, and is used throughout

the world today, particularly in Islamic countries. Unlike the conventional method of transferring money through bank wires and ACH transfers, these are a network of *hawaladars* (dealers) who keep ledgers of both debits and credits where payment can be settled in cash, property, or services.[18] There is no way to determine how many trillions of dollars pass through this system. Kingdom warriors, *we* need to develop a parallel "redemptive" system of commerce for the days of peril to come!

2. Sovereign Wealth Funds (SWFs) are special purpose investment funds or "arrangements" that are owned by governments, created for macroeconomic purposes, investment in foreign financial assets, fiscal stabilization funds, etc.[19] In 2023 there were about $11.5 trillion in these instruments, mostly in non-western countries (including China). Despite the existence of the "Santiago Principles" of alleged oversight, the system is purportedly rife with lack of transparency, poor governance, and corruption.

What might God have in His sovereign plan for the righteous to have access to these mega-funds?

Kingdom Wealth Provision—'Where there is vision, there is provision'

This category of stewardship has to do with *how we give or disburse resources.* This may seem curious to some readers, but it is a critical part of honoring God with the wealth He has entrusted to us. This applies to provision from individuals and provision from collective or aggregated sources. Who do we trust? Has the ministry or organization been vetted? Is there anyone who can provide personal testimony about the efficacy of the work they do? Are the leaders of these ministries people of integrity and abiding faith in Jesus?

Discernment before Engagement

During this greatest transfer of wealth in human history, each person or collective unit will need to make informed, wise decisions regarding their assets and what they do with them. Some will be people of faith, others not. Some will have a clear financial plan, others not. And some will already know where or to whom they want to deploy, invest, or transfer these assets—many others, will not.

Identified leaders within various kingdom alliance centers of influence, who provide tools and resources which enhance personal spiritual discernment, will be trained and commissioned. Combined with proper financial planning and covering intercessory prayer, these elements will guide engagement before deployment of financial resources. There are plentiful consultant resources in this arena.

Individuals/Couple/Families

Allow me to shift back to my story of meeting uber-wealthy people at both the hunting and skiing venues. As mentioned, a few had a clear understanding and plan for the transfer of their wealth—some under the guidance of the Holy Spirit, others purely economic decisions. There were quite a few then, there are many now, and there *will be* exponentially more people in the future who desire tools for "discernment and engagement" relative to transferring their wealth. This is an important avenue for people with spiritual intelligence to bring clarity to the aggregation and acceleration of wealth, in the many kingdom alliances which will be birthed. But I absolutely do not want to overlook all those who do not possess the monetary wealth of this world, which frankly is the majority of people on earth. *God will use everyone* who is yielded to His will and purpose to be a repository of light and love, a pray-er, a listener, a sharer of the message of salvation, providers of cups of cold water or temporary places to sleep for those who have no permanent home . . . and more.

Institutions / Kingdom Alliances

In this category will reside the mega-funds for aggregated and accelerated kingdom service. This will certainly include many of the *existing* faith-oriented financial institutions. As I participated in such a meeting in Atlanta with one such ministry, we discussed the X billions they managed and the significant funds each client held in their donor-advised funds (DAFs). So many people with DAFs had no particular plan for their money. And, to avoid excise tax, private foundations are required to make minimum distributions equal to approximately 5% of the fair market value of their assets. There are many funds sitting unused in accounts, and there is *much* kingdom work to be done. People need an accelerated vision for what they can with enormous amounts sitting in their accounts. This is what, I believe, will arise within these strategically birthed kingdom alliances around the world—mega-funds, collectives of abundant new sources of money, people, and knowledge that God will use mightily.

Wise Provision by Organizations

Proper stewardship, covering prayer, discernment, and preparation are needed by those who receive money as well. I will highlight one ministry, to illustrate. Reflejo (https://reflejo.org) whose website is in Spanish, Portuguese, and English, identify themselves this way: "We are a group of Latin-American missionaries called to be forerunners to Gospel Movements among the unreached." *Reflejo* is Spanish for "reflection"—reflecting Christ as they fulfill their mission to the people of nations in which they minister. CEO Dave Mathews and development officer Dan Barry are both men of vision and prayer. Their strategy for reaching a particular unreached people group in the Middle East begins with mobilizing prayer. Then they develop a leadership team based on the particular needs in that field, identify and train the candidates for a three-year minimum commitment, raise the funds, then deploy them. Their website plainly states, "Oftentimes we are asked, 'Why does Reflejo focus on sending Latinos to the unreached?' The short answer is: 'Because we are called to fulfill the Great Commission too.'" When you investigate them, they will have a well-vetted, clear plan.

Mantle of Destiny—Women

It was my honor to speak at a 2023 Nations of Women global conference held in Cairo, Egypt. This company was founded by Dr. Tina Allton, a Ghanaian, currently living in greater London. My message to the assembled women leaders from every continent was "Your Mantle of Destiny". I am certain, beyond any shadow of doubt, that the King of the Universe has ordained a special role for women, *always*, but also and especially in these latter days. God created humankind, both male and female, in His own image—*equally*, with an ordained purpose for both.

Let me first address longstanding and allegedly biblical limitations placed on women, especially those in ministry. I commend to you the reading of the book *The Handmaidens Conspiracy* by Donna Howell.

> Women in ministry walk a tightrope. Many are led to serve, and do so in amazing, inspiring ways. But there is a line—especially in traditional, conservative churches—that they are never supposed to cross. Paul's first letter to Timothy seems to make it clear, "But I suffer not a woman to teach, nor to usurp authority over the man, but to be in silence" (1 Timothy 2:12 KJV). Okay, then. We don't let women preach or teach, unless it's to other women. If they try, we smack them back across that line—hard enough so they learn their lesson! Is that what Paul meant? Did you know about Deborah, who pushed a reluctant Barak (who told her, "If you will not go with me, I will not go") into leading Israel to victory over a large Canaanite army? The key to correctly applying that verse, and *every* verse in the Bible, is understanding what God *meant* by what He said, not just our interpretation of ancient words on modern paper. And reaching that understanding means first understanding the context in which it was written—culturally and religious.[20]

Most persons of faith reading this book will recognize these powerful and divinely called women in Scripture; there are many more:

- Miriam—prophet; saved her brother Moses, which shaped the arc of history
- Deborah—prophet, judge, exceptional military leader
- Lydia—highly successful businesswoman
- Phoebe—church leader and deacon
- Priscilla—businesswoman and evangelist to Ephesus

- Jesus' ministry—was inclusive of many women, in contrast to the accepted culture of that day. They provided much of the financial resources that he and his "team" needed—not the disciples, let alone the religious leaders or the synagogues.

What Is a Mantle? What Is Your Mantle?

Ancient door mantle

- A sturdy piece of wood or stone placed over the main entrance of a home or place of commerce (representing sturdiness and *a primary point of access* to the inhabitants)
- The largest layer of the earth's interior and 84% of earth's volume composed of solid ultramafic rock with porous channels to release built-up tension and heat coming from its core (moderator, mediator)
- A confirmation of family responsibility transferred from one generation to another (perhaps your mantle of responsibility is the go-to person or the expediter in your family)

- A cloak signifying the passing of prophetic authority (Elijah-Elisha, 2 Kings)
- A mantle is, most importantly, a symbol of the anointing of the Holy Spirit that God graciously gives to *all* His children.

Throughout history, in every corner of the world, women have been the backbone, the strength, the embodiment of stability in the *family*, the *farm*, the *fabric* of society, maintaining a *face* of resilience, and a consistent expression of the *faith* of our Father. Ladies, you have a specific mantle for the *future*! Here are a few contemporary illustrations of mantles of calling/destiny:

- The Esther Mantle—hundreds of thousands Esthers which gathered in Washington DC, October 12, 2024—"mama bears" fiercely protecting our children and families from today's Babylon culture of perversion (https://hervoicemvmt.com)
- *The Deborah Mantle*—book with the subtitle, "A Woman's Call to Arise and Slay the Giants of Her Generation" (https://nateandchristy.co)
- The Her Voice MVMT—a "Nehemiah 14" mantle: "Our kids are counting on us! We are a prayer movement. We are here to Free Her Voice so Save a Nation"

And since this chapter is focused on kingdom wealth, consider these important realities:

- Women represent 10.4% of the CEOs of the Fortune 500 (52 companies).[21]
- Women CEOs make up between 56% and 63% of the charity sector in the US.[22]
- The National Christian Foundation (and other wealth management foundations) is led by a woman overseeing billions in managed assets.
- "An unprecedented amount of assets will shift into the hands of US women over the next three to five years, representing $30 trillion."[23]

These are valuable statistics for wealth managers, consultants, and big corporations. But they also provide critical spiritual intelligence for the *ekklesia* in every respect, especially in birthing new centers of influence in a global kingdom alliances network. At some point *soon, I pray that a strategic network of Women's Councils, in the marketplace sector, in multiple countries will arise to take the Lord's mandate to aggregate and accelerate to an entirely new level!*

Mantle of Destiny—Africa

Over the years I have had the joy of working, teaching, and traveling in thirty-nine of Africa's fifty-four countries. In my Christian humanitarian work, for sure, I have seen much suffering.

Ralph's 39 Africa countries of engagement

But Africa is a rich continent that includes people, land, natural resources, economic power, and its distinct destiny! I have had many opportunities for close observation of the economic, social, and political transformation on the continent. The DRC currently imports 95% of its food, while at the same time has 82 million hectares of rich soiled land which can be cultivated. It is a sleeping giant in agriculture and many other sectors. Most cell phones and other electronic devices contain the mineral tantalum, which comes from the ore of coltan (columbite-tantalite), which is used to produce scores of products including capacitors, electric vehicle batteries, etc. The DRC has 80% of the world's reserves for this mineral. *The destiny of Africa in the decades ahead is off the charts in importance!* Let's briefly address five benchmarks for the continent:

People—There are 1.5 billion people in Africa, growing continuously (as it is everywhere). Roughly half its population is under seventeen years of age.

Land—Africa comprises 17.21 million mi². Few people realize that the continent of Africa is larger than China, India, most of Europe, and the contiguous US combined!

Natural resources—Imagine the economic value to the people of the Congo (let alone the rest of Africa) if their 82 million hectares of fertile, uncultivated land was properly developed. The kingdom world does not fully comprehend their petroleum; hydropower; rare earth minerals; critical non-rare earth minerals such as silicon, cobalt, and lithium; precious metals; gems; water; and more and how this can be righteously developed. The curse of resource-rich countries is the proliferation of armed conflicts and corruptions of militia groups and neighboring countries. *God is going to change this!*

Economy—Africa is the last emerging mega-market on our planet. They have, as of early 2024, twenty-one billionaires, 342 centi-millionaires, 135,200 millionaires and $2.5 trillion in liquid investable wealth.[24] This is just the beginning. Africa, economically, will explode!

Destiny—Africa and Africans are mentioned more than 1,400 times in the Bible, particularly Egypt, Ethiopia, Libya, and Sudan, as well as names like Mitsrayim, Adamo, Sheba, Cush, and Abia

State in Nigeria to name a few. Africa is described distinctly as a "place of refuge" in the book of Jeremiah. It most certainly will be a refuge in the days of tribulation! Also, African Christian churches are rising up as a strong bulwark against the perversion and cultural decline of many western church denominations.

Like every other topic in this book, this is a huge and important one. Redemptive change is happening all over this amazing continent. Many of the corrupt postcolonial leaders are being replaced (some by persons of strong faith in Jesus). *Please pray* for the fourteen former French colonies who still pay France collectively $500 million annually, dubbed a "colonial tax." This allows France to expropriate 85% of their annual income—outright thievery. Asian, European, and North American countries purchase huge quantities of natural resources for export, then manufacture them into finished products to realize exponential profits. Africa must control its resources from raw material to production to sale of finished products, and become the megamarket it is destined to become!

Africa has been given a destiny and the present circumstances are changing! This massive continent has a large, youthful workforce. It has unbelievable wealth in resources. It has the fastest growing Christian population, and one that adheres to the tenants of the Gospel. Africa is where the cradle of civilization began. Now, in these coming times of peril, Africa *will* serve as a place of refuge—a continent containing many sheep nations, strategic global sources of food, water, minerals, spiritual moorings and so much more. God has prepared Africa, with this precise bounty of human, financial, and intellectual capital, to become prosperous and bless the world in many ways according to his will and purpose. Luke 23:26 (TPT) describes both a historical event and this prophetic foretelling of Africa's destiny. "As the guards led Jesus to be crucified, there was an African man in the crowd named Simon, from Libya. He had just arrived from a rural village to keep the Feast of the Passover. The guard's laid Jesus' cross on Simon's shoulders and forced him to walk behind Jesus, carrying his cross." *I am certain*, that the people of Africa will be a divinely pre-positioned refuge and resource for so many . . . when much of the rest of the world is shackled by totalitarian dystopia.

Be assured also, God has set aside enormous kingdom wealth in every continent and region of the world, from sheep nations and covenant nations through the creation, transfer, and provision of these resources, *for such a time as this*!

§   §   §   §   §

[*Special Note*: One entire chapter, titled Covenant Communities, was removed from this book to accommodate word count space limitations. I anticipate this will be included in a sequel to this book. The content provided tangible examples of alternative communities (past and present) who developed self-sustaining systems to live independently from oppressive external circumstances including the use and movement of monetary resources. It also provided a listing of digital platforms that were developed to circumvent tyrannical systems of control and influence over free expression.]

But keep reading . . . the final chapter!

CHAPTER 16
Occupy Until I Come (Back)

BEHOLD, I AM coming quickly!

I bring my reward with me to repay everyone according to their works.

I am the Aleph and the Tav,

The First and the Last,

The Beginning and the Completion. . . .

I, Jesus, sent my angel to you to give you this testimony to share with the congregations.

I am the bright Morning Star, both David's spiritual root and his descendent.

"Come," says the Holy Spirit and the Bride in divine duet.

Let everyone who hears this duet join them in saying, "Come."

Let everyone gripped with spiritual thirst say, "Come."

And let everyone who craves the gift of living water come and drink it freely.

"Come."

(Rev. 22:12–13, 16–17, TPT)

"Look, he is coming with the clouds, and every eye will see him"

From the beauty and authority of Scripture just cited, now hear these words from the hearts of humankind. . . .

- "Some may come and some may go. We shall surely pass. When the One that left us here returns for us at last. We are but a moment's sunlight fading in the grass."[1]

- "A couple of months ago I looked around and realized that many of my friends are not finishing well. I pray that when I get to heaven some of those who've gone before us will say, 'Why is your left leg all bloody and your pant leg all tore up?' I want to be able to say, 'I was sliding into home plate.'"[2]

- "Every expression of love or kindness . . . pierces the darkness . . . and reminds the enemy his time is short."[3]

- "You can't perfectly follow the eightfold path of Buddhism, the five pillars of Islam, the Ten Commandments, or even your own moral conscience. We can't be who God intended without a relationship with God—so God paid the ultimate price to forgive us and restore relationship with every *willing* person." [4]

- Before Nelson Mandela left prison he said, "As I walked out the door toward the gate that would lead to my freedom, I knew if I didn't leave

my bitterness and hatred behind, I'd still be in prison."[5] Forgiveness
does not make you weak; it sets you free.

- Father Forgive . . . the hatred which divides nation from nation, race
  from race, class from class.[6] We each must shed the hurts which binds
  us and apply the "seventy-seven" (plus) rule. Appendix 3 has the full
  "desert fathers" prayer "Father Forgive."

I want very much for you, the reader, to at least understand, if not also
appreciate, my three motivations for writing this book. *First,* I wanted to
emphasize that there is a spiritual dimension, more vast, more important,
and more directly related to our temporal, time-bound, and earthbound
life than we fully realize. God abides in this dimension. "For God is a
Spirit, and he longs to have sincere worshippers who adore him in the
realm of the Spirit and in truth" (John 4:24, TPT). Everything, everyone,
every institution on earth either honors God or at least is moving toward
him; *or conversely,* does not honor God, opposes his precepts, and will find
themselves in alignment with our mortal enemy. The final judgment will
result in: either we spend eternity in God's presence, or we are removed
from His light and love for that same eternity. Please, *please* understand,
these are the only two options!

Second, for all those with spiritual discernment, but especially for those
still being awakened who are asking, "How did we get here?", I wanted to give
tangible, documentable information to answer this primordial question. The
truth is, the enemy has infiltrated everything in his domain of temporary
authority on earth. Lies, perversion, and corruption have undermined and
compromised much more than most of us fully understand.

Third, this is the season, the generation that the prophets of old spoke of
and desired to see—a time when the mysteries of the ages are being fulfilled,
hastening the day of the return of the Lord. "But that day of the Lord will
come like a thief. . . . That day will bring about the destruction of the heavens
by fire, and the elements will melt in the heat. But in keeping with his
promise, we are looking forward to a new heaven and a new earth, where
righteousness dwells" (2 Peter 3:10, 12b-13). Until then, these immediate years
ahead will evidence enormous wealth transfer, innovative wealth creation,
and a season of restoration and revival. *It is a time to be bold and to take down
the strongholds of evil, everywhere they exist!*

A young prophetic couple, Nate and Christy Johnson, offer this word: "To the remnant—we are in a 222 moment." Daniel 2:22 reads, "He reveals deep and hidden things; he knows what lies in darkness, and light dwells with him." Here are excerpts from a much longer word of encouragement to us living in this present age:

- We are in a moment where God is wanting us to pick up our authority again where we have forfeited it.
- We are in a moment of breaking powerlessness and defeat we have settled in and violently shaking off bonds of weariness around us.
- We are in a moment of occupy and increase, and not a season of maintenance.
- We are in a moment of recovery and recompense.
- We are in a time of the unlocking of places, resources, and areas that have been locked up and out of access for some time.
- We are in a time of entering promises we have been contending with for 3, 7 and 10-year periods.
- We are in a *kairos* time of obtaining what has felt unattainable in the past. The doors that have looked the most shut are about to fling open wide.
- We are entering a season of deep revelation and encounter where God pulls back the curtain and reveals where we are going.
- We are entering a season of endless dreams and visions.
- We are entering a time of deep calling into deep and God resettling hearts that have been out of sync.
- We are in a time where God is unveiling hidden troops that have been in waiting.
- He is revealing his plans for the days to come which will be manifested through nameless and faceless people set aside for this moment.
- We are in a period of major exposure to the enemy's tactics and plans and their far reaches.
- It is a deliverance moment where blinders are breaking and those who have been brainwashed are waking up.
- God is evicting principalities and powers in cities and regions, and releasing an army to occupy those places.

- New leaders and spearheads are rising up around the earth to strike the ground. Empires of wickedness are going to keep being exposed and crumble.
- This is a moment where we will see such an uprising of true justice and Kingdom light released on earth . . . and the Glory of God will be revealed in (all) the earth.[7]

What does it mean, *practically*, for each of us as individuals to "occupy" until the Lord Jesus returns? God created every one of us for a purpose. Yes, the "chief end [purpose] of man is to glorify God and enjoy him forever."[8] But he also created us with a special and unique opportunity for kingdom service *that only each one of us individually can fulfill*, in precisely the place and time in which we live. On my office wall are various items of remembrance and encouragement. Few are more important than this verse from the shepherd king of Jesus' lineage: "You keep every promise you've ever made to me. Since your love for me is constant and endless, I ask you, Lord, to finish every good thing that you've begun in me" (Ps. 138:8, TPT).

In portions of this book I have shared, candidly, my journey and some of my struggles. Yet, I have an abiding sense of what the Lord has ordained for me to do to occupy until he comes back. And that "mantle" of my destiny is found in Chapter 13—kingdom alliances. But what about you? Many reading this book already know clearly what God has called you to do to "occupy" until Jesus returns. Others will be blessed by the declarations and decrees that were made earlier in this "222 Moment." Fully expect that the Holy Spirit *will* reveal, unlock, and increase the specific purposes He has *for you*, which will occupy you until you are with Him. Believe for it— and declare it!

With regard to the seven "mountains of trouble (plus one)," *these are a few suggested areas that need to be occupied by kingdom warriors.* If any of these apply to you, thanks be to God!

Religion (of Abrahamic origin)

- The vast majority of people who will enter the kingdom of God before the Lord returns will not cross the threshold of a church. Pray for workers to go into the harvest, and if you are called, please respond. It may simply be in your extended family, neighborhood, or workplace.

- Support organizations and ministries that specifically labor in the domains of our greatest existential threats: jihadist Islam, humanism/globalism, communism/totalitarianism.
- Worship, disciple, and fellowship with true followers of Jesus and leave your social club called a church, *if* that is what the Lord prompts you to do. Time is short.

Family

- Protect our children—vehemently. Not on our watch, not in our community, will we allow the promoters and perpetrators of sin and perversion to capture them any longer.
- Defend the traditional family, one male husband and one female wife, in a monogamous union which honors God.
- Support organizations and ministries that disrupt and oppose sexual deviance, human trafficking, pornography, abortion, and all things in opposition to the Word of God.

Education

- There are two tracks of engagement, depending on your circumstances and calling:
    1. Work within the nationalized education system, join local school boards, become superintendents of districts, advocate for universal school choice with portable funding accounts, get involved everywhere and slowly but surely reverse decades of diminution.
    2. Create new faith-based and values-based private schools, new homeschool networks, wholesome curricula, truthful history lessons; establish an entire alternative educational

infrastructure to the present system in as many states and regions as possible.

Government

- We do not have the luxury of creating a two-track process to fix our government. We the people, people of faith and freedom, must first *pray*, then take back our constitutional republic, one district at a time. Rather than moving out of or staying away from "government" and military service, we must get involved in a significantly greater measure. Politics is a dirty, dirty business. *So, we have to clean it up—* one dog catcher, one city council member, one county supervisor, one congressperson, one senator, one president at a time! Start with the 2024 national elections and every one following.

Business

- Here is another two-track opportunity. The coming kingdom age we are now entering, as we have already described, is a season of an outpouring of creativity and abundance—of intellectual, human, and financial wealth. Spirit-led people will respond to open doors and new business opportunities. And again, we must aggregate and accelerate those plans and businesses. But for the many who will remain in "corporate America," "corporate Australia," "corporate Asia" . . . you get the picture . . . everywhere, we must be salt and light! Every wackadoodle philosophy that now permeates virtually all of our businesses (we don't need to list them again) needs to be opposed. Also, exercise the power of the purse and take the time and intentionality to shop and invest your values.

Media and Technology

- We identified in Chapter 10 the corporate conglomerates which control the commanding heights of this important mountain of societal influence. We free-thinking people need to use alternative media platforms and create more—then, when intrusive technologies shut these down, create even more alternatives. Don't be fooled by the "fact checkers" and aggregators of nonsense that throw around accusations of sites being racist, misogynist, homophobic, Islamophobic, white nationalist, etc. We the people are too well informed to believe these pathological liars who call us pathological liars.

Arts and Entertainment

- Cancel, stop purchasing, don't watch or listen to anything that dishonors God.
- Buy, support, promote anything that honors God.
- Redraw the boundary lines of restraint and caution around your eyes and heart. We have been seduced by the enemy. "Indeed, the safest road to hell is the gradual one—the gentle slope, soft underfoot, without sudden turnings, without milestones, without signposts."[9]

A New World Order

- This is a *big* one. How can "little ol' me" do anything about something this globally complex and devious? First, become aware and stay aware.
- Second, *Pray*.
- And above all else, "Trust in the LORD with all your heart and lean not on your own understanding; in all your ways acknowledge him, and he will make your paths straight." (Prov. 3:5–6)

Kingdom Alliances

And I covet your prayers and support in this way:
- That God will raise up key intercessor networks to pray for forty days to raise up one, two, then many "redemptive communities" / "centers of influence" / "apostolic hubs"

- That the people God has called and prepared for this area of kingdom service will come forth and be in communication with each other
- That God will fulfill and complete his calling placed on me, Ralph Plumb, in this "large assignment" that has been given me. I *am* an "innovator" and "solutionist"

Without question, since the days ahead will be a season of intense spiritual warfare, the most important element of our being "occupied" until He comes back is in putting on the whole armor of God and being covered in prayer. Here are some important reminders regarding matters you already know and declare from Scripture:

Five motivating reasons to pray:

- Prayer builds my relationship with Yeshua.
- Prayer is crucial in determining El's will.
- Prayer helps us overcome temptation.
- Prayer accomplishes El's work.
- Prayer is a weapon of spiritual warfare.

El is our armor—for divine protection:

- He is our strong protection (2 Chron. 16:9).
- He encamps about us (Ps. 34:7).
- He is like a hen to her chicks (Ps. 91:4).
- He is like high mountains that surround us (Ps. 125:2).
- He is like a wall of fire (Zech. 2:5).
- He is our defense (Ps. 5:11).
- He is our rear guard (Ex. 14:20).
- He is our fortress (Ps. 144:2).
- He is our rock of defense (Ps. 18:2).
- He is our hiding place (Ps. 31:20).
- He is our place of refuge (Ps. 46:1).
- He is our shield (Ps. 84:11).

So many of these Scriptures come from the heart of David through his Psalms. David and his mighty men took the stronghold of Jerusalem. This was a pivotal moment because this is where the temple would be built and the people would worship—Zion—the city of David.

This event holds profound spiritual significance beyond its military conquest. For David, capturing Zion wasn't merely about expanding his territory or securing his reign; it was a symbolic act of bringing God's presence into the heart of his kingdom. The City of David would become the center of worship, a place where God's people could gather to seek His face and experience His presence. But the location was only symbolic. God's presence is found wherever his people seek him.

Zion represents the spiritual stronghold—the place where we encounter God in a profound and transformative way. Just as David longed to bring the ark of the covenant to Zion, we are called to invite God's presence into the core of our being, making Him the center of our lives. The strength of Zion lies not in its walls or fortifications, but in the presence of the Lord which dwells within it. When we abide in God's presence, we find refuge, strength, and security.

In His presence, there is fullness of joy.

In His presence, there is peace that surpasses understanding.

In His presence, there is strength to face whatever challenges may come our way.

As believers, we are called to dwell in the presence of the Lord continually—not just in times of celebration or crisis but in every moment of our lives. Like David, we must seek to establish Zion in our hearts, allowing God to reign supreme and His presence to permeate every area of our existence. The strength of Zion is not reserved for a select few, but is available to all who earnestly seek God with a sincere heart.[10]

With the Lord's presence within us we can embrace freedom in times of peril! This is His promise and his provision. Amen and amen.

APPENDICES

The Incredible Lightness of Barack Obama

Victor Davis Hanson
November 9, 2023

JOE BIDEN IS caught in a quadfecta of corruption, cognitive decline, a failed agenda, and eroding polls. Amid this apparent vacuum, an opportunistic Barack Obama — who used to be more discreet in managing his third term—is reentering the arena.

Last week, he came out as the overseer of the Biden administration's AI agenda, even as his foundation's "Democracy Forum" was warning Americans about the need for "inclusive capitalism" and the pathologies of "material consumption"—all this from a multi-mansioned multimillionaire.

Now, Obama is weighing in on the Gaza war by undercutting his third-term presidential proxy.

Yet just as he seems somewhat clueless about the contradictions of an erstwhile "community organizer" turned into a hyper-capitalist, consumption-addicted elite, so too Obama has little self-awareness about how much of Biden's unpopularity derives from his continuation of Obama's own agendas on the economy, border, crime, race, foreign policy, and energy.

His apparent obliviousness continues with his most recent odd assertion that, "The occupation and what's happening to Palestinians is [sic] unbearable."

But Obama surely concedes that Gaza has been autonomous and free of Israelis since 2005, and governed by a "one man, one vote, once" Hamas clique since January 2006.

Obama added that, "If you want to solve the problem, then you have to take in the whole truth, and you then have to admit nobody's hands are clean – that all of us are complicit to some degree."

In truth, Obama's blanket accusation is absurd.

Over the last 17 years, an autonomous Hamas has managed to create both a hierarchy of billionaires ensconced in luxury Qatari hotels, and the most sophisticated subterranean tunnel city in the world—but little else except corruption, poverty, and violence for all concerned.

Obama again seemed unaware of his own confession when he lectured, "nobody's hands are clean" and "all of us are complicit".

Not quite, Barack.

Those most culpable for the current catastrophe are Obama and his team, who invited in Robert Malley to be their point man on Hamas; cooked up the "Shiite crescent" misadventure; snubbed the grass-roots Green Movement that sought to overthrow the Iranian theocracy; invited the Russians back into the Middle East after a 40-year hiatus; fled Iraq and fueled the ISIS caliphate; lifted sanctions on Iran, giving it a multibillion-dollar war chest that armed to the teeth Hezbollah and Hamas; estranged the U.S. from Israel; and created the media echo chamber that empowered the disastrous Iran Deal.

The rest was history.

Cerilon Kingdom Fund

1 Why: What is on my heart

I WAS CHALLENGED by the question of why. Why am I doing what I am doing? Why am I persevering? Why do I make an effort? Why do I take on things that seem impossible? Why do I stand up every morning and get to work? Many years ago, a friend of mine tested me to say: "Stop doing what you are doing, go and work for someone else, and have a comfortable life." My response was clear from my heart and is still clear in my mind; "If I do that, I will die." If I do not do what has been the calling on my heart, I will spiritually die. This is not the direction I want to go in; I want to live a life guided by the Holy Spirit, colaboring with our Father every step of the way. My prayer is the following: "God help me to fulfill what You have planned for me, for us, no matter how hard it is. Let You will be done for our lives. Father thank You for the opportunity to partner with You. We walk in faith following Your guidance Holy Spirit. Let it be so. This journey of making a difference in us and through us is painful but also an amazing privilege. We ask this path into sonship to be honoring to You. in Jesus's name. Let it be so. Amen."

1.1 Vision

To **change nations for the glory of God**. This starts with change in us, our families, communities, cities, countries, industries, and the world. Let God's will be done on earth as it is in heaven.

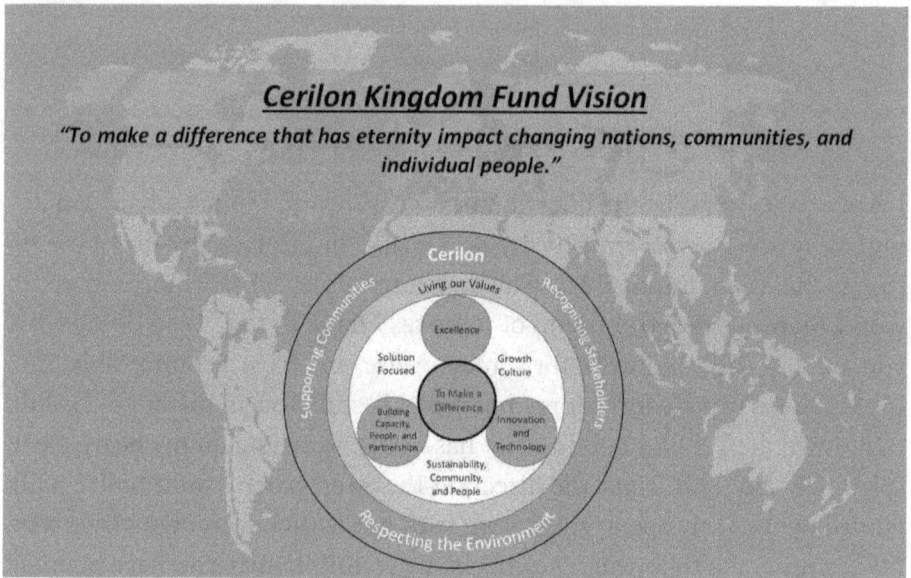

Cerilon Kingdom Fund Vision

"To make a difference that has eternity impact changing nations, communities, and individual people."

Matthew 25:37-40 New International Version (NIV).

37 "Then the righteous will answer him, 'Lord, when did we see you hungry and feed you, or thirsty and give you something to drink?38 When did we see you a stranger and invite you in, or needing clothes and clothe you? 39 When did we see you sick or in prison and go to visit you?'

40 "The King will reply, 'Truly I tell you, whatever you did for one of the least of these brothers and sisters of mine, you did for me.'

When we visited a church in Stony Plain, Alberta, Canada, I received a prophetic word from Charlie Robinson for large quantities of oil in my life. A few weeks later, the Holy Spirit gave me a picture of an oil vortex fed from hidden sources. This is a picture of the oil vortex. Rather than pulling down inside it is washing clean, producing oil and living water. The touch, impact, and exposure to the heavenly oil will bless people, communities, and countries.

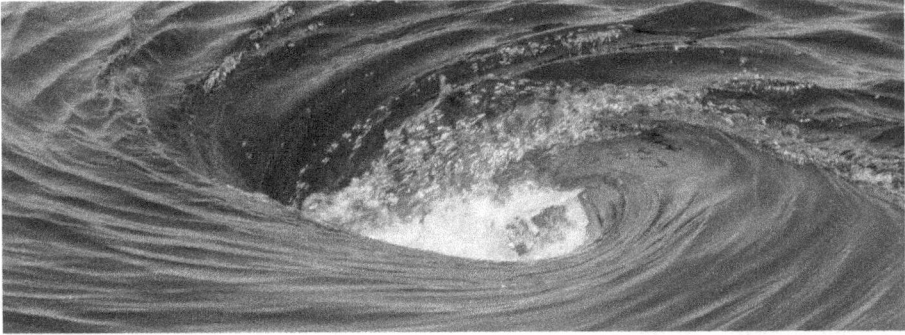

1.2 Mission

To be ambassadors of our heavenly Kingdom and warriors walking with our Father *to make a difference that has eternal value* by ministering to the world through our businesses and expertise.

In Josiah 1:3 it says, "I will give you every place where you set your foot, as I promised Moses."

Walking out life, taking territory for the Kingdom, standing our ground, as Kingdom warriors, is a calling for each one of us in every walk of life. We are called to bring the light into the world to glorify our Father.

Mathew 5:14-16 "You are the light of the world. A town built on a hill cannot be hidden. Neither do people light a lamp and put it under a bowl. Instead, they put it on its stand, and it gives light to everyone in the house. In the same way, let your light shine before others, that they may see your good deeds and glorify your Father in heaven."

We are called to disciple the world according to Mathew 28:19-20 "Therefore go and make disciples of all nations, baptizing them in the name of the Father and of the Son and of the Holy Spirit, and teaching them to obey everything I have commanded you."

Let us be the healers, the ambassadors, the warriors, and the teachers to disciple the nations as sons and daughters in all spheres of life.

1.3 Focus

I feel that business can enter places where other will not have the audience and ability to speak life into. Global need, local need, all comes from places of gaps between the intended life and the realities people are facing. Many situations are stemming from worldly distort from Gods plans and purposes for nations, communities, families, and people.

My calling and purpose are to lead in many areas like we all do but primarily in business. Insight into the combination of Holy Spirit guidance and business strategic intelligence, Spiritual Intelligence (SI) or SQ, and how a relationship with our Father provides SI/SQ, in a Volatile, Uncertain, Complex, and Ambiguous (VUCA) world. This further provides the Emotional Intelligence (EQ), Intelligence (IQ). God is the master planner and as we integrate the day to day with the preceding spiritual alignment, living with purpose is much easier.

My intention is to build based on the culture and persevere by a dedicated team for more than fourteen (14) years of intercessory prayer and guidance intertwined with business to the level of discernment that miraculously opens and closes doors or provides insights beyond normal understanding and to expands that to all business opportunities we open in any place in the world. These are the seeds we want to sow into global business opportunities that will be followed with the other step sin the Kingdom value chain.

1.4 Kingdom Stewardship Principles

We are called to take *ownership* of our dreams, destinies, challenges, and opportunities, have the courage and intentionality to step into *leadership* to act on the opportunities and challenges, and provide *stewardship* regarding dreams, destinies, challenges, and opportunities presented to us. We are being generational stewards of what is being entrusted to us. Being obedient is the act of worship, fulfilling what we are destined to bring to this broken world! Beauty to ashes, love to hate, hope.

God provides the complete answer to life, how, when, and with what guidance we should live.

We are called to complete obedience in body, soul, and spirit. Complete surrender and transformation to be Christlike. This also applies to the relationships with God, us, families, and externally. When we anticipate bringing change to the nations, it is a complete answer with solutions covering all the areas (body, soul, and spirit). It means complete in our roles as an individual, relationship as a child, father or mother, spouse, in our vocation, as a brother, sister, or friend. Complete in our relationship with the Father, Son, and Holy Spirit.

1.5 Kingdom Guiding Principles

The CKF Kingdom's guiding principles are ensuring we have the correct perspectives from God, being guided by the example of Jesus, enabling, governing, and establishing the correct position and perspective. We will enable, collaborate, and act to make a difference.

The key principles are:
1) We follow a Kingdom perspective and worldview;
2) We are guided by the Holy Spirit;
3) We are part of one body of Christ, one Kingdom;
4) We love people to Jesus;
5) We are stewards of God's resources;

1.6 Kingdom Value Chain

The Kingdom Value Chain is for me build on several factors and stages that will be addressed.

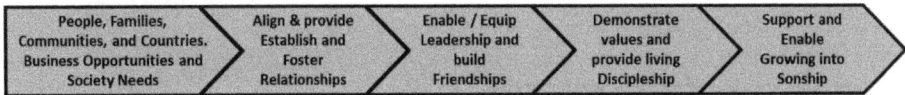

People, Families, Communities, and Countries. Business Opportunities and Society Needs	Align & provide Establish and Foster Relationships	Enable / Equip Leadership and build Friendships	Demonstrate values and provide living Discipleship	Support and Enable Growing into Sonship

Key factors are that we identify the nations and countries where opportunity exist to bring redemption where it is needed the most. Where we align what we can offer through ourselves or partnerships to bring the Kingdom to nations, communities, and people. There is not blueprint for any of the plans. We identify the local man of peace, start the process and see what the best way is forward as the Holy Spirit leads us. Ownership of the problems, working with anyone to own and commit to the process or the solutions will be key. We will play several roles depending on the situation or the need. Sometimes, it is soundboard, strategic advisor, on-the-ground delivery, funder, facilitator, or the conductor of the program to be delivered in all areas of government, arts/entertainment, media, education, business, religion, family, or community.

The Kingdom Value Chain moves from needs and gaps to relationships, then to Friendships, and then to Discipleship, and is followed by Sonship for all sons and daughters who are stepping into their rightful place.

1.7 Structure

The following structure is established to deliver Kingdom impact.

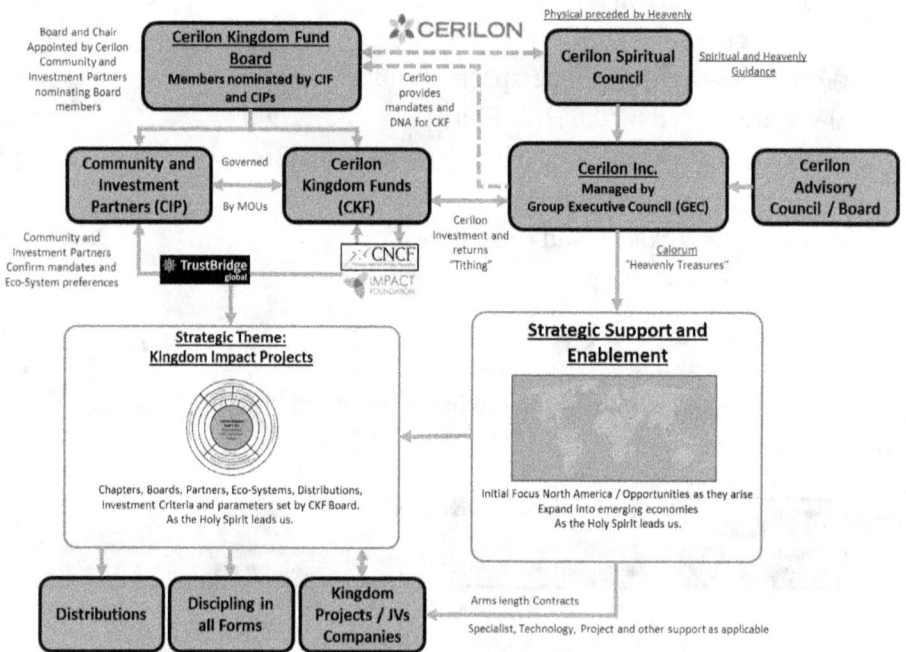

Chapters and Partners Structures as follows distributing funds to impacts as directed by the CKF board and committees as directed by the Holy Spirit according to the CKF Fund guidelines.

Leverage global partnerships with entities and people with a passion for certain functions and services to the Kingdom playing an integrator role playing to the strengths of each of the groups and people but optimizing on overheads and effectiveness.

What we have realized is that the singular approach with one Donor Advisor Fund (DAF) in Canada is going to be difficult to manage across various jurisdictions and to build a USA DAF for ease of transfer of funds from our first USA business generating USA income. This is in progress to be developed further.

1.8 Business as a Mission

This is something to be addressed on multiple levels.

1. Company Values. The company values are Ownership, Leadership, Stewardship, Excellence, and Friendship leading to Worship. As we step into who God created us to be, we worship Him in recognizing he called us for a purpose, and we live a life unto Him, to be sons and daughters of the almighty God, shining light in a dark world bringing glory to God in how we do business.

2. We impact the communities and people in the locations where we do business. Our presence must bless the communities, and they must see a different light shining in their environment.

3. We improve the environment with the products we provide and how we develop and operate businesses.

4. We take ownership of the sector of the industry God gave us to work in and do it with honor and dignity, adding value to all.

5. We provide a business platform to transfer communities and difficult locations as we add value in countries with no or difficult access with honor and respect.

1.9 Questions

This provides a few questions and answers.

The vision and strategy lead to a structure that anticipates a global change in the energy industry and opportunities to replicate, integrate, and support communities and people in much more and in many places.

1. How does this project lead to ministry?

There is a governing relationship between the Cerilon Kingdom Fund (CKF), and the Cerilon GTL Inc. The Cerilon GTL project and the following projects are providing clean, environmentally friendly transition energy and opportunities to support nations all over the world, especially in developing countries.

I have committed at least ten percent (10%) of my shareholding to the CKF and Kingdom projects in various parts of the world. This will support various ministries in providing necessary business, infrastructure, education, relief, medical aid, water, food, and discipleship in all forms necessary. We support all the Kingdom mountains to make a difference with eternal value.

The intention is to equip people on a body, soul, and spirit level and build a personal relationship with our heavenly Father. This will teach them how to look to Jesus and build their own capacity to be self-sufficient in a Godly manner.

The ability to lead with business, apply Kingdom values and principles, sow love, and establish relationships provides a global platform in a massive, growing niche market. Ministry is strategically and intentionally set up from relationship, to business, to friendship, to brothers and sisters in the

Kingdom. We don't want to lead everything. We want also to enable other organizations to bring their visions to life as we are there to enable them.

2. What is the financial return toward the ministry from this investment?

Apart from investment, the heart and mission of the founder and majority shareholder of Cerilon Inc., the holding company, is to enable an equipment ministry or Kingdom-focused endeavors.

We are establishing Kingdom principles in business with the opportunity to portray and flavor this growing niche industry segment with a moral mindset and values that will differentiate it from many other industries.

The ministry opportunities to establish business in developing nations with Kingdom principles and values create the opportunity and platform to minister and disciple people in many nations. Having a sustainable business platform to support smaller facilities and leverage know-how enables ministry growth that is not possible on just small-scale GTL and ministry-focused projects. The business-led ministry has a higher chance of sustainable results.

Ministry endeavors would change as directed by the board and teams.

For the key investors, the opportunity is to sit on the CKF board to guide future Kingdom ministry investment leveraging initial investment.

3. What is the financial return from this investment other than the ministry? The anticipated return is on many levels.

Firstly, a return on the capital deployed with recurring dividends from the investment.

This further allows tax benefits to accrue to investors as we will have more than $100 million in the USA Inflation Reduction Act (IRA) Investment Tax Credits (ITCs).

The returns could be tax-optimized in Canada via the Canadian National Christian Foundation (CNCF), where the Cerilon Kingdom Fund is registered. The same optimization will be done in the USA with Novo and Impact Foundation Cerilon Kingdom DAF.

The other intangible returns will be the opportunity to leverage the Cerilon teams' know-how to support other projects and developments like energy, water, mall-scale GTLs, petrochemical facilities, renewable projects, and relationships to reduce the time to market for other projects planned by investors.

Regards
Nico

Father

Forgive . . .

The HATRED which divides nation from nation race from race, class from class	**Father Forgive**
The COVETOUS desires of men and nations to possess what is not our own	**Father Forgive**
The GREED which exploits the labors of humankind and lays waste the earth	**Father Forgive**
Our ENVY of the welfare and happiness of others	**Father Forgive**
Our INDIFFERENCE to the plight of the homeless and the refugee	**Father Forgive**
The LUST which uses for ignoble ends the bodies of men and women	**Father Forgive**
The PRIDE which leads us to trust ourselves and not in God	**Father Forgive**

Acknowledgements

To – The Eternal Three-in-One, Blessed are you, Lord our God, King of the universe.

On each day that I would write portions of the manuscript, I began with this in my prayer:

Holy Spirit – guide and inspire every word I write today. Grant me divine inspiration to speak truth in the midst of darkness. May all the proceeds from my effort be pleasing to you and be in alignment with your will and purpose.

To – My daughter Chelsea Plumb Cejas, who was *always* available, at all hours of the day or night, to help me with a myriad of things that I never got quite right like formatting, pagination, converting pdf to jpg, double and triple checking things, preparing the inserts of photos, maps, charts, and so much more. With all my heart I thank you for lightening the journey!

To – An amazing friend and man of God, George Bell. You provided key elements of content in a few sections of the book where you are mentioned by name. Thank you also for two riveting real-life stories of surviving your early days in the music and entertainment business while staying out of the clutches of the Illuminati. Your wisdom and encouragement throughout the development of this book are greatly appreciated.

To – Kay Edwards and your team at Outsight Network for your stellar research on many topics. Both your data and counsel brought tangible clarity to many important subjects. Her company's moniker validates what they will deliver to any of you who resonate with this goal: *Helping leaders find clarity in complex times.* My only regret is one entire chapter ofyour valuable research didn't make this publishing, but for sure will be included in a sequel.

To – My friend Danney Alkana who encouraged me to research more carefully and to understand the importance of the Biblical account of God's creation of our universe, planet earth, and humankind. So much of alleged 'science' is based on projections and postulates, often by people hostile to faith.

To – *So many* thought leaders, bold communicators and prophetic voices who have been mentioned in nearly every portion of this book. God speaks to and through different people in different ways. I sincerely believe that every name referenced throughout, added redemptive value to the central message that everything in our earthly sojourn is either with God or moving toward Him OR is aligned with the enemy.

To– And finally, I want to thank the entire talented team at Illumify Media Global who also own the subsidiary publisher McHenry Press. You really are a professional and creative group. Sincere appreciation to my friend and CEO Michael, Jennifer, Geoff, Karen and Debbie for the fantastic cover design. It has been a sincere pleasure working with you.

Recommended Resources

Allen, Joe
Dark Aeon: Transhumanism and the War Against Humanity. New York: Skyhorse Publishing. 2023.

Allen, Scott David
Why Social Justice is Not Biblical Justice: An Urgent Appeal to Fellow Christians in A Time of Social Crisis. Grand Rapids, MI: Credo House Publishers, 2020.

Bonnke, Reinhard
Faith: The Link with God's Power. New Kensington, PA: Whitaker House, 2014.

Cahn, Jonathan
The Harbinger II: The Return. Lake Mary, FL: Charisma House Book Group, 2020.

The Return of the Gods. Lake Mary, FL: Charisma Media. 2022.

Clark, Randy
There is More: The Secret to Experiencing God's Power to Change Your Life. Minneapolis, MN: Chosen Books. 2013.

Dice, Mark
The Illuminati in Hollywood: Celebrities, Conspiracies, and Secret Societies in Pop Culture and the Entertainment Industry. New York: The Resistance Manifesto. 2016.

Dreher, Rod
Live Not by Lies: A Manual for Christian Dissidents. Penguin Random House. 2020.

Duval, Daniel
Kingdom Government and the Promise of Sheep Nations. Katy, TX: Bride Publications. 2015.

Gibson, Rosemary, and Singh, Janardan Prasad
China RX: Exposing the Risks of America's Dependence on China for Medicine. Guilford, CT: Prometheus Books. 2018

Gilliam, Jonathan T.
Sheep No More: The Art of Awareness and Attack Survival. New York/Nashville: Post Hill Press,2017.

Hanson, Victor Davis
The Dying Citizen: How Progressive Elites, Tribalism, and Globalization are Destroying the Idea of America. New York, NY. Basic Books. 2021

Hegseth, Peter
Battle for the American Mind: Uprooting A Century of Miseducation. New York, NY: Harper Collins Publishers. 2022.

The War on Warriors: Behind the Betrayal of the Men Who Keep Us Free. New York, NY: Fox News Books. 2024.

Hibbs, Jack
Living in the Daze of Deception: How to Discern Truth from Culture's Lies. Eugene, OR: Harvest House Publishers. 2024.

Horner, Christopher C.
Red Hot Lies: How Global Warming Alarmists Use Threats, Fraud and Deception to Keep You Misinformed. Washington, DC: Regency Publishing, Inc. 2008.

Horowitz, David
Dark Agenda: The War to Destroy Christian America. West Palm Beach, FL: Humanix Books. 2018.

Howell, Donna
The Handmaidens Conspiracy: How erroneous bible translations hijacked the women's empowerment movement started by Jesus Christ and disavowed the

rightful place of female pastors, preachers, and prophets. Crane, MO: Defender Publishing.2018.

Jarrett, Greg
The Russia Hoax: The Illicit Scheme to Clear Hillary Clinton and Frame Donald Trump. New York: Harper Collins. 2018.

Kelly, Julie
January 6: How Democrats Used the Capitol Protest to Launch a War on Terror Against the Political Right. New York, NY: Bombardier Books. 2022.

Kennedy, Robert F.
The Real Anthony Fauci: Bill Gates, Big Pharma, and the Global War on Democracy And Public Health. New York, NY: Skyhorse Publishing. 2021.

Charles Kraft and David DeBord
The Rules of Engagement: Understanding the Principles That Govern the Spiritual Battles in Our Lives. Eugene, OR: Wipf & Stock Publishers. 2000.

Levin, Mark R.
American Marxism. New York, NY: Threshold Editions. 2021.

Unfreedom of the Press. New York: Threshold Editions. 2019.

Liberty and Tyranny: A Conservative Manifesto. New York. Threshold Editions. 2009.

Lindsay, James
The Marxification of Education: Paulo Freire's Critical Marxism and the Theft of Education. New Discourses Publishers. 2022.

MacDonald, Heather
The Diversity Delusion: How Race and Gender Pandering Corrupt the University and Undermine our Culture. New York, NY: St. Martin's Press. 2018.

Maginnis, LTC. Robert L.
Alliance of Evil: Russia, China, the United States and a New Cold War. Crane, MO: Defender Publishing. 2018.

Mandel, Bethany and Markowicz, Karol
Stolen Youth: How Radicals are Erasing Innocence and Indoctrination a Generation. Nashville: DW Books. 2023.

Mandery, Evan
Poison Ivy: How Elite Colleges Divide Us. New York, NY. The New Press. 2022.

Miles, Lucas
Woke Jesus: The False Messiah Destroying Christianity. West Palm Beach, FL: Humanix Books. 2023.

Mitchel, Guy K.
Global Warming: The Great deception – The Triumph of Dollars and Politics Over Science and Why You Should Care. Richmond Hill, GA. Literary Management Group. 2022.

Nettleton, Todd (with The Voice of the Martyrs)
When Faith is Forbidden: 40 Days on the Frontlines with Persecuted Christians. Chicago: Moody Publishers. 2021.

Ngo, Andy
Unmasked: Inside Antifa's Radical Plan to Destroy Democracy. New York: Hatchet Book Group. 2022.

Orta, Pedro Israel
The Broken Whistle – A Deep State Run Amok: Memoir of a CIA Whistleblower. United States: Pedro Israel Orta Productions, LLC. 2024.

Patel, Kash Pramod
Government Gangsters: The Deep State, the Truth, and the Battle for Our Democracy. New York: Post Hill Press. 2023.

Pillsbury, Michael
The Hundred-Year Marathon: China's Secret Strategy to Replace America as the Global Superpower. New York: St. Martin's Griffin. 2016.

Shrier, Abigail
Irreversible Damage: The Transgender Craze Seducing our Daughters. Washington, DC: Regnery Publishing. 2020.

Sund, Steven A.
Courage Under Fire: Under Siege and Outnumbered 58 to 1 on January 6. Asland, OR: Blackstone Publishing. 2023.

Walsh, Michael, Ed.
Against the Great Reset: Eighteen Theses Contra the New World Order. New York/Nashville: Post Hill Press. 2022.

Endnotes

Introduction

1. Randy Clark, *There is More: The Secret to Experiencing God's Power to Change Your Life* (Minneapolis, MN: Chosen Books, 2013), 206.

Chapter 1 – God's Original Intent and Grand Design

1. Elizabeth Howell, Andrew May, *What is the Big Bang Theory? July 26, 2023.* www.space.com/25126-big-bang-theory.html.
2. Stephanie Olson, Malte F. Jansen, et al, NIH National Library of Science & Medicine, *The Effect of Ocean Salinity on Climate and Its Implications for Earth's Habitability* May 28, 2022, www.ncbi.nlm.nih.gov.
3. James Tour, *Dr. Tour Exposes the False Science Behind Origin of Life Research.* October 4, 2022, www.youtube.com/.
4. Wikipedia, https://en.m.wikipedia.org
5. Art Lindsley, *Made in the Image of God – The Basis for our Significance*, Institute for Faith, Work & Economics, December 11, 2012, https://tifwe.org.
6. Bereshet Prophecy (Note multiple spellings: Beresheet, Bereshit, Bereishith) *Is the End of Days Prophesied in the First Word of the Bible?* J.D. Lovett, Rock Island Books, 2018, https://rockislandbooks.com.

Chapter 2 – The Forever Loser and Liar

1. Charles H. Craft, *The Evangelicals Guide to Spiritual Warfare: Scriptural Insights and Practical Instruction on Facing the Enemy* (Chosen Books, 2015) 75-76.
2. Karl Marx (1843): *A Contribution to the Critique of Hegel's Philosophy of Right*, translated by A. Jolin and J. O'Malley (Cambridge University Press, 1070).
3. Ibid n.p.

4. Karl Marx, Economic and Philosophical Manuscripts of 1844, https:// www.marxists.org.

5. Oxford Languages, www.languages.oup.com.

6. Jonathan Cahn, *Return of the Gods* (Lake Mary, FL: Charisma Media, 2022) 119.

7. Ibid.

8. Ibid.

9. Carrie Ann Murray, *Diversity of Sacrifice: Form and Function in Sacred Practices in the Ancient World and Beyond* (New York: State University of New York Press, 2017) *106*.

Chapter 3 – Perversion, Corruption, Treason

1. Diana Larkin, A Watchman's Journal, *Caught in the Act*, September 12, 2023. www.youtube.com/@awatchmansjournal

2. Diana Larkin, A Watchman's Journal, *The Downfall and Destruction of Darkness*, April 23, 2024. www.youtube.com/@awatchmansjournal

3. Oxford Languages www.languages.oup.com

4. Oxford Languages www.languages.oup.com.

5. The Federalist – *Report: CIA Started Russia Collusion Hoax by Asking Foreign Governments to Spy on Trump Campaign*, Tristan Justice, February 13, 2024.

6. *Steele Dossier*, accessed May 22, 2024, https://en.wikipedia.com.

7. Interim Staff Report of the Committee on the Judiciary – U.S. House of Representatives, *An Anatomy of a Political Persecution: The Manhattan District Attorney's Office's Vendetta Against President Donald J. Trump* April 25, 2024.

8. Christian Post, Ryan Foley, *10 Evangelical Reactions to Trump's Guilty Verdict: A Very Sad Day*, May 31, 2024.

9. Kash Pramod Patel, *Government Gangsters: The Deep State, the Truth, and the Battle for Our Democracy* (New York: Post Hill Press, 2023) xi-xiii.

10. Kash Patel Foundation Newsletter, April 2024.

11. Fred Lucas, *Total Vindication for FBI Whistleblower Who Questioned Wray's Narrative on Jan. 6*. June 4, 2024. https://dailysignal.com.

12. Mollie Hemingway, The Federalist – *Jan. 6 Committee Hid Trump-Exonerating Evidence*, March 8, 2024.

13. United States Committee on Oversight and Accountability, publicly recorded James Comer Press Conference, April 2, 2024. https://oversight.house.gov.

Chapter 4 – For Those Who Discern

1. Amir Tsarfati, Amir and Barry Stagner, *Bible Prophecy: The Essentials* (Eugene, OR: Harvest House Publishers, 2022), 11.

2. At the Finish the Task (FTT) conference held in California in December 2012 Paul Eshleman enjoined the group to agree on their understanding of the meaning of *ta ethne* found in Mathew 28:19 from which we derive the Great Commission. For clarity the term *ethnos* is used 161 times in the Bible, with 4 different words translated into English: 84 times as "Gentiles", 63 times as "nations", 6 times as "people" and 6 times as "pagans" and 1 time each as "country" or "heathen". www.missionfrontiers.org.

3. Oxford Languages www.languages.oup.com.

4. Ibid.

5. Heather Riggleman, Who Were the Major and Minor Prophets in the Bible? Christianity Today, September 16, 2019, https://Christianity.com/author/heather-riggleman/

6. Hugh Ross, *Fulfilled Prophecy: Evidence for the Reliability of the Bible*, August 22, 2003, www.reasons.org.

7. Ibid.

8. Cindy Jacobs, *2024: The Year of Shakings and Open Doors.* Passcode required link to January 1, 2024, www.partners.generals.com.

9. Tim Sheets, filmed live at The Oasis Church, June 6, 2022 and May 5, 2024 https://oasiswired.org

10. Diana Larkin, A Watchman's Journal, February 8, 2023; July 18, 2023; March 5, 2024, https://dianalarkin.blogspot.com.

11. Wanda Alger, Wanda's Weekly Newsletter, November 29, 2023; January 10, 2024, https://wandaalger.me.

Chapter 5 – Mountain of Trouble – Religion (of Abrahamic Origin)

1. Greg Laurie, Harvest Christian Fellowship televised message, July 30, 2023.

2. The Christian Post, CP Daily, February 13, 2013, https://newsletter@christianpost.com

3. John Burke, *Imagine Heaven*, (Grand Rapids, MI, Baker Books, 2015) 161.

4. Amy Mek. RAIR Foundation USA, digital newsletter June, 2024, https:// rairfoundation.com.

5. Reinhard Bonnke, *Faith: The Link with God's Power* (New Kensington, PA: Whitaker House, 2014) 102-103.

6. Saul D. Alinsky, *Rules for Radicals: A Pragmatic Primer for Realistic Radicals* (New York: Vintage Books, 1971), introductory quotes, n.p.

7. Jason Mandryk, *Beyond Asbury: Six Other Places Where Revival is Happening Now*, March 13, 2023, https://premierchristianity.com.

8. Pew Research Center. *Global Christianity: A Report on the Size and Distribution of the World's Christian Population*, 2021, www. pewresearch.org.

9. Oxford English Dictionary. www.oed.com.

10. C.S. Lewis, *The Screwtape Letters* (New York: Macmillan Publishing, 1959).

11. James Emery White, Church and Culture blog, Vol 18 No 12, 2022, www.churchandculture.org.

12. Scott David Allen, *Why Social Justice is Not Biblical Justice: An Urgent Appeal to Fellow Christians in a Time of Social Crisis* (Credo House Publishers: Grand Rapids, MI, 2020) back cover.

13. Ibid, 2-4.

Chapter 6 – Mountain of Trouble - Family

1. The Annie E. Casey Foundation, Kids Count Data Center (by topic), https://datacenter.aecf.org/data/tables.

2. Town Hall, Report on New York City's Annual Drag March, June 29, 2023. https://townhall.com/columnists/calthomas/2023/06/29/pride-vs-shame-n2625086.

3. All Karl Marx Quotes About "Children", Inspiring Quotes, www. inspiringquotes.us.

4. *Cambridge Dictionary Modifies Definitions of "Man" and "Woman"*, As reported on X and Fox News, December 14, 2022, https://foxnews.com.

5. Grace Melton and Jay Richards, The Heritage Foundation. *UN Report Castigates Religion for Stymieing the Sexual Orientation-Gender Identity Agenda*, July 10, 2023, https://dailysignal.com.

6. *A Proclamation on Lesbian, Gay, Bisexual, Transgender and Queer Pride Month*, June 1, 2021, www.whitehouse.gov.

7. *New Supplier Diversity Voluntary Data Collection in Cal eProcure*, California Department of General Services, May 6, 2022, CADGS@ public.govdelivery.com.

8. *Texas Father: "My children are now subject to being chemically castrated in California",* National Center for Youth Law, 2014, www. teenhealthlaw.org.

9. *Network Goes All-In on Trans Day of Visibility; Makes No Mention of Easter,* Daily Wire, April 1, 2024, https://dailywire.com.

10. The Economist: Independent Journalism, *As NHS England Report Reveals Weak Evidence for Gender Surgery for Minors, the World Should Take Heed of Their Warning,* April 12, 2024, https://economist.com

11. Cureus: Publishing Beyond Open Access, Alexander Muacevic and John R. Adler, *Suicide-Related Outcomes Following Gender-Affirming Treatment: A Review.* Marh 15, 2023. www.ncbi.nlm.nih.gov.

12. Tucker Carlson Interview of Vivek Ramaswamy, Tucker Carlson Today, August 17, 2023, https://tuckercarlson.com.

13. Kirk Cameron, Sky Tree Book Fairs, https://skytreebookfairs.org.

14. World Prayer Network, Tony Perkins interview, WPN Prayer Call 157, August 3, 2023, https://wellversedworld.org.

15. The Christian Post, *Franklin Graham warns Christians about 'Respect for Marriage Act',* Presented by Westside Christian Fellowship. November 28, 2022, https://christianpost.com.

16. New York Times / Opinion Section, Nicholas Kristof, *The One Privilege Liberals Ignore,* September 13, 2023, https://nytimes.com

17. The Briefing: A Daily Analysis of News and Events from a Christian Worldview, Part 1, The Liberal Theories, Conservative Lives: Liberal Authors Make Brave Argument About the Breakdown of the Nuclear Family, September 19, 2023, https://albertmohler.com.

18. Gitnux Market Data, *Pornography Industry Statistics and Trends in 2023,* https://blog.gitnux.com.

19. Everyday Health, *Is There a Price to Pay for Promiscuity?* Chris Iliades, MD, July 15, 2010, www.everydayhealth.com.

20. United Nations Program on HIV/AIDS UNAIDS, *The 8 March Principles for a Human Rights-Based Approach to Criminal Law Proscribing Conduct Associated with Sex, Reproduction, Drug Use, HIV Homelessness and Poverty,* April 18, 2023, https://unaids.org.

21. Charlotte Lozier Institute: Fact Sheet, *Reasons for Abortion, Research Confirms 95.9% of Abortions are Killing Babies as Birth Control, Just .4%*

for Rape. Elsye Gaitan, Mia Steupert, Tessa Cox. May 24, 2024, https://lozierinstitute.org/fact-sheet-reasons-for-abortion.

22. Christian Post, Samantha Kamman, *Pro-life activist Lauren Handy to serve nearly five years in prison for DC facility blockade*, May 14, 2024, https://christianpost.com.

23. International Justice Mission, Appeal Letter, *The number of children trafficked and abused daily could fill State Farm Stadium 189 times*, Mark Herzlich, February 10, 2023, https://ijm.org.

24. Lausanne Global Analysis Vol. 11, Issue 4, *Human Trafficking*, Loun Ling Lee, July 2022. https://lausanne.org/lga.

25. Live Action News, Sex trafficking, porn and abortion, Laura J. Lederer and Christopher A. Wetzel, accessed on May 22, 2024, https://liveaction.org.

26. Moving.com, Top 10 Largest U.S. Metropolitan Areas by Population in 2023, May 23, 2023, www.moving.com, (with individual research on the mayors of each city).

27. City Mayors, *African American Mayors*, Tann vom Hove, accessed September 1, 2023, www.citymayors.com.

Chapter 7 – Mountain of Trouble - Education

1. Pete Hegseth with David Goodwin, *Battle for the American Mind: Uprooting a Century of Miseducation*, (New York, NY: Broadside Books, 2022) 8.

2. Ibid, 19.

3. Ibid, 109-110.

4. Ibid, 88.

5. Ibid, 94.

6. Ibid, 38.

7. USAFacts and Edunomics Lab as reported in U.S News and World Report, Chris Gilligan., August 26, 2022, https://usafacts.org.

8. Research.com, *U.S. Public Education Spending Statistics for 2023*, Imed Bouchrika, July 28, 2023. https://research.com/education/public-education-spending-statistics#4.

9. Associated Press, *Feds Say U.S. Colleges 'Massively' Underreport Foreign Funding*, Collin Brinkley, October 20, 2020, https://apnews.com.

10. New York Post, *U.S. Universities Including Cornell, Harvard, and MIT Raked in $13B in 'Undocumented Contributions' from Foreign Donors: Report,* David Propper. November 8, 2023, https://nypost.com.

11. WiseVoter.com, *Education Rankings by Country,* accessed March 4, 2024, https://wisevoter.com/country-rankings/education-rankings-by-country.

12. Public School Review, *Average Public School Reading / Language Arts Proficiency,* Accessed March 19, 2024, www.publicschoolreview.com.

13. Senate Bill No. 107, Gender-affirming health care, , Introduced by Senator Wiener, January 5, 2021, Amended in Assembly August 25, 2022.

14. United Teachers Los Angeles, Position Paper. *The Same Storm, but Different Boards: The Safe and Equitable Conditions for Starting LAUSD in 2020-21,* July 2020.

15. Orange County Register/Opinion Section, *California's schools are reviving the loyalty oath,* Ethan Blevins and Daniel Ortner, June 13, 2022.

16. The Daily Wire. *LGBTQ+ Liberation': Los Angeles Schools Create Guide for Elementary Rainbow Clubs,* Spencer Lindquist, August 9, 2023, https://dailywire.com.

17. Washington Stand, *Over 1,000 School Districts Hiding Students' Gender Identities from Parents,* S.A. McCarthy, August 21, 2023, https://washingtonstand.com.

18. American Enterprise Institute. Eye on the News. *Education, The Social Order,* Max Eden June 16, 2023.

19. Budding Roses, Winner of the 2018 Spirit of Portland Award – Non-profit Initiative of the Year, www.buddingroses.org.

20. ACLU of Illinois, *SB 818: Keeping Youth Safe and Health Act,* August 22, 2021, https://aclu-il.org/en/legislation/sex-ed#.

21. Just the News, *CDC Urges LGBTQ Curriculum be Integrated Within Schools,* October 2020, https://justthenews.com.

22. Pete Hegseth with David Goodwin, *Battle for the American Mind: Uprooting a Century of Miseducation,* (New York, NY: Broadside Books, 2022) 18.

23. Ibid, 13.

24. George Washington University – Program on Extremism Lorenzo Vidino. *The Hamas Network in America: A Short History,* October 2023.

Chapter 8 – Mountain of Trouble - Government

1. Public Policy Institute of California, *California Voter and Party Profiles*, Mark Baldassare, Dean Bonner, et al, August, 2023, www.ppic.org.

2. Breitbart News Daily, Mike Slater broadcast, April 11, 2024, https:// breitbart.com.

3. Edmund Clarence Stedman and Ellen Makay, *John Winthrop, A Model of Christian Charity*, (New York: A Library of American Literature: Early Colonial Literature) 306-307.

4. The U.S. National Archives and Records Administration (NARA), *Declaration of Independence (1776)*, https://archives.gov.

5. The U.S. National Archives and Records Administration (NARA), *President George Washington's First Inaugural Speech (1789)*, https:// archives.gov.

6. Town Hall, *There's a New Player in the Government's Censorship Game*, Katie Pavlich, August 30, 2023, https://townhall.com/tipsheet.

7. Niall Ferguson and Victor Davis Hanson, *The History of Socialism and Capitalism*, Excerpted from The Human Prosperity Project, Hoover Institute, Stanford University. October 1, 2020, https://resources. hoover.org.

8. The Epoch Times, Letter from Jan. 6 prisoner to Americans: 'Don't Do Nothing', April 16, 2022, https://m.theepochtimes.com-exclusive-letter-from-jan-6-prisoner.

9. Jim Hoft, Ben Wetmore and Patty McMurray, Guns, *Burner Phones and Fake Registrations – The Buried Michigan Voter Fraud Scandal: GBI Strategies Director Gary Bell had 70 Organizations Operating in 20 States in 2020-Tied to Joe Biden Campaign*, August 9, 2023, https:// thegatewaypundit.com.

10. The Washington Stand, *Multiple FBI Offices Targeted American Catholics*, S.A. McCarthy, August 10, 2023, https://washingtonstand.com.

11. The Daily Wire, *100% Transparent: Jordan Peterson Says He Will Move to Broadcast Mandated Social Media Training*, Leif Le Mahieu. September 1, 2023, https://dailywire.com.

12. Reader's Digest, *114 Inspiring Leadership Quotes*, Emma Taubenfeld. November 17, 2021, www.rd.com.

13. AMAC Newsline, *10 Shocking Examples of Wokeism in the U.S. Military*, Aaron Flanigan, August 2, 2023, https://amac.us/newsline.

14. Hillsdale College, Imprimis Newsletter, June/July 2022, Volume 51, Issue 6/7, *The Rise of Wokeness in the Military*, Thomas Spoehr, https://impris.hillsdale.edu/the-rise-of-wokeness-in-the-military.

15. World Prayer Network, Frank Gaffney interview-WPN Prayer Call 157, *An Air Force in a Death Spiral*, August 3, 2023, https://wellversedworld.org.

16. The Daily Wire, *Biden Admin Opposes Merit-Based Military Promotions, Wants Provisions for Race and Gender* Virginia Kruta. July 11, 2023, https://dailywire.com/news/biden-admin-opposes-merit-based-military-promotions-wants-provisions-for-race-and-gender.

17. UCSB: The American Presidency Project, *Franklin D. Roosevelt, Prayer on D-Day,* Gerhard Peters and John T. Woolley, https://presidency.ucsb.edu//documents,prayer-d-day.

18. Caroline Keane, *The Best JFK Quotes of All Time,* September 11, 2017, www.townandcountrymag.com.

19. Democratic Socialists of America. DSA Political Platform, www.dsausa.org.

Chapter 9 – Mountain of Trouble – Business

1. *Largest American companies by market capitalization,* https://companiesmarketcap.com/meta-platforms/marketcap/.

2. Forbes Media, *The Top 10 U.S. Hedge Funds of 2023*, Rebecca Baldridge, Sept 29, 2023, https://forbes.com/advisor/iinvesting/top-hedge-funds.

3. Sovereign Wealth Fund Institute, *Rankings by Total Managed AUM*, 2023, https://swfinstitute.org/fund-manager-ranking/asset-manager.

4. Investopia. *Top 5 Biggest Mutual Funds*, Sheila Olson August 2, 2022, www.investopedia.com/investing/biggest-mutual-funds/.

5. *Pensions and Investments Online, Pensions and Investments*, accessed in March, 2024, www.pionline.com/pi-1000-laergest-retirement-plans/2022-full-list.

6. Creflo Dollar, *Take Authority over the Spirit of Mammon*, August 29, 2018, https://worldchangers.org.

7. ESG Analytics, *Where Did the Term ESG Come from Anyway*, Qayyum Rajan, March 29, 2022, https://esgananalytics.io.

8. Heritage Action for America Newsletter, Jessica Anderson, October, 2023.

9. Fortune, *Elon Musk Blasts ESG*. Christiaan Hetzner, June 15, 2023, https://fourtune.com.

10. The Epoch Times: Nation Section, *A Quiet Revolution Against 'Woke'*, Darlene McCormick Sanchez, June 21-27, 2023.

11. Sullivan & Cromwell LLP, S&C Memo, *Treasury Department Releases Principles for Net-Zero Financing and Investment*, September 22, 2023. www.sullcrom.com.

12. *What are the California Climate Credits?* April 8, 2022, www.sce.com.

13. Town Hall, Katie Pavlich, *Greta Thunberg Finally Admits What Climate Change Activism is Really About,* November 3, 2022, https://townhall.com/tipsheet/katiepavlich/2022/greta-thunberg.

14. The Wall Street Journal, Michael Buschbacher and Taylor Myers, *Electric Cars Emit More Particulate Pollution,* March 3, 2024.

15. GreenCars, Dave Nichols, *How EV Batteries Are Made*, June 2023, https://greencars.101.

16. EVBox Blog, Electric battery weight explained, February 17, 2023, https://blog.evbox.com/ev-battery-weight#

17. Russ Poldrack, *On Carbon Footprints and Biased Judgements.* Russ Poldrack. December 15, 2010, www.russpoldrack.org/2010/12/on-carbon-footprints-and-biased.html.

18. Global Climate Intelligence Group, *World Climate Declaration: There is No Climate Emergency*, August 14, 2023, www.clintel.org.

19. NTD News: *Over 1,600 Scientists Sign 'No Climate Emergency Declaration',* Naveen Anthrappully, August 29, 2023, https://ntd.com/over-1600-scientists-sign-no-climate-emergency-declaration_938916.html

20. The Epoch Times, *Meteorologists, Scientists Explain Why There is No Climate Emergency,* Katie Spence. September 13, 2023, https://theepochtimes.com/article/meteorologists-scientists.

21. The Epoch Times, *Two Princeton, MIT Scientists Say EPA Climate Regulations Based on a Hoax,* Kevin Stocklin. August 12, 2023, https://theepochtimes.com/business.

22. Birch Gold Group, *Globalists are Engineering a Financial Shock, and Here's the Proof.* Brandon Smith, July 5, 2023, https://birchgold.com.

23. YouTube, Robert F. Kennedy Jr address to Hillsdale College, *Anthony Fauci and the Public Health Establishment* (minutes 12:50 to 14:22), April 8, 2023, www.youtube.com/.

24. *The Real Anthony Fauci: Bill Gates, Big Pharma, and the Global War on Democracy and Public Health.* Robert F. Kennedy Jr. (New York, NY. Skyhorse Publishing, 2021), xiv.

25. Ibid, viii.

26. Daily Signal, Tyler O'Neil, *'Anti-Science': Former Health Officials Slam FDA Duplicity on 'Puberty Blockers' in Light of New Evidence*, August 13, 2024.

Chapter 10 – Mountain of Trouble - Media / Technology

1. *Summary: The Psychology of Totalitarianism: A Guide to Mattias Desmet, Mechanistic Ideology & Mass Formation,* Leo Aprendi (Apprendi Academics, Bari, Italy, 2022) 12.

2. Elon Musk. X@elonmusk, November 28, 2022.

3. Pete Hegseth with David Goodwin, *Battle for the American Mind: Uprooting a Century of Miseducation*, (New York, NY: Broadside Books, 2022) 14.

4. Breitbart News, *University Study of AI Powerhouse ChatGPT Reveals Clear Leftist Bias*, Allum Bokhari, August 17, 2023.

5. WebFX, *The 6 Companies that Own (Almost) All Media.* May 2024, https://webfx.com.

6. The Media Research Center. *George Soros: Media Mogul.* n.d., www.mrc.org.

7. The Media Research Center, *MRC Study: Soros Funded Groups Backing Big Tech*, accessed on May 15, 2024, www.mrc.org.

8. Warner Brothers, *Who We Are and Our Values*, 2024, https://wbd.com.

9. The Media Research Center, *Journalists Denying Liberal Bias, Part One.* Brent Bozzell, Accessed on April 26, 2024, www.mrc.org.

10. Turning Point Action, *Is This Build Back Better?* May 14, 2024, https://twitter.com@realsnoopbailey.

11. Free Beacon, *US Intel Agency Wants to Ban Terms 'Radical Islamists' and 'Jihadist' Because They're Hurtful to Muslim Americans*, Adam Kredo,. March 27, 2024, https://freebeacon.com.

12. University of Oregon - Center for Institutional Courage, *What is DAR-VO?* Jennifer J. Freyd, April 2023, https://dynamic.uoregon.edu/jjf/defineDarvo.HTML

13. House Judiciary Committee Press Release. *New Report Details How the Federal Government Partnered with Universities to Censor American's Speech*, November 6, 2023.

14. The Free Press. *New Hate Speech Laws Threaten Freedom Across the West*, Rupa Subramanya, March 5, 2024, www.thefp.com.

15. Websites to discover more about GARM - https://wfanet.org/leadership/garm/about-garm, https://judiciary.house.gov/media/

in-the-news/garm-exposed-house-judiciary-report-says-ad-coalition-likely-broke-law-silence, https://www.weforum.org/projects/global-alliance-for-responsible-media-garm/.

16. The Daily Wire, *CIA Whistleblower Alleges Federal Agency Paid COVID Discovery Team to Alter Wuhan Lab Findings*, Brandon Drey, September 12, 2023, www.dailywire.com.

17. The Washington Stand, *Artificial Intelligence: Real Ignorance, and our New Idolatry*, Jared Bridges, December 28, 2022, 2, https://washingtonstand.com.

18. Daily Mail, *How Google AI Depicts Nazis and Vikings*, Peter Hess and James Gordon, February 25, 2024, https://dailymail.co.uk.

19. Scientific American, *AI's Biggest Challenges are Still Unresolved*, Anjana Susarla, Casey Fiesler, Kentaro Toyama & The Conversation US, January 24, 2024, https://scientificamerican.com/article/ai-rsquo-s-biggest-challenges-are-still-unresolved/

20. Oxford Languages, www.languages.oup.com.

21. Joe Allen, *Dark Aeon: Transhumanism and the War Against Humanity*, (New York: Sky Horse Publishing, 2023), 243.

22. The Washington Stand, *Artificial Intelligence: Real Ignorance, and our New Idolatry*, Jared Bridges, December 28, 2022, 5, https://washingtonstand.com.

Chapter 11 – Mountain of Trouble - Arts / Entertainment

1. The Daily Wire, *The Walt Disney Company*, Ben Shapiro, October 5, 2023, https://www.dailywire.com/.

2. Candace Owens Newsletter - Blexit, December 11, 2022, newsletter@pro-lifetoday.com.

3. National Review / Music. *Popstar Olivio Rodrigo Partners with Advocacy Groups to Distribute Abortion Pills at Missouri Concert*, Abigail Anthony, March 13, 2024, https://www.nationalreview.com/.

4. Naptah Face Book post, *Lady Gaga: I regret selling my soul to the dark forces of the Iluminati (Satanism)*, June 3, 2019, https://facebook.com/WhoRemembers/photos/lady-gaga-i-regret-selling-my-soul-to-the-dark-forces-of-the-illiminati-satanism/

5. *Bloodlines of the Illuminati*, Fritz Springmeier. (Portland, OR: Pentracks Publications, 2005) AND 298-page pdf, accessed November 2023.

Chapter 12 – A New World Order

1. Inside the Vatican, *Letter to America* (#185), Archbishop Carlo Maria Viganò. December 20, 2021, https://insidethevatican.com.

2. Dr. George Bell, Sermon Notes, August 9, 2022.

3. *Against the Great Reset: Eighteen Theses Contra the New World Order*, Michael Walsh, (New York/Nashville: Post Hill Press, 2022), 3-5.

4. Niall Ferguson and Victor Davis Hanson, *The History of Socialism and Capitalism*, Excerpted from The Human Prosperity Project, Hoover Institute, Stanford University. October 1, 2020, 18-19, https://resources.hoover.org.

5. Security and Human Rights Monitor, *A dialogue-driven approach to address the partisan dynamics of online misinformation*, Emillie de Keulenaar, November 17, 2019, https://shrmonitor.org.

6. Klaus Schwab, Thierry Malleret, *Covid-19: The Great Reset*, (Geneva, Switzerland: World Economic Forum Publishing, 2020) 11,72,89,113,165.

7. World Economic Forum, *Full Text of Klaus Schwab's Speech on The Belt and Road Forum*, May 11, 2017. https://cn.weforum.org/agenda/2017/05/oboren/.

8. Davos Manifesto 2020: *The Universal Purpose of a Company in the Fourth Industrial Revolution*, December 2, 2019, https://weforum.org.

9. Daily Wire, *The Real Story of the Great Reset*, Ben Shapiro, Accessed March, 2024, https://dailywire.com.

10. Mises Institute: Australian Economics, Freedom and Peace. *The Great Reset: Turning Back the Clock on Civilization*, Birsen Filip, June 15, 2022, https://mises.org/podcasts/audio-mises-wire/great-reset-turning-back-clock-civilization.

11. Translated from the Spanish language text appearing on the official government website for the President of Argentina. Address at the 54th Annual Meeting of the World Economic Forum, January 17, 2024, https://www.casarosada.gob.ar/international.

12. Washington Stand, *The 7 Most Outrageous Moments of the World Economic Forum 2024*, Ben Johnson. January 24,2024, https://washingtonstand.com.

13. Welcome to the United Nations, World Health Organization, https://un.org.

14. World Health Organization, Fourth Meeting of the Intergovernmental Negotiating Body to Draft and Negotiate a WHO Convention, Agreement or Other International Instrument of Pandemic Prevention, Pre-

paredness and Response, Provisional agenda item 3, *Zero draft of the WHO CA+[1] for the consideration of the Intergovernmental Negotiating Body at its fourth meeting,* February 1, 2023.

15. Daily Signal, *It's Going to Be Catastrophic: Why the Next Pandemic Will be Worse than COVID,* Rob Bluey, July 8, 2024, https://dailysignal.com.

16. The Brink: Pioneering Research from Boston University, *What's behind the Boom of Christianity in China,* Daryl Ireland, February 2, 20 23, https://bu.edu.

17. Journal for the Scientific Study of Religion, *Exceptionalism or Chinamerica: Measuring Religious Change in the Globalizing World Today,* Fenggang Yang, June 30, 2016.

18. Newsmax Money, *Prepare Before October . . . U.S. Dollar in Grace Danger,* June 17, 2024, https://Newsmax.com.

19. Gesara News, *Chinese, Russian payment systems consultations,* May 5, 2022, https://gesara.news/.

20. Michael Pillsbury, *The Hundred-Year Marathon: China's secret strategy to replace America as the global superpower,* (New York: St. Martin's Griffin, 2016), 178.

21. Fox News, *The Chinese Communist Party is rewriting the Bible,* July 17, 2023.

22. Family Research Council, *Escape from Xinjiang: The First Christian Family Speaks Out,* Tony Perkins, April 13, 2022, https://frc.org.

23. Straight Streets, More Than Meets the Eye: The Weekly, *"In less than eight minutes".* David Weston, April 12, 2022.

Chapter 13 – Kingdom Alliances

1. Conversation with Sam Metcalf at Starbucks, Tustin, CA, March 29, 2022.

Chapter 14 – Aggregate and Accelerate

1. Oxford Languages, Vocabulary.com, Collins Dictionary.

2. Oxford Languages, Merriam-Webster, Britannica.

3. *The Dream of the Three Coins,* Nate Johnston, May 2024, https://nateandchristy.co.

4. Email from Ron Maines, *Follow Up from Our Conversation,* February 13, 2023.

5.   Personal notes from meeting with Rick Warren, Lisa Pak, et al at Saddleback Church, Lake Forest, CA, February 25, 2021.

6.   Daniel Duval, *Kingdom Government and the Promise of Sheep Nations*, (Katy, TX: Bride Publications, 2015), 37-47.

7.   International Mission Board. *Persons of Peace*, accessed on April 5, 2024, www.imb.org/topic-persons-of-peace/.

8.   Email from Stephen R. Magnuson., Kansas City, MO, June 13, 2023.

Chapter 15 – Wealth Creation, Transfer and Provision

1.   Bride Ministries, Dan Duval message excerpts, *Trade, Economics and A Second Exodus*, March 8, 2023.

2.   AZ Quotes, accessed May 15, 2024, www.azquotes.com.

3.   Resource Development Council: Growing Alaska Through Reasonable Resource Development, *Alaska's Oil & Gas Industry*, https://akrdc.org/oil-and-gas

4.   Wall Street Journal, *New York Leads America Off a Renewable Energy Cliff*, Claudia Tenney, May 11, 2022.

5.   Congress Report, *U.N. Secretly Working with Banks to Crush American Food Industry*, March 26, 2024, https://congressreport.com/u-n-secretly-working-with-banks-to-crush-american-food-industry/.

6.   Global Finance: Global News and Insight for Corporate Financial Professionals, *China's US Debt Speculation*, Mark Townsend, May 30, 2024, https://gfmag.com/economics-policy-regulation/china-sells-us-treasuries-de-dollarization/

7.   Swiss America Trading Corporation, *The Secret War on Cash: What the 'War on Cash' is Doing to Your Money*, 3rd edition, Craig R. Smith & Lowell Ponte, (Phoenix, AZ: P2 Publishing, 2023).

8.   Paradigm Newsletter, *Biden to Order US Dollar Replaced with Trackable "Spyware" Version?*, Jim Rickards, March 3, 2023, https://pro.paradigmnewsletters.org.

9.   Ron M. Horner, *Building Your Business from Heaven Down: How to Receive Heaven's Input for Your Business*, (Pinehurst, NC: LifeSpring Publishing, 2020), iv.

10. Ibid, vii.

11. Bride Ministry Institute: 'A foundation to higher revelation', *Building Kingdom Business*, Christian Duval, accessed July, 2023, https://www.google.com/search?q=12.+Building+Kingdom+Business%2C+

Bride+Ministry+Institute%3A+Higher+Revelation&rlz=1C1CHBF_
enUS914US914&oq=12.%09Building+Kingdom+Business%2C+
Bride+Ministry+Institute%3A+Higher+Revelation&gs_lcrp=EgZjaH-
JvbWUyBggAEEUYOdlBCTE5OTdqMGoxNagCCLACAQ&sourceid=-
chrome&ie=UTF-8

12. Ibid, (research notes, July 27, 2023).

13. *BAM: A to Z: Mission / Quadruple*, Mats Tunehag, www.bamthinktank.org

14. Seek Capital, LLC: *Company vs. Enterprise vs. Corporation: Business 101*, December 1, 2020. https://seekcapital.com

15. Joy Corps: 2023 Annual Report, https://joycorps.org.

16. Merrill: A Bank of America Company, *Will the "Great Wealth Transfer" Transform the Markets?*, June 2024, https://www.ml.com/articles/great-wealth-transfer-impact.html.

17. Global Financial Integrity, *Transnational Crime*, March 27, 2017, https://gfintegrity.org.

18. Investopedia. *What is Hawala? Money Transfer without Money Movement*, Julia Kagan, December 17, 2023, https://www.investopedia.com/terms/h/hawala.asp.

19. International Working Group of Sovereign Wealth Funds, *Sovereign Wealth Funds: Generally Accepted Accounting Principles and Practices; "Santiago Principles"*, October 2008, https://www.ifswf.org/sites/default/files/santiagoprinciples_0_0.pdf

20. Donna Howell, *The Handmaidens Conspiracy: How erroneous bible translations hijacked the women's empowerment movement started by Jesus Christ and disavowed the rightful place of female pastors, preachers, and prophets*, (Crane, MO: Defender Publishing, 2018), vii-viii.

21. Fortune, *Women CEOs run 10.4% of Fortune 500 companies A quarter of the 52 leaders became CEO in the last year*, Emma Hinchliffe, June 5, 2023, https://fortune.com/2023/06/05/fortune-500-companies-2023-women-10-percent/

22. Pro Bono Economics, *Women and the charity sector*, Rachel Gomez, Daisy Harmer, et al, November 2023, https://www.probonoeconomics.com/women-in-charities.

23. McKinsey & Co, *Women as the next wave of growth in US wealth management*, July 29, 2020, https://mckinsey.com.

24. Henley & Partners, The Africa Wealth Report, *Benchmarking Africa's Wealth.*, https://henleyglobal.com.

Chapter 16 – Occupy Until I Come (back)

1. Youngbloods, Lyrics from *Get Together*, BMG Rights Management, Raleigh Music Publishing LLC, Royalty Network, Sony/ATV Music Publishing LLC, 1967.

2. Text Message from my friend and Kingdom warrior, David Weston. June 15, 2024.

3. Neb Hayden, *Walking with a Limp: Chasing the Truth a day at a time*, (North Carolina: McFarland Publishing, 2019).

4. John Burke, *Imagine Heaven: Near Death Experiences. God's Promises, and the Exhilarating Future that Awaits You*, (Grand Rapids, MI: Baker Books, 2015), 164-165.

5. Nelson Mandela -quote when he left prison on Robben Island February 11, 1990, Pass It On – Inspirational Quotes, https://passiton.com.

6. *Father Forgive* – one excerpt of a prayer from the "Desert Fathers", contemplative sign in some guest rooms at St Andrews Abbey, Valyermo, California. https://valyermoretreats.com.

7. Nate and Christy Johnson, *To the remnant: we are in a 222 moment*, June 2024, https://www.nateandchristy.co/to-the-remnant-we-are-in-a-222-moment.

8. The Westminster Shorter Catechism, https://ligonier.org.

9. C.S. Lewis,, *The Screwtape Letters*, https://goodreads.com.

10. Your Daily Prayer, *It's not about where you are, but who you are*, May 15, 2024, https://pray.com.